# AMAZON JOURNEY

D0160973

# AMAZON JOURNEY

## An Anthropologist's Year Among Brazil's Mekranoti Indians

# Dennis Werner

Prentice Hall, Englewood Cliffs, New Jersey 07632

Library of Congress Cataloging-in-Publication Data

Werner, Dennis.
    [Amazon journey]
    Journey : an anthropologist's year among Brazil's Mekranoti
Indians / Dennis Werner.
        p.   cm.
    Originally published: Amazon journey. New York : Simon & Schuster,
c1984.
    Bibliography: p.
    Includes index.
    ISBN 0-13-025453-3
    1. Mekranoti Indians--Social life and customs.  2. Ethnology-
-Field work.   I. Title.
F2520.1.M45W47  1990
306'.089'98--dc20                                      89-34800
                                                          CIP

Editorial / Production Supervision: Susan Alkana
Cover design: Jeannette Jacobs
Manufacturing buyer: Carol Bystrom

© 1990 by Prentice-Hall, Inc.
A Division of Simon & Schuster.
Englewood Cliffs, New Jersey 07632
Previously Published by Simon & Schuster.

Printed in the United States of America
10  9  8  7  6  5  4  3  2

ISBN   0-13-025453-3

Prentice-Hall International (UK) Limited, *London*
Prentice-Hall of Australia Pty. Limited, *Sydney*
Prentice-Hall Canada Inc., *Toronto*
Prentice-Hall Hispanoamericana, S.A., *Mexico*
Prentice-Hall of India Private Limited, *New Delhi*
Prentice-Hall of Japan, Inc., *Tokyo*
Simon & Schuster Asia Pte. Ltd., *Singapore*
Editora Prentice-Hall do Brasil, Ltda., *Rio de Janeiro*

I dedicate this book to three anthropological colleagues whose examples and encouragements have helped me over many professional and personal hurdles—to Carol Ember for her clarity and honesty, to Dan Gross for his enthusiastic persistence, and to Nancy Flowers for her ability to put things in calm perspective.

# CONTENTS

# Preface

I had many reasons for writing this book. Probably the more personal ones were the most important. My friends and family prodded me with questions about what is was like to live among a primitive tribe, somewhat amazed that I, who had always shunned the countryside, should decide to spend a year living in the middle of the Amazon jungle. I wanted to collect all the anecdotes I had been telling them. I also thought I should talk informally about some of my technical studies that they had never read. Maybe then they would understand why I was so interested in the Indians.

A second reason was the need for a book for introductory anthropology students. Usually I assign one of the popular accounts of travels among an exotic people written by journalists or explorers. These books are delightful reading and, by and large, well-rounded studies, but they do not talk much about how their authors actually gathered data. Yet books on field techniques tend to be too stodgy for beginning students.

The solution was to write my own personal account, showing what it was like to be confronted with hundreds of new people speaking a strange language and doing strange things. I tried to convey the bungling awkwardness of plopping oneself down, uninvited and ignorant, among a foreign people, and the sense of satisfaction in gradually growing to understand them. In the process I hoped to explain a few handy research techniques as well.

My third reason for writing the book was directed at my anthropological colleagues. While I was still in graduate school, a fellow student once complained that every time I opened my mouth numbers came out. Although she did not know me very well, she was aware that I used statistics and that was enough for her to brand me an insensitive technocrat. Like many social scientists, she felt it was dehumanizing to reduce people to lifeless numbers. How could one possibly sense individual passions, hates, anxieties, and humor in tables of sterile statistics? For her, quantification, at best, simply obfuscated the obvious. It seemed you needed to know the answers even before you asked the questions. At their worst, statistics seemed overly manipulatable. They merely confirmed the comment attributed to Mark Twain that there are three kinds of lies—big lies, little lies, and statistics.

I can understand these feelings. In their fascination with their statistical tables, many social scientists do forget about the individuals behind the numbers. Some researchers do spend their time, rather uncreatively, using ever larger samples and more refined statistical techniques to reach conclusions that have already been demonstrated in countless earlier investigations. And a few researchers have even been caught falsifying their data to make them conform to some cherished theory, while others have distorted their data or their conclusions in more subtle or unconscious ways.

Yet, despite these problems, I wanted to show that statistics could be an extraordinarily useful research tool. Sometimes the numbers in my studies revealed things that otherwise I would not have seen. When I mention that Bànhõr is thought the most stupid man in the Mekranoti village, I know this, not because I am a particularly keen observer, but because I asked a random sample of adults to tell me who was stupid, and Bànhõr was named more often than anyone else. Knowing how he was viewed by the rest of the villagers, I was able to empathize more with him, and with the problems he faced in the village.

When I observed that "like many other *kupry* (single mothers who provide sexual services for the village's men) Ngrwa'o lost her mother while still a child," I am relying on a statistical correlation. The correlation told me something new about why Mekranoti women become *kupry*. In fact, when I gathered the information about the *kupry* and about people's childhood caretakers, I had not thought at all about a possible relationship between the two. It was only much later that I even considered looking for a correlation. I certainly did not know the "answers" before asking the questions.

Sometimes the statistics even revealed things that I had avoided learning. While in the field I paid only slight attention to the *kupry*, and entertained the notion that here was a society where people looked kindly upon "prostitutes" and did not discriminate against them. Yet a later analysis of data showed that the *kupry* were thought lazier, uglier, and less acceptable as work partners than were other women. They were also more likely never to have received a good ceremonial name. No amount of manipulation on my part could make these correlations disappear, although I did delay in publishing these results.

To make for smooth reading I do not report correlation coefficients or other statistics in the text. But they are there, backing up what probably look like casual offhand remarks. At the end of the book I provide a bibliography of publications in scientific journals for those interested in confirming the statements.

I have tried to remain as faithful as possible to the actual events of my stay among the Mekranoti, but I did take a few liberties with direct quotes, which would have been inexact after translation even if I had recorded them. Also, except for the few instances where I mention that someone told me a story, I did not collect myths, but relied on tales gathered by other anthropologists and missionaries among the Kayapó. In general where I speak of the Kayapó rather than the Mekranoti I am referring to customs that hold across the different Kayapó groups. To protect the Indians and others, I have also changed everyone's name, including the names of the outsiders who were with me in the Indian village. Only the names of Mekranoti ancestors and of my fellow anthropologist, Gustaaf Verswijver, have been left unaltered. I tried to make up Kayapó names much as the Indians do, by adding special prefixes and suffixes to the names of animals, plants and other objects in the Kayapó environment. Some Kayapó prefixes, such as Bep, Tàkàk, Ngrenh, Koko and Nhàk indicate "good" names among the Kayapó. In changing the names of Indians with these special prefixes I substituted one "good" name for another. This way scholars may "map" the special names if they wish. The Mekranoti may find some of the names inappropriate. If so, I beg their pardon.

My information on the Indians comes from many different sources, and I am deeply grateful to the Mekranoti and to all of the others who helped. These include especially Pykatire, Bebgogoti, Bepkum, Ajo, Nokàre, Ire'i, Pakyx, Bemotire, Nhàkti, Ngrenhkàjet, Gustaaf Verswijver, Ruth Thompson, Micky Stout, Kathy Jefferson, Raimundo Amaral, and Senhor Guilherme. I also thank Dan Gross, Nancy Flowers, Maddy Ritter, and Carol Ember for their encouragement throughout my studies, and Jean Langdon for her suggestions on the book. My sister Joyce and my friend Rafi helped me with practical and personal matters during the writing of the book. National Science Foundation grants BNS 76-03378, BNS 78-25295, and BNS 78-24706 generously supported the research on which the book is based.

# 1

# ORIGINS

The deep green of the Amazon jungle extends over more than 6,600,000 square kilometers, an area significantly larger than all the countries of Europe (except Russia) combined. But most of the vast forest is still unknown. Rivers and altitudes have yet to be mapped accurately. Thousands of exotic plant and animal species await identification. A few isolated Indian groups have escaped discovery by the outside world. Even with all our elaborate science, we are still humbled by the forest's secrets.

Brazilian peasants living precariously along the banks of the jungle's larger rivers do not disguise their awe at the forest's mysteries. They turn pale with fright at stories of strange river beasts, like *cobra grande*, the 200-meter snake that lives in a hole at the bottom of the river and hypnotizes people with its blue eyes. Some of the fishermen report having seen the creature, and know of two children who were pulled into the river by the reptile and there turned into snakes. There is also the water jaguar that attacks people after flopping its ears loudly on the water's surface, the hybrid creature with a monkey's head and a snake's body, and the river porpoise that sometimes entices women into sexual acts, and whose penis serves as an infallible love charm. Some fishermen working in the flooded forest have even seen the

1

river's guardian, Mother Fish, in the form of a dark-skinned woman with a red dress sitting in the back of their boat before vanishing into the cool forest air. Enchanted places where past cities, like Atlantis, have fallen into the waters threaten all who unwittingly venture nearby, attracted by the sounds of the bleating goats or laughing children imprisoned in the submerged world. Unkind woodland sprites, borrowed from Indian folklore, lurk hidden among the trees, like the goblins and elves of Germanic fairy tales.

After spending only a short time in the dense forest, you can easily understand this sense of mystery. No matter where you look you can see only a few feet away. There is no use trying to find a wider view. The trees are too tall and too close together, their leaves are too broad, and the lianas and vines that stretch between them give a thick and heavy feel to the forest canopy. If you are lucky you may come across a sylvan glade where a fallen tree has made a small clearing and allowed the sun to pass through. No matter where you go, all appears still. Only frail breezes work their way through the trees. The forest sounds—the barks of howler monkeys, the grunts of wild boars, the bellowing of swamp frogs, and the whistles of birds—seem to come from nowhere, or from everywhere. To the unaccustomed, and even to those who have lived in the forest for years, the sounds are mysterious. You can never tell if they are the calls of a bird, an insect, a small animal, or an Indian imitating these sounds.

Dangers and pleasures are ever present but hidden from view. Tarantulas scurry unexpectedly across the narrow jungle paths, and strange insects or even plant leaves may cause days of intense pain if you accidentally brush against them. Honey, delicious exotic fruits, and strange, delicate orchids also lie obscured among the forest foliage until you are almost upon them. Everywhere is the overwhelming presence of the mysterious.

Some six hundred million years ago the South American continent looked different from today. The Andean mountains had not yet been born, and part of the land was under water. The seas gradually withdrew three hundred million years ago, exposing the land, its rivers flowing westward from the eastern mountains to the Pacific ocean. Gradually these early mountains eroded into hills, leaving behind the poor soils that characterize the region. Then seventy million years ago the great chain of mountains that became known as the Andes erupted. Rivers changed direction, now flowing eastward into the Atlantic Ocean. The great lake that lay at the eastern border of the Andes filled with the sediment carried from the new mountains, and the Amazon River began to take on its present-day look.

Today the mighty river spews twelve times more water into the ocean than the Mississippi, giving the seas one fifth of all the runoff water they receive every year. But the water's force does not come from its slope. A boat traveling up the Amazon can go far into Peru before ever coming across rapids or falls. As a result of the flatness, whenever the river floods its banks it covers vast areas of the forest floor. From the air you can sometimes see the water's shimmer under the trees in the few spots where there is enough of a clearing for the sun to reach the ground and reflect off the temporary swamp.

Wandering south from North America, the first human beings probably made their way to the southern continent more than ten thousand years ago. Some may even have arrived while glaciers still covered part of the Andean mountains, although evidence for South American ice-agers is poor. The first settlers shunned the Amazon valley. Instead, they clung to the mountains, following herds of wild animals far into southern Chile and then spreading out into what is now Argentina long before venturing into the Amazon forest.

When they finally did enter the Amazon valley they avoided the dark interior areas, preferring to live along the rivers that flowed out of the western mountains. Here the soils were more fertile because of the rich Andean silt deposited by the annual floods, and the waters carried more fish and supported more birdlife than in other areas of the forest. Even the swampy savannas of northern Bolivia were preferred over the Amazonian interior. When the first Europeans arrived on the continent, the Amazon forest, at least away from the rivers, was the most sparsely populated area of South America, probably having no more than 0.2 persons per square kilometer.

In the lowlands, it was the dense populations on the Brazilian coast and along the Amazon River that most fascinated the first European explorers. These explorers saw the Indians either as enemies to be destroyed or as pawns in their battles with other Europeans vying for the new land. Few were interested in their cultures. Hans Staden, a humble German sailor working for the Portuguese, was captured in 1554 by the Tupinambá Indians near the present site of Rio de Janeiro. Several times he narrowly escaped being eaten by the cannibals in one of their rituals. After living with the Indians for more than nine months he finally escaped to describe his adventures "for the glory of God." His detailed accounts are among the first written descriptions of South American Indian cultures.*

*Hans Staden made two trips to Brazil, one in 1547 and the other in 1550. It was on this second trip that he was captured by the Tupinambá Indians. His accounts, originally published in 1557 in German, Flemish, Dutch, Latin, French, English, and Portuguese, have been republished several times over the centuries. A recent Portuguese edition includes detailed notes by historians and anthropologists: *Duas viagens ao brasil*. Editora da Universidade de São Paulo. Livraria Itatiaia Editora Ltda. 1974.

A popular Brazilian film entitled *Como era gostoso o meu frances* (How Delicious Was My Frenchman) is based on Hans Staden's accounts and occasionally appears in New York and other U.S. cities.

The Tupinambá lived in fortified communities surrounded by a double row of palisades. The heads of their enemies were placed on poles at the village entrance. Wearing carved stones hanging from the holes in their lower lips, they fished with spears and nets in the ocean, and went off on warring expeditions in their long bark canoes. Using spears, arrows, and the smoke from burning pepper to drive out their enemies, they brought their captives back to their villages to be mocked by the women and children. Sometimes they gave the prisoners wives, who guarded them and took care of them until the day when they were sacrificed and eaten. Any children born of these marriages were raised as any other village children until the day when they too were killed and eaten. The cannibalistic feasts were rituals of anger against the enemy.

The Tupinambá were not the only group to intrigue the first Europeans in Brazil. From the Indians, Hans Staden had already heard about the women warriors to the north. When Carvajal went up the Amazon River in 1542 he observed these female "captains," who held the front positions in battle and clubbed to death any of the men who dared turn their backs. The event was impressive enough to give the entire area the name of the mythical Greek women who also excelled in war. The narrow strip of rich Amazon floodland was heavily populated in those days by two Indian civilizations, the Tapajós and the Omagua. The Tapajós lived farther downstream in villages tightly arranged next to each other. At the mouth of the river named after them was their capital, a city that could muster 60,000 warriors. The Omagua, with their foreheads flattened since childhood by boards tied to their heads, lived farther upstream in large villages with houses made of cedar planks. They raised tortoises captured from the Amazon River, and raided the sparse interior tribes for children, whom they treated as slaves. Their earthly ruler was called the same as "god."

As highly developed as these societies were, they could not survive the onslaught of the European invasion. Many Indians died in battles with the newcomers, and even more succumbed to illnesses for which they had no resistance. Over the years, epidemics of smallpox, measles and even the common cold ravaged their lands. From what was probably a native population of five million when Europeans discovered the area, the Amazonian population has tumbled to a fragile 500,000 Indians today.

It was the simpler interior groups that survived into the twentieth century. They lived in small villages or in houses dispersed throughout the jungle and hunted paca, tapir, and deer to add to the food from their simple gardens. Outsiders were not very interested in what seemed to them uninteresting cultures and an inhospitable place to make a living, but eventually civilization began to invade even these groups. In some areas, it was the presence of wild forest products like rubber or Brazil nuts that attracted the invaders. Elsewhere it was pasture for cattle, or agricultural land for growing coffee or cocoa. Almost half of the Indian groups in contact with one of these economic frontiers in 1900 were extinct by 1957. Even among those that avoided direct contact, 20 percent became extinct, mostly because they fell to the epidemics that made their way into their territory even before the invaders.

The fights between the encroaching outsiders and the Indians were so severe that, among the rubber gatherers along the southern tributaries of the Amazon, one man had to stand guard with a rifle in case of Indian attack while another drew out the latex sap. Agriculturalists sometimes put gun traps around their houses and fields in case any Indians wandered nearby, or they poisoned the water with strychnine and gave the Indians the contaminated clothes of smallpox victims. In some places, even in the twentieth century, captured Indians were sold as slaves. And professional Indian-killers hired by farmers or by construction firms became regional heroes. Sometimes these killers sold war "trophies"—parts of their victims' bodies—as a sideline. Sometimes they turned one Indian group against another to let the Indians do the killing. As recently as 1963 an airplane swooped over one Indian village, using a machine gun and dropping dynamite to exterminate the villagers. Some Indians were remarkably passive in the face of these massacres. One group was so timid that ranchers began to see the Indians as harmless animals they could kill for sport in their free time.

Other Indians fought back. At first they attacked with bows and arrows while hidden in the forest, but soon most stole enough guns to make their attacks more murderous. As they tried to hide deeper in the forest, some groups dug holes and filled them with pointed stakes hoping the deadly traps would discourage the invaders, or they mined the paths with sharp sticks.

Even their resistance eventually wore down; there were just too many foreigners. Seeing their enemies multiply, one Indian group reasoned that whites must regenerate after they are killed. How else could their increasing numbers be explained? They decided to cut off the heads and genitals of their victims in the hopes that this would prevent their coming back to life. But the onslaught continued even so. As the old coffee plantations lost their fertility, the agriculturalists had to look for new frontiers. With their rubber trees chopped down, the latex gatherers also had to move on. And the ranchers had to look for greener pastures.

The southern part of Pará was labeled by some anthropologists in the late fifties and early sixties as the last frontier for Brazilian expansion. The headwaters of the area's rivers had little to interest early settlers. The land was thought less fertile than lands farther west. It was flooded during several months every year, and the rivers were not easily navigable. Also, the area was inhabited by fierce Indians known as the Kayapo. Eventually even this area would be invaded by gold prospectors and cattle ranchers living along the Araguaia River to the east and by latex- and Brazil-nut-collecters from the north and west slowly putting a squeeze on the Indians' lands.

The region soon became known for the fierce battles between natives and whites, and the Kayapo groups that lived there earned a reputation as the most hated and feared Indians of all Brazil. Sensationalist headlines in São Paulo and Rio de Janeiro proclaimed the savagery of the forest tribes. Some of the violent stories were more mythical than real. The area's "civilized" residents delighted in exaggerating the assassinations of their hated enemies. According to one account, a man, alone in the forest, once killed an Indian who insulted him only to find himself confronted with a hundred angry warriors. For protection, he used a suitcase as a shield and began shooting at the Indians, until, single-handedly, he had massacred almost all of them. Actually, the man who supposedly carried out this extraordinary feat denied having ever seen any Indian footprints, let alone Indians, during his sojourn. But he told another story about a massacre he witnessed when a group of Indians were invited to a white man's feast in which an ox was killed for the revelers. When the Indians went to sleep at least twenty of them were killed by the whites.

Not all of the violent stories were exaggerations. The Kayapo were, indeed, one of the fiercest groups in all of Brazil. For years the Indians assaulted rubber-gatherers in their area, sometimes taking away captive women and children to join to their group. They attacked unexpectedly and quickly ran back to the forest. A nomadic people who wandered about in the vast area between the Araguaia and Tapajós Rivers, they were difficult to find, and seemingly more dangerous because of their unpredictability.

In the early part of the twentieth century there were a few honest attempts at pacifying the Kayapo, but these were not very successful. The first missionary to search out the Indians lost the wife of one of his Indian helpers to the Kayapo attackers. Later, a bishop managed to shout to the Indians from a distance before they fled to the forest. In 1935 three English missionaries, known as the "Three Freds," sailed up the Fresco River in an ill-fated adventure they knew would cost them their lives. In a letter written before their departure they revealed that they knew they would die, but asked not to be criticized, for they were on a religious mission. They were more interested in proving their worth in the eyes of God than in actually helping the Indians.

Later, another English missionary attempted to verify the disappearance of the "Three Freds." A young man with a love of the Indians, he managed to make peaceful contact with the Gorotire-Kayapo, and eventually set up a mission in which the Indians were treated equally with whites. The locals expected him to be killed, but to the astonishment of all his mission flourished.

Not all contacts with the Indians were so successful. Several Kayapo groups became extinct after pacification. At the end of the nineteenth century a group of priests at the present site of Conceição do Araguaia convinced the Brazilian settlers in the region to build a church that would also serve as a fortress against Indian attacks. Recognizing their military inferiority, one group of Kayapo, the Pau d'Arco, finally decided to cooperate with the whites. But the Pau d'Arco did not last long. Epidemics soon swept over their village. Once a proud tribe of fifteen hundred, they were rapidly reduced to a few isolated souls working on nearby ranches. Some of the priests who worked with the Kayapo thought it was better to let the Indians die in Brazilian hands than to allow them to return to the forest where they could not receive baptism and last rites.

Some native groups fared better than others, mostly by putting off contact as long as possible. By fleeing farther and farther from its navigable rivers, one Kayapo horde—the Mekranoti—avoided whites until 1953. Already in 1949 they had begun accepting gifts of metal knives, scissors, and other tools from Claudio Villas Boas, the famous Brazilian Indianist, nominated several times for the Nobel Peace Prize. But the contact between the two cultures was brief, only a shout across a river. Claudio was using the standard method to contact warring Indians, invented years before by General Cândido Mariano da Silva Rondon. On dangerous ventures out from a fortified base, Claudio laid out presents wherever he found traces of the natives in the forest—on the river bank where the Indians came to bathe, in favorite hunting spots, and in abandoned villages.

For four years Claudio patiently continued putting out presents for the Indians, achieving nothing more than an occasional glimpse of the natives as they scurried back into their forest retreat. Only in 1953, while the Indians were on trek near the Xingu River, far from their main village, did a few brave young men accept Claudio's invitation to accompany the Indianist to his campsite.

After this first peaceful encounter, part of the Mekranoti decided to remain with Claudio, where they could gain more presents. But when a cold epidemic struck, the other half ran off again to the forest interior. Here they remained until 1957 when another well-known Indianist, Chico Meirelles, sent a few pacified Kayapo as peace ambassadors to bring the Mekranoti west to the Curuá River. Knowing they would receive bountiful presents, the Indians accepted the offer, but quickly returned to their hiding spot.

It was only in 1966 that a missionary finally moved into their village and persuaded the Mekranoti to cut an airstrip from the forest. From that time on their relations with modern civilization have been more peaceful, although they still have no qualms about killing unwelcome foreigners who venture into their territory.

Like other Indians, the Mekranoti fought fiercely with rubber workers and Brazil-nut-gatherers and were decimated by colds, measles, and malaria. But they were blissfully ignorant of all the other treacherous cruelties their relatives had suffered, and they were rapidly recuperating their lost numbers. A proud people, they saw in their history not victims of progress, but fierce warriors who maintained their own in the dense forest, and even "pacified" the whites who from time immemorial had lived to the east and occasionally made timid forays into their habitat.

According to the Mekranoti, long ago the Indians once lived in a world above the sky where everything one could want was plentiful—sweet potatoes, corn, manioc and bananas. One day a man, hunting in the forest, discovered an armadillo's hole. Resolving to bring the game back to the village, he dug and dug until nightfall, but could not reach his prize. After several days of burrowing into the red earth, he finally sighted the giant armadillo. But in his excitement he punctured the celestial ceiling and the animal fell through the hole to another earth below. That world was just like the one above, full of palm trees, savannas, and rivers. The man returned to his village to tell the others of his discovery. After much discussion the Indians decided to move to the new world. Gathering together all the cotton cords they could find in the village, they made a giant rope to descend to the forest below. First went the young men, then the women with children on their hips, and finally the fathers and elders. Some people were afraid to come down and so remained in the world above. A child cut the rope, and then it was no longer possible for anyone else to descend to this world.

There are many other people on this lower layer of the universe as well—bat people, piranha people, and whites. This last group, too, has its origins in the mythical past. Whites were born when an Indian woman had sex with a monkey. This explains why they have so much hair on their bodies and faces. Because of the metal tools they use, whites are an especially impressive and dangerous people, although they are not very strong. Whites have curious habits like chopping down the trees in vast areas of the forest and placing giant animals on the land, eventually eating their pets. Sometimes they dig deep into the earth to find rocks they like. And sometimes they send people to live among the Indians, to gather arrows and other weapons to hang on their walls, or simply to visit out of curiosity.

# 2

# A FIRST GLIMPSE

The plane had been flying for two and a half hours over the Amazon valley. During the first half hour I occasionally saw cattle ranches on the ground, but afterwards there was only the quiet green of the forest interrupted now and then by a shimmering stream cutting across what looked from the air like a shag rug. The scenery had lulled me into a dreamy state. But as the tiny plane swooped down over the grassy airstrip, my stomach jumped into my chest. I caught my first glimpse of the Indians I would be studying for the coming year.

Naked children romped playfully among the tall grasses that almost hid them from view. Several women, wearing at most a few beads around their waists or necks, carried nursing infants like shoulder bags in woven straw slings. The men wore either swimming trunks or tiny grass sheaths that tied off their foreskins and made their penises point upwards. One woman held aloft a large black umbrella shading her from the bright sun. A man with a large red wooden disk stretching his perforated lower lip, and a baseball cap skewed to one side on his head, leaned nonchalantly against his shotgun. Somewhat stunned by the whole situation, I could not help thinking that they looked like characters from a Fellini movie.

I had been excited about this trip for more than a year before finally arriving in Brazil to do anthropological fieldwork. Now, as I was finally arriving at my destination, I began to think of all the events that led up to my coming to the middle of the Amazon jungle—years of university classes, papers on South American Indians, and finally, stressful grant applications.

While anxiously wondering if funds would come through, I pestered my friends with incessant talk of the possible adventure. In an attempt to assuage my anxieties one friend persuaded me to consult the I Ching to foretell the future. Although magic had never appealed to me before, I felt unexpectedly relieved when the sticks gave me the ideograph for "The Traveler."

Only years later would I understand this reaction. As people do in most societies, I was using magic to relieve anxiety about a subject that was unpredictable, uncontrollable, and important—research funds. But I would have to live a bit more with magic to realize its importance.

The grant was approved only a few weeks before the project was to begin. Together with two other anthropologists going into the field with me, I hectically made the rounds of New York camp-goods stores, and visited a few South Americanists to get practical advice on living in the Amazon. "Take along a lot of freeze-dried turkey tetrazzini," suggested one fish-hating anthropologist who had worked with river-dwelling Indians. "Don't buy serrated knives you can't sharpen," an experienced camper recommended. "And be sure to change dollars into cruzeiros before leaving the U.S.," warned a South Americanist familiar with the artificial exchange rates in Brazil. Heavy-laden with camp goods and valuable advice, my two companions and I boarded a 747 in the middle of February 1976, destined for Brazil.

Sunny Brasília was a welcome change from the cold New York winter, and a learning experience in itself. Built as a stimulus to development in Brazil's interior, it is one of the world's few planned cities. The climate is perfect—never too hot or cold, and there is not too much rain. The natural savannas that surround the city give a pasturelike look to the area, even though cattle have never grazed on much of the acidic grasses, where not many years ago Indians hunted deer and paca. But the vast majority of Brazilians detest the city. It is just too orderly, there is no action in the streets, and all the buildings look alike.

I once heard a peasant from Manaus complain that the city had copied its architecture from the poor along the Amazon River. "Houses in Brasília are all built on stilts just like our own," he pointed out. The entrance to virtually every apartment complex is an open landing with columns supporting the six floors of living space above. Unlike Amazonian huts, houses in

Brasília have basements for cars, and usually five or six bedrooms, including one for the maid. The poor live outside the city or else squat in the rat-infested apartments under construction. The designers neglected to think about them.

I waited more than two months to get permission from the Brazilian Indian Foundation (FUNAI) to go into Indian lands. Worried about bad foreign press, the government had declared off-limits to non-Brazilians all Indian communities within a hundred kilometers of any border, and I wondered if they were planning on a few other restrictions as well. While poring over documents about different Indian groups in the FUNAI library, I met Gustaaf Verswijver, a young Belgian anthropologist who had spent a couple of months among the Mekranoti-Kayapo of southern Pará. He suggested I go with him to the Mekranoti village. This way we could share the expenses of the plane trip. I had been thinking about the Kayapo and Gustaaf's reports about the Indians settled the matter. Like most anthropologists, I felt a little uneasy about "sharing" a group with an anthropological colleague, but my research would be fairly specific so I knew there would be plenty of things for both of us to study. Besides, it would be somewhat comforting to go into a village with someone who had a little experience.

Gustaaf, who seemed to know everybody in FUNAI, helped me get my permission, and told me what to buy for the Indians. Shotgun shells were good, but it was illegal for foreigners to buy any. The Indians also liked good-quality machetes—no one would want anything that was shoddy. Everyone liked small, dark blue beads or large white ones, but any other size or color would be rejected, Gustaaf pointed out, adding that a few pots might also be helpful.

Transportation plans were somewhat complicated. We started the trip on a bus headed for Belém near the mouth of the Amazon. It took a little maneuvering to get the driver to accept our many heavy bags. We also needed to get off at an unscheduled stop in a frontier town called Miranorte. When we arrived early in the morning in the dusty little village, several people noticed the rich "gringos" and made offers to take us to the next step in our journey, but no one seemed to have a vehicle with enough space for all of our things. Finally, we found someone with a truck who was willing to take us to Araguacema, a small town on the Araguaia River, just upstream from Conceição do Araguaia, the site of the ill-fated mission for the Pau d'Arco Kayapo. We were lucky it was the dry season. In the wet season the bridges wash out and the road is too muddy. After picking up additional passengers along the way, the driver, five hours later, left us sweaty, dirty, and tired in Araguacema.

Araguacema is an old town, by Brazilian frontier standards. Originally a river port, it now connects with the outside world through the road to Miranorte. Sometimes wealthy businessmen from São Paulo or Rio fly their private planes there to fish on the Araguaia River. Now, in the dry season, some of the broad river's beaches stretched out to connect with sandbars in the middle of the watercourse. Even now the river was a powerful stream, but with the rains its strong current discouraged even the local residents from venturing out in rowboats. One group of Indians tells a story of how, when fleeing from whites, it was river porpoises who showed them how to cross the dangerous waterway.

We had to wait a day or two for our pilot to schedule a trip to the Mekranoti village. We took advantage of the time to talk to some of the locals. They were impressed that we planned to work with Indians. "Wild ones, or tame ones?" they always asked, expressing their own view of how the "animals" ought to be treated. Most of them had already met some of the pacified Kayapo on the other side of the river, and some had heard of fights with warring groups. Looking at their own houses of mud walls and thatched roofs, I could not help thinking that their prejudice stemmed from a desire to separate themselves from the Indians, whose villages looked all too much like their own.

The hotel where we stayed had humble but delicious food. Typical for Amazonia, dinner always included fish, fowl, and a mammal (beef, wild pig, armadillo, or paca). We could bathe only at night because water was pumped with electricity available in town only from seven o'clock until ten o'clock each evening. During the hot day a swim in the Araguaia River was irresistible, so I decided to join some children splashing about in a small inlet. I noticed that some of them had large ugly scars on their legs, obviously from stingrays, but I reasoned that with so many people in the river the rays must surely have left the spot where I was swimming. I was in the water for only a few minutes when I overheard the children talking about a poisonous snake they had seen swim into some weeds two feet from where they were playing. I promptly decided I was not quite as hot as I thought and splashed out of the water.

It was with apprehension that Gustaaf and I finally boarded the small plane for the Mekranoti village. Part of our anxiety was for the fieldwork we would be doing, but part came from worries over money. The pilot told us we had to pay for the thousand-dollar trip even if we failed to land or to find the village. Weather was the main problem. With too much rain the grassy Mekranoti airstrip is too slippery for landing. With too many clouds, no one can see the village. (It was only months later that a satellite photo would clarify the village's location—54 degrees 13 minutes west longitude, 8 degrees 39 minutes south latitude.)

An hour after our plane crossed the Xingu River, Gustaaf spotted a garden at the point where the Rio Rasgado flows into the Sabují. The tiny garden looked only slightly different from the unending forest—a more yellowish, lighter green with lower trees. We felt relieved knowing that the Mekranoti village had to be nearby. As our plane passed over a small hill, a small circle of thatched houses surrounding an earthy gray plaza came suddenly into view. It would have been easy to miss. No wonder there are still undiscovered Indians in the area.

From the air the village, even though tiny, looked like a bastion of civilization in the endless jungle. The central plaza was clean and the neat thatched roofs stood out, carefully isolated from the trimmed nearby forest. Only a few papaya trees near the houses interrupted the smooth village clearing. Already we could see some of the Indians rushing out of their houses to look at the airplane above.

As we circled several times while the pilot tested the wind, I grew queasy. Now that there was no way of turning back, the scene below was more fearful. The village looked awfully small. I though of how I would need to depend on its people for food, shelter, and company for a year. There would be no way to call for help if I needed it. As I watched the naked Indians run to the nearby airstrip to greet us, all of the self-doubts I had avoided up to now rushed uncontrollably into my head. What if they didn't like me? How would I carry out any of the studies I wanted to do if they refused to talk to me? Or worse, they could decide not to feed me, or could even kill me outright as they had done in the not too distant past with those who displeased them.

As the plane taxied to a halt, I tried to gather my senses. When the plane stopped, I sat up straight and watched more attentively as the Indians drew closer to peer in at the goods we had brought. At first I thought some of them were wearing clothes. But then I realized they were simply painted with delicate black stripes that looked strangely like leotards and tights. The black genipap dye came to an end at the sternum, looking like a T-shirt with a low neckline, and the unpainted feet and hands gave the appearance of a cuff. Some of the Indians had shaved the tops of their heads, making them bald on top, and both men and women had plucked out all of their facial hair, including eyebrows and eyelashes.

Gustaaf was the first to step outside. Several women, holding their forearms across their bowed heads, wailed loudly. Seemingly unperturbed by the piercing shrieks, their babies continued suckling contentedly on their mothers' breasts while holding loosely onto the sitting sling hanging from their mothers' shoulders. This keening, I later found out, could mean many different things, including the death of a loved one. But on this occasion the wails were simply welcoming cries for Gustaaf's return. Gustaaf reciprocated with heavy backslaps to some of the men, who shouted loudly to each other, as they passed the news of our arrival in the village. The expansive welcomes made me feel awkward.

The Indians seemed to know exactly what to do. With little hesitation or discussion the young men loaded our heavy goods onto their backs, and marched single file out of the airstrip. Surrounded by curious Indians trying to talk to me in a language I could not understand, I followed the group along the broad grassy path, elegantly lined with tall papaya trees. Within a few minutes we had reached the village plaza.

From the ground the village looked less exotic. The houses had a more lived-in look, and the plaza was not quite as clean as it appeared from the air. The "men's house" in the village center looked even more worn than the other buildings. The walls of split saplings placed vertically side by side let the sun pass through the slats, tracing stripes of light and shadow on the ground from the afternoon sun. There was an opening on each side of the rectangular structure, and men seemed to walk constantly in and out. But I had little time to look around before being shuffled into the house of the FUNAI medical attendant.

We would be spending the night here, Gustaaf informed me. Later, the Indians would prepare us a house of our own. The FUNAI house was like most of the other houses in the village. A thatch roof covered a mud-walled structure with a clay floor. But unlike other Mekranoti houses, the FUNAI dwelling had walls to separate bedrooms, a kitchen, and a pharmacy. It also had windows—really just holes where mud was not thrown into the interstices of the wattled walls, giving the spaces a delicate latticed look. At the moment, the only other outsider in the village was Ronaldo, the FUNAI medical attendant. (Later, other visitors would come and go—two missionaries, other FUNAI personnel and even a Brazilian peasant family—but I would be too busy with the Indians to pay much attention to them.)

Ronaldo asked us for our papers as soon as we arrived. We had landed on April 30th, a day before our permissions allowed, but no one saw any problem with this. Still, Ronaldo had to start up the rickety gasoline generator located in a separate hut behind his house to give him the electricity needed to send off a radio message telling his superiors of our arrival. A short young man from Belém, Ronaldo had been with the Mekranoti for three years. He had worked previously in other Indian villages, and felt secure with the Mekranoti during the many months he'd spent alone with them. Ronaldo seemed pleased to have us for company, and talked excitedly about everything.

We were quickly filled in on some of the recent events in the village. A young man had died the day before our arrival. The man had been in poor health for more than a week before his death, and Ronaldo tried to get his superiors to send in a plane to take the patient to a hospital. Every day FUNAI made promises but failed to come through. As happens all too often in this isolated part of the world, the plane arrived only after the man's death. The Indians complained about the worthlessness of their *kuben* (foreign) tutors and threatened to go back to their warlike past. Ronaldo had heard these laments before and hoped they would soon pass. Our arrival seemed to calm some of their nerves.

Even as our goods were being unloaded in one of the extra rooms, Indians came by to give us presents of yams, bananas, manioc flour, and papaya. One man mumbled a few words and shoved us some meat through a window before disappearing into the crowd. "It's jaguar," Gustaaf reported. We handed the food to Ronaldo, who gave it to a young Indian to cook. Gustaaf and I hung up our hammocks amidst the curious stares of a roomful of talkative and laughing Indians. Some of the women simply plopped themselves down against the mud walls of the room, their babies lying across their laps. The dirt floor must have been cold against their naked skin, but they seemed not to mind at all. They were not going to miss anything that these curious white men would do. Toddlers waddled back and forth between the women. Older children stopped to stare wide-eyed at the bizarre outsiders, before rushing off again to play. A few of the men also sat along the walls or even in the center of the room. And from the outside less aggressive Indians looked on through the wooden grates of the windows.

Some of the Indians simply sat quietly, observing everything, while others chatted loudly. I understood nothing of what they said, but I could tell they were making jokes at our expense. Sometimes they pointed to us with their noses, or even walked up to touch us, or our clothes, but the laughter seemed good-humored so I really didn't care.

After years of reading anthropological accounts, I had expected this undue attention and was even content with the feeling that everything was going "as planned." The Indians obviously enjoyed our presence, even if only to make jokes about us. Gustaaf laughed at my troubles in setting up a mosquito net around my hammock. But a young Mekranoti, feeling pity for me, eventually took charge of the whole operation and set it up in no time. His helpfulness assured me that my stay would be fine.

Our next order of business, according to Gustaaf, was to take some gifts to Tàkàkrorok and Pãxkê, the two main chiefs in the village. I decided to present an ax head to each. To establish a good reputation, Gustaaf also thought it would be wise to give Tàkàkrorok a number of smaller items to redistribute to the rest of the villagers. So, as the Indians crowded around me, I searched through my bags for combs, cups, small knives, rubber sandals, and beads to give away. Unfortunately, the small items I needed were not on top, so I had to unpack everything to get to them. The Indians examined carefully every item I brought out. Gustaaf complained that I should not reveal my trade goods and insisted I be more careful in the future. I was not quite sure why I should hide these articles from the Indians, as everything would eventually end up in their hands anyway. But I reasoned it was best to trust in Gustaaf's judgment since he had already spent time in the village. Eventually I got a collection of presents together, and the two of us headed off for the structure called the *ngà* (men's house) in the center of the plaza.

The Indians who had been watching us since our arrival followed behind. The procession we created attracted the attention of the other villagers, and soon we were surrounded by a noisy mob as we all stepped into the darkness inside the men's house. The crowd opened up for Tàkàkrorok to pass through. A tall, lean man with wavy black hair and a large smooth face, Tàkàkrorok looked a lot younger than his sixty-odd years. Unlike most of the other men he did not wear a lip disk, but had only a small hole in his lower lip where he was punctured as a child. Physically, he was not at all what I expected of an Indian chief. I anticipated an ancient man with a pipe in his mouth and a serious demeanor—something like the Indian chiefs from all the cowboy movies I had seen. There were a few men in the crowd who fit this image well. But Tàkàkrorok looked sportier than this. His wry smile verged on impishness, and his gait was fast and determined.

In the dark of the overcrowded men's house, Tàkàkrorok received our gifts and spread them out on a woven straw mat placed on the ground before him. Squatting on the dirt floor behind the mat, he picked up the various articles, and mulled over them in silence. Then, after looking briefly at the people in the crowd, he announced a name and held an item in the air. Returning his glance to the goods on the mat, Tàkàkrorok could not even see the person who picked up the gift from his hand. The other Indians chatted and joked good-humoredly with each other while awaiting Tàkàkrorok's pronouncements.

I thought the whole process took an extraordinarily long time and felt guilty about wasting people's energy on such cheap trinkets. But the Indians themselves seemed pleased with the presents. At least no one complained to us, and most people smiled.

After this spree, we walked over to Pãxkê's hut, behind the first row of village houses and closer to the FUNAI building. A gruff burly man, Pãxkê had none of Tàkàkrorok's elegance. His chin had a large unsightly hole where once he had worn a lip disk. Like several of the men, he had FUNAI surgeons sew the aperture partly shut, but the hole never really closed. Since a few days after his birth, when his lip was first pierced, his mother had been stretching the opening so that it would eventually accommodate a balsa wood disk three or four inches in diameter. A few men still wore the brightly painted red plates that stood tightly against their noses when they smiled, or vibrated threateningly in front when angry. The disks still had an exotic charm about them, but after operation the holes that remained were ugly deformities from which saliva constantly dripped.

The hole in Pãxkê's lower lip looked even more unkempt than usual because of the stray chin hairs he failed to pluck off his broad face. Wearing only a pair of unwashed shorts, Pãxkê smiled as we approached him, somewhat surprised at our visit. He accepted our gifts and then returned quickly to his house with only the fewest of words to Gustaaf, asking how long our visit would be.

There were still some Indians with us when Gustaaf and I returned to the FUNAI building, but the darkening skies sent many people home. Ronaldo was busy helping a young man prepare our dinner. The wind would alternately put out the fire on the makeshift clay stove or fan it into dangerous flames that could burn down the entire village if ever they caught on the thatch roof. "It's important to get the right kind of wood to burn," Ronaldo informed me. "Otherwise the fire is too irregular and can get out of control."

Our food was simple but good—the jaguar boiled in salted water and served with manioc flour, with canned guava paste for dessert. The meat tasted like a greasy stewing beef or oxtail, and seemed familiar. But the manioc flour was different from any I had tried before. Made by toasting the grated root of the cassava plant, manioc flour if usually finely ground to give it a consistency (and flavor) like sawdust. But the Mekranoti do not bother to remove all of the fibers or to grind the final product into tiny granules. Instead, they simply leave the flour in the form of hard stonelike pellets that are impossible to eat unless soaked in juice or saliva. When I first tried the finely ground Brazilian flour I thought it tasted terrible, but eventually I grew to like it. I was confident I could like the Mekranoti version as well.

I had not minded the crowds during the day, but now I was beginning to get annoyed at all of the stares. The Indians stood against the walls with their arms folded over their chests. They were obviously planning on staring at us all night. Watching everything we did, the young men sometimes commented to each other about our actions, and then laughed. They made no effort to hide the fact that we were the subject of their conversation. I could not help thinking they were mocking our table manners.

Eating, like other body functions, has a personal quality to it, and doing it in front of the Indians made me feel embarrassed. Things might have been different if the Indians ate with us, but they didn't. Occasionally Ronaldo or Gustaaf would talk a bit to one of the onlookers, but I understood nothing that was said. I felt especially awkward when Ronaldo gave a few Indians a piece of guava paste from his plate.

Several of the day's events had made me feel like an eighteenth-century English explorer who had arrived uninvited in one of the crown colonies and ordered the natives to work for him. First, there was the line of Indians carrying our bags on their backs to FUNAI headquarters. Then we made a show of generosity in giving out cheap trinkets. Later we were served by Ronaldo's helper at the table. Now we were giving the Indians crumbs from their masters' table.

Ronaldo and Gustaaf did not seem to notice the class distinctions we were setting up. As with many Brazilians, they were accustomed to maids and found nothing strange in being served by so many Indians. But I was not at all interested in setting myself apart from the people I came to study. I hoped soon to become a more normal part of the community.

The crowd of onlookers began to shrink after nine o'clock and by ten there was no one left. The Mekranoti usually go to bed between eight and nine, a custom I found difficult to accept at first. New York City's nightlife had given me a sleeping schedule quite different from theirs. But the calm of the evening, the lack of electric lights, and the exhaustion I felt after the day's excitement made going to bed at ten seem like a reasonable idea. I had never actually slept in a hammock before, but I knew enough to arrange myself diagonally across the sling in order to make a flatter bed. Since the night was cool I needed a few blankets, both underneath and on top. It took a bit of struggling with the hammock, blankets, and mosquito net to get myself comfortable, but once everything was in order I felt good. Gustaaf blew out the kerosene lamp, and I was left to think through the day's activities. A few bats whizzed past my ear, trying to get as close as possible without touching. But I felt snug and secure wrapped in my blankets and surrounded by the mosquito net.

In the distance I could hear the wistful sound of a flute. The tune was simple and hypnotic. The flute-player trilled slowly the two upper notes, a whole tone apart, and then sensuously touched a third tone, a whole step below, before falling to a mysterious, dark diminished fifth. The music floated gently like a breeze in the cool night air. I imagined the Indians' lives would be as simple and complex as that far-off lilting melody, so enticingly unassuming and yet so hard to capture, or remember.

The music was soothing. Living with the Indians would be good, I felt, as I reflected briefly on the day's events, before falling off into a good night's sleep.

# 3

# SETTLING IN

Awakened by the sound of giggling voices around me, I opened one eye. At first, I could see only the delicate patterns of light and shadow on the floor as the bright sun filtered through the latticed windows. Gradually I left my dreams behind and realized I was actually living in a far more fantastic place than the one I had been dreaming about. Glancing up from my hammock, I could see several Indians watching me from the windows. Using their noses, they pointed to different things in the room and then laughed to each other. When they saw I was awake they smiled a friendly greeting. I wanted to greet them in return, but had no idea how. I simply smiled back, and gathered my senses while remaining inside the mosquito net.

Surrounded by curious onlookers, Gustaaf and I got dressed and went off to enjoy a breakfast of leftovers from the previous night. There were fewer Indians watching us, but they made more attempts to communicate. Gustaaf translated. "They want to know what you're going to give them. Just say '*adjym*,' " he advised. "It means 'later.' " I tried the new word a few times but was met with cold stares. The Indians were familiar with the trick and did not approve. Gustaaf warned that I would be plagued with requests throughout my entire stay in the village.

After breakfast Ronaldo had to attend to his medical duties, and Gustaaf went off to make arrangements for our house. This left me alone with the Mekranoti for the first time. Frustrated with their requests for goods, a few Indians tried to talk about other matters. Unfortunately, I could understand nothing else. A fat young woman with a jolly face pointed to objects in the room and slowly pronounced Kayapo words. Thankful for the opportunity to learn Kayapo, I tried to repeat her speech, but encountered laughter after everything I said. On second and third tries the laughter grew more and more intense and I soon realized I would never learn the language like this. The Indians were out for amusement; they cared nothing about my linguistic abilities. Still, the laughter was far preferable to the cold stares I got at breakfast, and I began to feel more at ease with the Indians.

Gustaaf returned shortly afterwards with information about our future lodgings. We would be living in the village's rice granary, near Tàkàkrorok's house. The structure was smaller than most Mekranoti dwellings, but after years of sharing studio apartments in New York City, it looked large to me. Some of the bachelors gathered saplings that they lashed into the walls to keep out dogs and chickens. Others took a wheelbarrow to the river to bring back mud for the floor. With a latrine in back and a makeshift clay stove, our house would be complete in a few days.

In the meantime, we decided to make some visits to people at home. Before leaving Brasília I had copied Gustaaf's census data, so I already knew the names of many Mekranoti and even some of their kinsmen, but I could not connect any of the names with faces. Visiting people at home seemed like a good way to meet them in an environment where I would remember them.

The Mekranoti houses were dark, windowless structures up to thirty feet long and fifteen feet wide, with high vaulted ceilings giving a cathedral-like feel to the spacious single room below. Blackened with the thick tar from years of household fires kept burning day and night, the thatched roofs housed myriads of harmless and not-so-harmless arthropods. Giant forest roaches crawled over the beams, and once in a while an eight-inch tarantula fell to the ground. Snakes sometimes made their way into the grassy ceilings, looking for the mice that infested many of the houses and could be heard or seen late at night.

On long cords hanging from the ceiling the Indians stored their bags or baskets of shotgun shells, beads, and prized ceremonial ornaments made of mollusk shells, reeds, and feathers. Usually a bunch of ripening green bananas also hung from the ceiling in the house's corner, along with baskets of cassava roots or grated manioc flour. Sometimes pet macaws or parrots paced back and forth on the house beams or on the high shelves the Indians liked to build along the mud-wattled walls to store their water pots or prized garden fruits like papaya, pineapple, or pumpkin.

When we entered the houses we found people sitting on the floor or on one of the many sleeping platforms built from split saplings and covered with straw mats. The beds were built just high enough off the ground to be out of jumping range of the fleas that infested the mud floors. Usually a single large platform was reserved for mother, father, and young children. Old women sometimes shared one of the hard beds with their unmarried daughters. A few families had Brazilian hammocks stretched across a corner, but these were used mostly during the day for lounging about. Only the older boys who had to spend the nights in the men's house in the village center slept in hammocks, although a young man would sometimes set up his bedding in his girlfriend's house for a night of sexual adventures.

Between the platforms women tended the small fires used for cooking during the day and for warmth at night. The smoke-filled air made my eyes water, and because the ashes on the floor were overrun with annoying fleas, I learned quickly not to sit, but rather to squat, leaning slightly forward with the weight on the balls of my feet. We received gifts of food everywhere we went. Usually people offered us fresh meat, but sometimes we got partially eaten scraps from the banana leaves people were using as plates when we walked in on them. Apparently having nothing else to give, they seemed embarrassed at their offerings.

I met many new people during those first few days, but because I could speak very little Kayapo, there was little we could talk about. Not remembering anything they said, I was nowhere close to remembering the 285 new faces. But I did remember a few people, like Mrytàmti, the old man who talked so quietly that even if I had spoken Kayapo I would not have understood him. He was sitting alone staring into space when we walked in on him, but greeted us with a gentle, friendly smile and offered us some meat. Mrytàmti fit my image of a tribal leader much better than Tàkàkrorok. With an ancient, quiet face that appeared full of wisdom, he seemed absolutely sure of everything he said. At night he sometimes gave speeches to the villagers, but he was not, I was told, one of the main leaders. The other people stuck much less well in my memory. I needed to talk with them first. It would be months before I could get them all straight, and even then I would never learn all of the children.

Frustrated with both the language and people's names, I resolved to gather some data that required my knowing neither. Although I had no good reason for needing it, I decided to make a map of the village. I could at least occupy my time until I figured out how to handle the more important matters. So using a compass, a ruler, and a measuring tape, I spent the next few days calculating angles, and pacing from the men's house in the village center to each of the twenty-four residences surrounding it. When I had just about finished, Gustaaf asked me how I had been handling the dogs. "Why?" I asked. "Well," he answered, "they usually attack people near the houses. Haven't they bothered you?" Up to that point I had had no trouble, and wondered what he meant. But the next time I went out I found out.

Although the Mekranoti love their dogs, mourning their deaths and threatening people who might inadvertently harm them, they keep the pets half-starved and beat them mercilessly. This makes for good hunting animals, but also creates vicious, psychotic personalities. Whenever one dog begins an attack, the other village curs join in. Sometimes there is nothing to attack at all, but the dogs make a mad rush out of the houses and bark at the air just the same. On my next mapping trip I found myself surrounded by at least twenty snapping and snarling animals. Fortunately, the villagers rushed to my aid, grabbing their dogs and taking them back to the houses. I never figured out how I managed to escape attack during those first few days. Maybe my own naiveté protected me from the beasts at first; then they later picked up on my nervousness. Maybe the Indians simply watched me more closely at first and kept their dogs away from me. In any case, from that day forward I always carried a stick to protect me while crossing the village. I was bitten only once.

We conversed little during those first few weeks, but the Indians gradually came to recognize me as part of the community, and soon I received a new name from one of the elders. He simply walked by my hut one day and in front of the others declared that I was to be called Beproti. The name was a "good" name, usually awarded only with a special ceremony sponsored by one's parents, but I was given it as an honorary distinction. Since Gustaaf had only a "common" name, the Indians felt obligated to award him a special name as well. He was christened Bepita, and we both became respected members of the community.

I could not help thinking that this bestowal of honors had a great deal to do with all of the goods we brought in. The constant haranguing for presents began to wear on me. Sometimes I felt like a battered vending machine that gives out goods when kicked hard enough. At one point an old woman went into a screaming rampage. She had been giving me food and firewood since I arrived, she complained, but I always refused her requests. Instead, I gave to people who never gave me anything at all.

I was tempted to give everything away at once and trust to people's generosity. But I remembered an anthropologist who lavished all of his trade goods on the Indians as soon as he arrived in their village. Soon afterwards he found himself without food, and was forced to go out hunting every day to fend for himself. Hunting alone, or with only a child to keep an eye on him, he was able to learn very little. I wanted to avoid that mistake.

True, the village missionaries freed themselves of all their goods as soon as they arrived among the Mekranoti. But they gave only to those who had "earned" the articles during their previous visits. After years of the missionaries' comings and goings, the Indians knew they could count on their benefactors, but I was new in the village and the Mekranoti had no reason to trust me. Also, I needed to interview everyone, and could not play economic favorites like the missionaries who worked with only a few people. I would have to come up with a system of my own.

After several weeks of harassment, I finally hit upon a solution. Whenever anyone brought me anything I wrote it down on a five-by-eight card that I had prepared for that person. Later, when asked for a present, I could look at this card before deciding whether to give or not, and could record my gifts there as well. If people complained about unfairness, I cited examples of what they and others had given me, and what I had given them. The Indians soon caught on to my record-keeping. By the end of my stay they would ask what they could give in order to receive one of my trade items. In a deal, I could trade a large metal pot for two hunks of meat, a load of firewood, and a formal two-hour interview in my hut. The arrangement was more mercantile than I might have wanted, but it worked. Instead of being a vending machine, I became as human as any town storekeeper.

My days gradually became routine. On awakening I joined the men in the cool early morning air, as they dragged themselves half asleep to the men's house in the village center, and then curled up on the bare floor, with legs and arms wrapped around each other for warmth. At first I found their intimacy surprising. I expected warriors to be coldly formal, but here they were looking like lovers, stroking each other's skin and whispering into each other's ears. Sometimes they formed tight clusters, one man lying behind the next, legs and arms in a confusing tangle.

Several times Gustaaf and I joined the men on the floor, but the fleas bothered us too much, so we usually remained seated or squatting. The morning conversations were slow and usually ended rapidly as the men ate the breakfast of cold leftovers brought them by their female relatives, and then went off hunting.

Most of the mornings and afternoons we visited people in their houses, or received them in our own hut. At these times the men's house was nearly empty except for a few elders weaving baskets, sleeping mats, or handicrafts to sell to FUNAI. The large open structure was more lively at night. Then, while some of the men lounged on the hammocks of the boys who slept there, the older men excitedly recounted their day's hunting activities. Sometimes an elder would grab his bows and arrows or a club, and begin a long animated story about some past war adventure. He would act out all the parts—the fearful enemy, the brave Kayapo warriors, and the screaming children. The accounts were dramatic and well acted, but I understood little of what was said. I grew ever more frustrated at the communication gap.

Besides the isolation caused by the language problem, I also began to feel claustrophobic. The surrounding forest blocked out any kind of view. Since arriving among the Mekranoti, the farthest away I had ever looked was from one end of the airstrip to the other. The view across the village plaza was even more restricted. The inner circle of twelve houses was so tightly packed that only a few inches separated some of the roofs. I longed to get out and see something, but there was nowhere to go. Finally I resolved to visit some gardens. Getting out of the village would be a good change from the daily routine. Maybe I could even gather some useful information. After arranging with a young man to accompany us, Gustaaf and I set off through the forest.

Keeping up with our guide required running at times. The path was narrow and branched off at various points, so I was determined to keep up for fear of getting lost in the jungle. Just outside the village the secondary growth was thick around us, but as we entered the virgin forest the ground became clearer. Huge trees towered above us, blocking the sun and inhibiting the growth of underbrush. A few lianas connected some of the large branches and sometimes dangled just above our heads where they had been hacked off by an Indian on an earlier trip. Once in a while, when the path descended into a hollow, we saw thick trees with their roots high above the ground like the flying buttresses of a cathedral. In the rainy season, when the land was flooded, the open-air roots kept the tree high above the water. Occasionally I had to stop at a stream to take off my shoes and socks, but ended up getting everything wet anyway. Eventually I just gave up and walked right through the streams.

Along the way our guide pointed to various plants and pronounced names for each of them. I tried to take notes, but my efforts were utterly useless. I could come nowhere close to identifying the plants and we moved so fast I could write nothing down—not even in poorly understood, phonetic Kayapo. Finally, we climbed a rocky hill and arrived at the garden's edge.

I was struck by the difference in temperature between the cool shaded forest and the hot open gardens. I began to resent the heat, which up to this time had never bothered me. The gardens were planted in concentric rings: in the center was a patch of sweet potatoes, surrounded by a circle of manioc, then circles of bananas and papaya on the outside. To get to the low sweet-potato vines in the center, we had to squeeze through the dense six-foot manioc plants. We hacked our way from one garden to the next. I tried to write down the names of the garden plot owners as our guide told them to me. I also tried to draw the gardens on a crude map, although I had little confidence in my mapping abilities.

Finally we came to forest again. As our guide started off on a trail, I asked if we were going to visit more gardens. He announced we were on our way home. I was hoping to check my crude map on the return trip through the gardens, so I asked if we could return by the same route. When the guide announced that this *was* the return trail I was crestfallen. I thought we had been trudging in a straight line from one garden plot to the next, when in reality we had made a circle around to our starting position. I despaired of ever getting an accurate count, let alone a map, of Mekranoti gardens.

On our return to the village I decided to ask people about their fields rather than visit the plots in the forest. I figured out how to say "Where are your gardens?" and "How old are they?" and went around from one household to the next asking questions. Since the women did most of the agricultural labor, I thought they would be the best informants But the responses I got were incomprehensible. The Indians' ideas about ownership were very different from the ones I was used to. Several women would claim the same gardens as their own, and it was impossible to sort out the mess. Also, I had neglected the whole problem of defining what a garden was. The Mekranoti cut clearings from the forest and planted gardens that lasted several years afterwards. As weeds began to take over, the forest returned, bit by bit, leaving nothing but a few banana trees and eventually nothing at all. Just when a garden ceased to exist was impossible to determine.

It was only months later that I finally solved the problem. I did not really need a map. I needed to know only how many gardens there were. Since the Mekranoti were clear about who cut garden plots from the forest, I simply found out how many gardens were cut each year, and from there could calculate how many gardens of different ages there were altogether. After measuring garden productivity of a few gardens I could then figure out the total Mekranoti garden yield.

Having gathered no apparently useful data during the first few weeks in the field, I began to feel anxious about my work. But, in retrospect, these early weeks did acquaint me with daily routines and with people.

One of the first Indians I got to know was Kukrytbam, a young man whom Gustaaf saddled into helping us set up house. For a while Kukrytbam fetched water and firewood and even did the cooking on the stove he had made. He also repaired things and put the finishing touches on our house, adding tables and finely carved hardwood benches as we needed them. A friendly and open young man, he tried to talk to me and I learned a few words for things around the house.

A robust young man with curly hair, Kukrytbam was one of the older members of his age-grade, and also one of the smartest. He rarely got angry and was well liked by the others. During our stay he built up a reputation as a hard worker. Some suggested that perhaps he was growing interested in securing a wife.

At night Kukrytbam's friends often visited us in the house. They were all members of his age-grade, a group of young men from fifteen to twenty-five years old who had passed puberty, but still had no children. Collectively known as the *norny*, they loved to look at the pictures we had brought in, especially the pictures of other Indian groups and of young women. They commented extensively on them, joking about sexual details with each other. At the time I understood little of the conversations, but I didn't really mind since the men were pleasant company just the same.

The *norny* were a close group, always traveling around together during the day and sitting beside each other in the evenings on a log in a corner of the men's house. At night they hung up their hammocks, one beside the other—hammocks that were tucked away out of sight under the roof rafters during the day but cluttered the men's house at night. In the past, young men had remained *norny* until they were older, and they were an even tighter group than today.

Once they even formed their own separate village after a fight with the elders. The *norny* had been saddled with the job of constructing a new men's house. After they finished, some of the old men complained that the building was poorly made. This angered the *norny*, who began furiously to tear down their structure. A few of the elders then attacked the young men with clubs and soon everyone was involved in the fray. The *norny* decided to take their "wives" and run off to the forest on their own. It was months before a few of the repentant elders began searching for their sons and daughters.

One of the most important people I came to know at this time was Tàkàkrorok, the village chief. His hut was next door to ours on the inner circle of houses. He dropped by several times a day, mostly for coffee, but sometimes for other imported foods, like pasta, which he adored. Later, I learned how to discourage Tàkàkrorok when I wanted to keep my food. I simply told him I was eating deer, which was taboo for people who had been given "good" names as children. But at the beginning of my stay I welcomed the chief's presence. He cautioned me against giving away too many gifts when the other villagers became overly aggressive, and he even made a speech one night in the central plaza telling people to be good to Gustaaf and me. The speech was thrown in as part of one of his nightly harangues.

As Tàkàkrorok preached, the villagers lay hidden from view in their houses, next to the small fires they had built for warmth. I could hear their chatting and wondered if anyone was paying attention as Tàkàkrorok sauntered about outside of the men's house and rambled on with his stilted haranguing voice and grandiose gestures. To accentuate important words the Kayapo sometimes stretch them out and glide into a falsetto voice, adding elaborate arm movements. When haranguing, Tàkàkrorok also emphasized words starting with "n" or "ng" by preceding them with a guttural thrust which, as described by one *Washington Post* reporter who had visited the Mekranoti, made him sound as if he had just been punched in the stomach. Tàkàkrorok would occasionally pound the club he was carrying into the ground to bring home an important point.

Although I greatly appreciated Tàkàkrorok's speech, it seemed to have little effect on the villagers. Requests continued as before. At one point a few people even complained that Tàkàkrorok had been unfair in redistributing the goods we gave him on our first day in the village. Tàkàkrorok had given things only to "his own" people, they explained. Gustaaf and I should feel obligated to correct the matter by giving out more gifts to those who were left out. But even if Tàkàkrorok's speech wasn't all that helpful, it still felt good to know that someone was looking out for us.

Tàkàkrorok was a self-made man. His mother was killed soon after he was born, and his father died when Tàkàkrorok was still a young boy. In some respects Tàkàkrorok was lucky to be still alive. Sometimes when a mother died leaving a baby behind, the Mekranoti buried the baby with the dead mother. But fortunately, Tàkàkrorok had others to care for him and his younger brother and sister. Some years later when he was much older and a fight split the Mekranoti village, Tàkàkrorok's sister accompanied her husband to go off to another area with a dissident faction of Tàkàkrorok's village.

She died there along with her two children, one of whom was poisoned. With no resistance to the common cold, Tàkàkrorok's brother also succumbed to an epidemic about the same time. He left three children who Tàkàkrorok thinks are still alive in another Kayapo village far away, even though he is not very interested in meeting them.

Apart from these family members who perished while he was still young, Tàkàkrorok had few close kinsmen. His position in the village probably stemmed more from his personal qualities. A highly intelligent man, he was recognized as an authority on many different subjects, from ceremonial etiquette and myths to shamanistic cures, Kayapo history, and the customs of foreign peoples. An expert craftsman, he was one of the few people in the village who knew how to weave the straw sleeping mats the Kayapo place on top of their beds while at home or directly on the cleared earth while out in the forest. He was also recognized as an expert warrior, an important role in recent Mekranoti history, and was known for his generosity. A few other factors may also have helped his career along. He had five sons in the village, and although they were too young to be of much help when he first became a chief, they may have enhanced his position once he got started. At the time I knew him, Tàkàkrorok was the oldest man in the village (over sixty years old) and one of the tallest—a full five feet eight inches, of which he was very proud.

Tàkàkrorok's position gave him few, if any, privileges in the village. He worked just as many hours as anyone else. His house was also like that of other people. A little more crowded than some, and with whiter walls, but essentially the same—a windowless, dark, rectangular structure. He had separated a room for himself and his present wife, Kamerti. His daughter by Kamerti and her husband also slept in this room with their two infants, while Kamerti's nieces with their husbands and children took the rest of the dwelling. In addition, a girl stolen as a baby from an enemy tribe slept in the house and helped Kamerti with chores.

As a distinguished elder, Tàkàkrorok was expected to give speeches in the late evening hours or just before dawn. He also served as spokesman for the group in dealing with FUNAI or other outsiders, and had several ceremonial duties as well. People asked his advice about dance steps, about the timing of ceremonies, and about the assigning of people as sponsors for Mekranoti festivals. Tàkàkrorok also knew the lore surrounding different rituals. Twice during my stay I heard him singing alone in his house in the middle of the night while others slept. He chanted soothing melodies in an even voice and regular cadences, quite unlike the usually highly energetic and aggressive Kayapo tunes. Tàkàkrorok was singing to bless the valuable "gifts" people in the village had received from outsiders—gifts like shotguns from FUNAI or hardwood for bowstaves. He sang of how the gifts would be used and how effective they would be. His wife, who slept beside him on the floor beside her daughter's sleeping platform, sang along when she knew the words, but usually she just listened, occasionally making requests for favorite tunes. When I recorded these songs several Indians came by to ask me to play them. Since only Tàkàkrorok knew the words and he sang only at night, few people had actually heard more than a few bars.

My good relations with Tàkàkrorok also had their drawbacks—particularly with his ex-wife, Nhàkry. When Tàkàkrorok was still a boy, Nhàkry's parents chose him to marry their daughter during an initiation and naming ceremony. These betrothals usually amounted to nothing in Mekranoti society, but in this case, when Nhàkry came of age, she began having sex with Tàkàkrorok. The steadiness of the sexual ties eventually confirmed the marriage and Nhàkry bore Tàkàkrorok six children. One girl died while still an infant but the other five survived into adulthood—three sons and two daughters who still live in the village. About 1945 (according to my estimated reconstruction of Kayapo history), after more than fifteen years of marriage, Nhàkry left him to move in with her brother and her first son, who now share a huge household that includes her son's wife's nieces and all of their children. Nhàkry still refers bitterly to Tàkàkrorok as "my husband," but Tàkàkrorok cannot bring himself to mention Nhàkry's name. He calls her "that woman over there" and changes the subject if anyone brings up Nhàkry's name. Nhàkry disliked talking to me and tried to avoid referring to Tàkàkrorok at all.

Kamerti, Tàkàkrorok's current wife, was also difficult at times. Originally from another Kayapo village on the other side of the Xingu River, Kamerti lost her father when she came as a war refugee to live with the Mekranoti some forty years ago. Her mother died during the same epidemic that killed Tàkàkrorok's brother, and her two sisters died several years later. Widowed from her first husband, Kamerti depended on other relatives for support—her sister's children who lived with her in the same house, and her son who went off to live in his wife's house.

Kamerti loved to flaunt the fact that she was now the chief's wife, and sometimes used this excuse to make unreasonable demands on me and others in the village, although most people paid little attention to her bossiness. One of the missionaries nicknamed her "hatchet face," because of her chronically disagreeable expression.

Probably because no one else gave her much company, Kamerti had a pet capuchin monkey that rode around on her head, and came down to play mischief with people's goods. The monkey was cute as long as someone else was taking care of it. But Tàkàkrorok got angry when the pet ruined the feather ornaments he had saved up for ceremonial occasions. The gadgets in my house were much too tempting for the animal. He came in to steal important pieces of paper, pens, and silverware. For a while I appreciated his eating the spiders on the roof and walls, quickly grabbing the bugs and rubbing them in his hands to squash them, but I was irritated when he threw my eggs on the ground to break them. After I beat him once for this he returned every day while I was gone for my bath to throw more eggs on the floor. Like people, monkeys carry grudges, it seems. Kamerti refused to take responsibility for the monkey's actions, but was very upset if anyone threatened the animal.

Tàkàkrorok's relationship with Kamerti was not as warm as it might have been. He openly preferred his second wife, who had died some ten or twelve years before in a measles epidemic, and he confided to me that the girl Kamerti raised as his daughter was not really his. She was much too short, he argued. The real daughter Kamerti had given him died several years earlier. She was tall, with wavy hair, and looked like a chief's child. This one was short and chubby and so could not possibly be his, he explained.

At one point I walked into Tàkàkrorok's hut and asked Kamerti where her husband was. Busying herself stringing beads, Kamerti muttered a few words about not having a husband. I was surprised and a bit embarrassed to have broached such a touchy subject, but I wanted to know more. "Where's Tàkàkrorok?" I asked, trying to phrase the question in a noncommittal way. "With his wife," Kamerti clipped. I could not resist pursuing the question and eventually discovered that Tàkàkrorok had been having an affair with Nhàkkàre, another woman in the village. Since the Mekranoti have no firm marital contracts, neither I nor anyone else could determine at the time whether Tàkàkrorok was married or not, and if so, to whom. But eventually it became clear that Kamerti would hold on to her husband, and I would be stuck with the claims of "hatchet face" to special privileges as the chief's wife.

There were also a few other people I began to know through Tàkàkrorok. One was Kaxre, Tàkàkrorok's youngest son by his favorite wife. Kaxre and his full brother, Tàkàkngo, had married two sisters and lived with these two women in their mother-in-law's house. By Kayapo standards Kaxre was an exceptionally handsome young man. Long, silky, jet-black hair, smooth skin, strong muscles, and a proud, aristocratic bearing made him one of the sexual favorites of Mekranoti women. Kaxre was well aware of his attractiveness. He loved the mirror I had put up in my hut and would come in periodically to admire himself. He never said a word to me, but just opened the door and went straight to the mirror. He would spend up to twenty minutes shaking his hair around, peering back over his shoulder and going through various other poses I always associated with U.S. fashion models. He never said a word to me, or even acknowledged my presence, but simply went into a final pose and then left as quietly as he had entered.

Recognizing individual personalities where I had originally seen only a faceless mob was a sign of progress, but I had a long way to go before I could really do serious fieldwork. Most of my attempts to gather useful information had been patent failures so far, and I could figure out no way to improve matters. My biggest problem was language.

When I first arrived in Brazil I spoke no Portuguese at all, but I did know Spanish and French and was able to carry on a broken conversation in Portuguese with Brazilians after only a few weeks. Feeling good about my language abilities, I was unprepared for the difficulties of Kayapo. I soon realized I would have to spend more time on the language then I originally planned.

# 4

# LEARNING KAYAPO

I enjoyed listening to their giggling as the boys chattered excitedly around the table. Their Kayapo sounded even more musical than usual. The words rolled out evenly with clipped staccato t's and k's and an occasional phrase punctuated with a guttural thrust into an m or a long slide into a falsetto voice. The boys were joking pleasantly with me, and since I understood nothing, I could fantasize they were saying anything I wanted. But my reveries were broken by a sudden silence. With wide-eyed attentiveness the boys all stared at me waiting for me to say something. They could joke as much as they wanted, but now I had to respond. I would have liked to say something clever, to join in the fun, but I could only look at them stupidly.

The boys made a few more jokes to each other and got up to leave. They would have more fun trapping small birds or chasing rabbits. Maybe an uncle would take them out on a hunting or fishing trip. Or at the very least they could play with their toy guns made of papaya stems that made popping noises when a stick was pulled through them. I realized that if the boys were unwilling to amuse themselves with me, the adults would be worse. I would have to make a greater effort to learn Kayapo.

On my second or third day with the Mekranoti, Gustaaf introduced me to a middle-aged man with a bright red hat in the shape of an army cap. "You'll need him to learn Kayapo," he said matter-of-factly. "He speaks a little Portuguese." I smiled to Kentỳxti but said nothing. I hadn't yet realized how dependent I would become on him. I thought I could learn Kayapo with anyone, and even entertained the thought of using several informants to get a more "balanced" perspective on the language. But now, after more than a week in their village, I knew that Kayapo was going to be more difficult, and that Kentỳxti would be indispensable.

It was late afternoon when I found him lying down in the men's house. The building was crowded at this time of day. A few men were weaving baskets but most were lounging about in their hammocks or sitting on mats on the floor. I recognized Kentỳxti because of his hat. Everyone else was watching closely, but Kentỳxti seemed to be ignoring me. Even after I said his name he continued to stare in the other direction, but he did respond with a drawn out and none-too-enthusiastic *"mỳj-ne"* (what?). In Portuguese I explained that I would like him to help me learn Kayapo. He spoke back in a fairly fluent Portuguese. I was delighted at being able to really communicate with one of the Indians for the first time. But Kentỳxti's rather cold answer was bothersome. "I'll have to think about it," he said, while continuing to look in another direction.

I left the men's house wondering what I had done wrong. Gustaaf explained later that Kentỳxti was probably upset because I failed to ask him for help on the day we were introduced. Now I was a little worried that the only person who could help me learn the language would refuse to cooperate. I wished I had chosen another village where I could get by with Portuguese.

The next morning I was surprised to see Kentỳxti, smiling and coquettish, amble up to my house and ask me when we were going to start. I grabbed my papers and a pen and blurted out, "Right now!"

"I suppose you want me to tell you how to say different things," Kentỳxti offered. He'd done this kind of thing before with some Protestant missionaries from the Summer Institute of Linguistics (formerly the Wycliffe Bible Society), and knew well what was involved. The missionaries had spent years going over the fine points of Kayapo grammar with Kentỳxti and still depended on him now and then when they came across a difficult biblical passage to translate into Kayapo. One missionary described him with the words "intelligent, quick, lazy, a wheeler-dealer, and a ladies' man." Kentỳxti knew his worth. Perhaps his coldness the night before was simply a way for him to strike a better deal with me.

The missionaries had written a couple of articles on Kayapo. These seemed useless while I was in Brasília, but now they were a tremendous help.

The articles described clearly the Kayapo sound system, so I wouldn't have to spend much time on that. I had a bit of trouble hearing the difference between words using various back vowels—like *àr* (to bake), *'ỳr* (almost), and *'yr* (to weave), which all sounded like moans to me. (The ' sign indicates a glottal stop.) But, in general, Kayapo phonemics were fairly easy.

Many people think the way to learn a language is simply to point to different objects in a room and find out what they're all called. This works for a while, but eventually you need to say things like "It's under the red leaf on your left," or "If you had to do it all over again what would you do?" No amount of pointing will help with these locutions. The real trick is to use substitution exercises. Start with a word, a phrase, or a sentence, and then change one part of it at a time to see what happens. I began with simple phrases suggested by an S.I.L. manual. "How do you say 'I cry'?" I asked. "Now how do you say 'he cries,' 'they cry'?" Then "I sleep," "he sleeps," "they sleep."

Problems began almost immediately. I tried to write down the sound sequences as I thought I heard Kentỳxti say them, but every time I asked for a repetition everything sounded different. After about an hour I eventually settled on two different ways of saying "I cry" that Kentyxti agreed were correct. I wrote them down as *"ba muwa"* and *"ba nē ba muwa."* By the same token, "you [singular] cry" was *"ga muwa"* or *"ga nē ga muwa."* I also learned that "you [plural] cry" could be either *"gar muwa"* (for a small group) or *"ga mē muwa"* (for a large group). "We cry" could be translated five different ways!: *"bar muwa"* (small group of us not including you), *"ba mē muwa"* (large group of us not including you), *"gu muwa"* (you [singular] and I), *"gway muw"* (small group of us including you), and *"gu mē muwa"* (large group of us including you). It took a long time to get all of these pronouns straight, but once I figured them out, they seemed rather obvious.

Kayapo reminded me of the German I had learned in a college class-room. The guttural sounds gave it a tough military sound, and like German, it was full of long sentences consisting of phrases embedded inside of other phrases: "I want the game that Kutê'o, who is Ireti's brother, killed, to eat." Most difficult of all, Kayapo vocabulary was based on compound words and phrases, like *"no ma"* (understanding eye—meaning curious). I could under-stand the words individually, but could not make sense out of them when strung together. I never knew which words to ask about.

I expected Kayapo to be harder than other languages I knew because it was unrelated to anything else. I also suspected it might be harder than even such notoriously difficult languages as Chinese. After all, linguists had already written excellent grammars for Chinese, while I would have to figure out a Kayapo grammar myself. I was ready for these problems, but I was not ready for the difference cultural variation would make in learning Kayapo. Vocabulary affects even questions of etiquette. Among the Mekranoti the giving and receiving of gifts is so much taken for granted that no one would think of saying anything like "thank you." Usually, people said nothing at all. It wasn't until the end of my stay among the Indians that I finally felt comfortable with this way of receiving goods. Other matters of etiquette were also difficult. There was no way to say "hello," "how are you," or "goodbye." People simply walked in on me and I on them.

A few other cultural differences were also hard to get used to. Because they had no use for them, the Mekranoti hardly ever dealt with numbers. They loved to joke with me about the absurdity of judging the passing of the day in terms of hours and minutes. "You just look at the sky," they would try to explain. Sometimes they would ask me to look at my watch to tell them if it was night or not, and then all would laugh at the ridiculousness of it all. The Kayapo counting system reflects this indifference: The word for one is *"pydji,"* two is *"amajkryt,"* and three is *"amajkryt nē ikjêket."* Anything else has to be made up of these three words. Four is *"amajkryt nē amajkryt,"* five, *amajkryt nē amajkryt ne ikjêket,"* and six, *"amajkryt nē amajkryt nē amajkryt."* Few Mekranoti ever attempt to count above six.

Colors are similar. There are words for black, white, and red, as well as one word, *"ngrãngrã,"* to mean either blue, yellow, or green. Any other color has to be described by referring to something in the environment—the color of the *pêjati* bird's tail feathers, or the leaves of the *rik* palm. In a culture without dyes or mass-produced articles, generic color terms were unnecessary.

One linguistic difference that bothered me particularly was the lack of Kayapo distinctions for paper products. For the Mekranoti, writing paper, file cards, books, notebooks, cardboard boxes, photographs, and kites seemed like much the same thing and didn't really need to be distinguished. When little boys grabbed my data to make kites, my explanations about different kinds of paper were futile.

It was easy to restrict myself to one Kayapo word where English had many, but it was much harder to do the reverse. There were many situations where the Mekranoti had elaborate vocabularies for things I thought were all alike. One of my worst problems was plant names. When Kentỳxti first started naming plants I ignored them, assuming I had more important things to learn. But I soon realized that this was the stuff of everyday conversation. I would have to learn at least the most important plants—like *bô*, a palm leaf, used for thatching roofs, or *ngrwa' ô*, used for weaving baskets, designing ceremonial masks, making baby-carrying slings, and wrapping up freshly killed game. But first I had to figure out which plants were most important.

There were also many words for carrying things—*kutu* (to carry garden produce from a basket on a tumpline around the forehead), *kubỳ* ( to carry in one hand), *kumyn* (to carry in both hands), *kudjin o tẽ* (to carry game on a stick), *kunjun o tẽ* (to lift a boiling pot with a stick), and *djupjên o tẽ* (to carry a baby in a baby sling). There were also different ways to strike animals (and people)—*to ky arẽ* (to break the head with a club), *to ma' arẽ* (to kill with a gun or a club), *to tyk arẽ* (to hit in the head without breaking it), *to xãk arẽ* (to strike without killing), *to pup arẽ*, and *'o pok arẽ* (to puncture with an arrow or spear), and *to prik arẽ* (to cut something off, such as a head)—valuable distinctions to a hunting and warring people.

If I made too many mistakes in speaking Kayapo, people complained to Kentỳxti that he wasn't teaching me right, so Kentỳxti took my lessons seriously. He was an excellent teacher for the first hour of a session. He seemed to know exactly where my problems were and how to correct them, but eventually he grew more and more fidgety. The Mekranoti found the benches they had made for me uncomfortable, and were unaccustomed to sitting in one place for very long anyway. Kentỳxti was better than most at sitting still, but he would occasionally get up to see what kind of food people had given me, and nibble on some of it as he answered my questions. After an hour of talking, his responses became less and less comprehensible. He would deliberately give me overly complex sentences he knew I could never understand just to end the session. So, to vary things a bit, I sometimes talked to Kentỳxti about people in the village, the Mekranoti past, and Kentỳxti's amorous adventures.

With a boyish charm Kentỳxti made light of everything. Sometimes, for fun, he mimicked others in the village, but he was never nasty about it. He even imitated the missionaries as they studied linguistics. Once while in Belém, he tried to learn another Indian's language by going through the substitution exercises the missionaries had used with him. If he had had more time, he would probably have succeeded. He was curious about everything— ceremonial ornaments, new songs, medicinal plants, and big cities. For a while I tried to teach Kentỳxi how to read Portuguese. Although he learned very fast, we eventually quit when the others complained that they should all learn together. They did not want Kentỳxti to divorce himself too much from the community. Sometimes Kentỳxti came into my hut when he had no one else to talk to or when he got into trouble because of one of his sexual escapades. For a while I felt like his confidant.

Kentỳxti's mother died when he was only a toddler, and he knew nothing about her. His earliest memories were of the traumatic moment when his father and a large group of Mekranoti, angry about personal jealousies, decided to flee the main village. This event must have occurred in the 1940s, for Kentỳxti was a small boy at the time. Kentỳxti's father joined the faction of two influential men named Angme'ê and Kenti. Angme'ê was a good man, the Indians say, but Kenti had already acquired an unsavory reputation for bloodthirstiness. Some accused him of murdering his own brother.

The two dissident leaders traveled far in the Amazonian forest with their followers, living off wild yams, palm hearts, and Brazil nuts. At times they came across gardens planted by Kayapo Indians or Brazilian explorers years before, and they ate the bananas and manioc still there. But eventually, Kenti fought with Angme'ê, killing one of the kinder leader's followers. To avoid reprisals, the murderer, along with a small following of eight men and their immediate families, including Kentỳxti, fled as far west as the Tapajós River and the Mundurucú Indians, a tribe noted for its fierce warfare and blue facial tattoos. The Mekranoti looked on Kenti's faction as the most decadent people in their entire history. "They didn't even plant gardens," people commented with an air of moral repugnance.

Angme'ê and Kenti met a few years later in a vicious battle that killed off almost half of the people in each group. Kenti was fiercer, but many people in his group were sick at the time, so it was a good moment for Angme'ê's attack. Still a boy, Kentỳxti was stolen by Angme'ê, while his father remained with Kenti. According to the Mekranoti, Angme'ê's faction was more "civilized" than Kenti's. Angme'ê attempted to plant gardens and was even open to pacification attempts by the Brazilian government. Kenti so disgraced himself that when he tried to return to the village the Mekranoti banished him. "Perhaps he is still alive and well among the Mundurucú," some people conjectured, "but we will have nothing to do with him."

One year after this battle, Angme'ê's group accepted gifts of peace from Chico Meirelles, a well-known Brazilian Indianist. At the Brazilian's request, they soon moved to a river location where the Indianist had set up an encampment. From here Meirelles decided to continue contacting new groups, and sent off a few Indians to bring back the rest of the Mekranoti still wandering about in the forest.

Kentỳxti would probably have gone along with this group of older men, except that he got stung by a stingray and couldn't walk. So he stayed behind with Meirelles, who cared for his wound. It was at this time that Meirelles took a liking to Kentỳxti, and Kentỳxti grew to like whites.

Among the forest Mekranoti brought back to Meirelles's encampment in 1957 was Kentỳxti's father, anxious to see his son after so many years of forced separation. Unfortunately, their reunification was short-lived, for Kentỳxti's father died during an epidemic only one year after seeing his now grown son. While most of the Mekranoti at Meirelles's encampment returned to the forest after receiving gifts from the Indianist, Kentỳxti stayed behind with a few Brazilians from the now defunct Indian Protection Service (SPI). He no longer had any relatives among the Mekranoti and had little reason to return to the forest with them. It was during his stay with the Brazilians that Kentỳxti picked up his Portuguese and his knowledge of foreign ways. Perhaps others, in similar circumstances, might have learned Portuguese as well as Kentỳxti, but Kentỳxti's inherent curiosity about the world and his clear intelligence must have played a large part in his linguistic achievements.

Kentỳxti continued to help Meirelles, even when the going got rough. Once, the Indian Protection Service made a disastrous attempt to attract the forest Mekranoti to a new settlement by promising to give them already producing gardens. The Mekranoti trekked to the proposed new village site, but when they got there, they found that the gardens had been cleared but never planted. To help alleviate the plight of the newly arrived Indians, Kentỳxti made tons of manioc flour and transported it upriver to the site of the unplanted gardens. An epidemic followed the garden fiasco and most of the trekking Mekranoti returned to their forest village. But Kentỳxti continued to reside with Meirelles. It was only after the departure of his foreign mentor, who was feeling ill himself, and of the other Brazilians who worked for him, that Kentỳxti grew tired of the tiny settlement on the Baú River. Looking for a wife, he too decided to join the Mekranoti group he had lived with as a small child.

In the main Mekranoti village people admired Kentỳxti for his intelligence and his knowledge of foreigners' customs. They also thought he was fairly generous with the goods he acquired from the *kuben* who used his services as interpreter and teacher. I was surprised once to find that Kentỳxti had given an expensive tape recorder and a few smaller items to an Indian who helped him clear a garden one year. For a month and a half Kentỳxti helped me twice a day to transcribe tapes of conversations with other Indians. All I paid him was the tape recorder, and he gave it away immediately to someone who worked for three days on a garden.

When they needed to deal with outsiders the Mekranoti would turn to Kentỳxti for advice, and would accept his suggestions about what to do. They might have given him more influence in local matters, too, except for a few shortcomings. Kentỳxti's biggest handicap was that he had no relatives. His father and mother had come originally from another Kayapo village across the Xingu. Most of Kentỳxti's aunts and uncles had been killed in skirmishes with Brazilians, and his parents had had no relatives to bequeath to him. This made people distrustful of Kentỳxti's loyalties. For a few weeks in the middle of my fieldwork Kentỳxti avoided me altogether because people complained that he spent too much time with me, giving none of the others a chance to receive my presents.

Kentỳxti was also short on knowledge about native customs. Because of all the time he had spent with Brazilians, he never saw many of the elaborate ceremonies the Mekranoti stage to bestow names on their children, and he knew relatively little about them. His knowledge of native medicine was also limited. I often thought he contradicted himself when explaining how plants could be used for cures—in cold teas, as balms on the skin, or boiled in water for baths—but I wasn't sure until one day when one of the chief's sons caught him in the middle of one of his elaborate commentaries. Kentỳxti immediately silenced himself to let the chief's son continue with the "correct" information. After this embarrassment he was more careful about admitting what he didn't know, and about referring me to more authoritative sources.

Kentỳxti seemed to regret his ignorance about native affairs and was eager to learn more. Under the guise of teaching me Kayapo, he sometimes practiced the special speech of Mekranoti haranguers, with all of the requisite abdominal grunts and broad gestures. He was also the first to ask me about any esoteric information I got from Tàkàkrorok, such as the songs Tàkàkrorok sang to bless valuable gifts.

Another of Kentỳxti's problems may have been the reputation he shared with Kaxre, Tàkàkrorok's youngest son, as the village's Don Juan. I doubt this affected his political ambitions too much since Kaxre was more influential than he, and had, if anything, an even greater renown for sexual adventures. Besides, influential Mekranoti men were expected to be promiscuous. But Kentỳxti's romantic escapades created a different kind of problem. While Kaxre could depend on his celebrated good looks to find sexual partners, Kentỳxti had to rely on his personality and the gifts he gave his paramours. He was attractive enough, and had a charming boyish smile, but he lacked the long, straight black hair, smooth skin and well-defined muscles that made other men more appealing to the flirtatious young women who commented openly about their favorites.

Kentỳxti talked extensively about the sexual prowess of different Mekranoti women—this one "just lies there rigidly and doesn't do anything; she's no fun at all," that one "moans, squirms around, does it in sitting and lying positions, and digs her nails deeply into your shoulders." For young Mekranoti men, scratch marks on the shoulder are the ultimate sign of true passion and virile sexuality.

Kentỳxti's commentaries were a welcome relief from our more drab conversations about Kayapo parts of speech, but I resented being drawn into his love affairs. Many of the presents he gave his paramours came from things I had given him as compensation for his teaching efforts. Sometimes his lovers' husbands or boyfriends would ask me how their wives acquired their new beads from me. I could get in trouble no matter what I said. Kentỳxti forewarned me on several occasions and gave me stories to tell. "When he asks you where the aluminum plates came from, just tell him she brought you firewood. We already agreed that's what happened."

One time Kaxre became suspicious about a flashlight he found among his wife's possessions. I think he knew Kentỳxti gave it to her, and actually mentioned something about it to Kentyxti. Kaxre was no saint himself and knew he had no room for complaint, but his vanity was at stake; the others in the village were talking. When he finally came by my hut to ask me the inevitable, I was still undecided about what to do. But he asked the question in a perfunctory manner and seemed uninterested in my answer. I judged at that point that he would probably prefer me to lie. That way he could pretend nothing happened, avoid a fight with Kentỳxti, and preserve his honor. My judgment must have been on target, for the affair was never mentioned again.

Kentỳxti's wife, Kotjaka, also resented his affairs with other women. She herself was relatively faithful in this relatively promiscuous society. I thought she was a pretty woman, but by Mekranoti standards she was about average. Her major handicaps were her reputed stupidity and her laziness. Perhaps these evaluations were in part undeserved; it would be hard for anyone to match Kentỳxti's quick wit. And her laziness may have been a reaction to a heart problem a FUNAI doctor once diagnosed for her. Kotjaka especially resented Kentỳxti's affair with Ngrwa'ô.

Ngrwa'ô was one of the Mekranoti "*kupry.*" As with most Mekranoti women, *kupry* generally live in the same house as their parents, their sisters, and their sisters' husbands. They have sex with different men in the community, and receive gifts of game or other presents from their paramours. Unlike prostitutes in our society, *kupry* do not work for pimps and are not ostracized. They are considered a normal part of the community, and may hold any of the ceremonial or professional roles married women enjoy. But they are thought less attractive and lazier than others, are not particularly welcome as work partners, and, of course, have reputations for promiscuity. As with many other *kupry*, Ngrwa'ô's mother died when Ngrwa'ô was still a child, and she never received a "good" name that comes only from having parents sponsor a special ceremony.

Ngrwa'ô was no prettier than Kotjaka, and had a reputation for being even lazier, but she smiled and laughed a lot, and was fun to talk to. Kentỳxti spoke well of her sexual abilities and appreciated her affection. Kotjaka would probably have tolerated Kentỳxti's sexual escapades, but when Ngrwa'ô became pregnant and Kentỳxti claimed the child, Kotjaka felt betrayed. She fought with Ngrwa'ô and threatened to kill the baby even before it was born. Kentỳxti managed to calm her down, but the animosity between the two women never subsided.

With Kentỳxti's guidance I gradually became more proficient in Kayapo, and after a few months we stopped the lessons. But whenever I had a questionnaire to design, or a special interview on a complicated subject, I asked Kentỳxti for help again. At times he warned me that while most people would understand a given question he had translated for me, others would never figure it out. We then had to try out the questions on the people Kentỳxti thought least likely to understand. One phrase was particularly difficult. I needed to ask about an imaginary situation, and had to use what, in English, would be called the conditional tense: "If you could..., would you..." An anthropologist friend of mine had tried to figure out the same expression for a related Indian language, but gave up, concluding that the Indians could not say it.

I was more persistent, and eventually found a solution. Kayapo has two words that make things imaginary. "*Amijo*" means to make oneself into something else—as to put on a monkey mask. "*Ren*" makes any phrase imaginary. The more I learned of the language, the more I realized there was to learn. Ever since, I have been suspicious of scholars who conclude that people have no way of saying something, or that a given language is easy to master.

As the months went by, I began to try out more gracious ways of saying things I had stumbled over before. Verbally adept Mekranoti, for example, like to emphasize points by asking rhetorical questions: "Were the Kreen Akrore weak during that battle?" The answers to these questions are always an emphatic "No," usually never stated but simply understood. The first time I tried out this linguistic turn I failed miserably. I had just come back from Brasília and wanted to emphasize the fact that Brasília was even bigger than Belém, a city some of the Mekranoti had seen. Unfortunately, I knew no way to say "bigger" or "more" in Kayapo. I could only say that Belém was smaller than Brasília, and so would have to begin with an emphatic statement that Brasília was very big. I wanted to use the rhetorical question, but asked it improperly. Switching "big" to "small" and the emphatic "yes" to "no" was too much for me. I simply asked, "Is Brasília big?"

I knew I'd blown it as soon as I said it. Everyone stared, looking puzzled. Finally, Tàkàkrorok broke the silence. "Well, at least he's trying," he consoled. "He's almost as good as the missionaries." I was embarrassed but flattered. The missionaries had lived for six years with the Mekranoti and spent most of their time learning the language and figuring out its structure. The Mekranoti often commented that they were "almost Indian."

Even after four or five months of living with the Indians, I still felt frustrated with my Kayapo. I had learned to speak Portuguese better after only two weeks. I realized I would have to organize my data collection carefully, beginning with tasks that required a minimum of language skills and gradually working my way to more complex matters. Later in the year, I would also need to review much of the information collected earlier, just to be sure I had understood things correctly. Despite all my frustrations, I grew to like the sound of Kayapo with its punctuated syllables, moaning vowels, and long-drawn-out falsetto emphases. I also learned to appreciate the irony of some of its locutions, like the word for money, "*pi'ôk kaprĩ*." The translation is "sad paper."

# 5

# JAGUARS
# AND SCORPIONS

"Beproti, Bepita, come quick." Grabbing notebooks and pens, Gustaaf and I rushed outside, not knowing what to expect. Led straight into the men's house, we were stunned at the sight of a jaguar about to pounce on a man sitting inside the door. The wily, spotted cat had its mouth agape and its claws extended in a threatening pose. Propped up on sticks, it looked alive and still dangerous. But old Mrytàmti, seemingly oblivious to the menace in front of him, chanted calmly and every now and then, after finishing a long phrase, he shook a gourd rattle to emphasize his words. It took me a while to realize that the animal was dead—the scene had been well staged.

The Mekranoti have great respect for the jaguar, and the killing of one, even in these days of shotguns, is cause for a ceremony. The jaguar is an important animal. It gave fire and bows and arrows to the Indians. "A long time ago, before any of us were around," Mekranoti elders like to begin their story, "there was neither fire, nor manioc, nor sweet potato, nor banana. Those were the days when animals could talk, and when Indians ate rotten wood, tree fungus, and raw meat." Everyone knows the rest—a man went out one day with his wife's younger brother looking for macaw eggs. Finding a nest on top of a steep cliff, the two males built a ladder for the younger one to climb up. When the boy reached the top he threw down some of the prized food, but the eggs were enchanted and turned to rocks before reaching the ground. The older brother-in-law broke his finger trying to catch one of these enchanted eggs and angrily tore down the ladder, abandoning his wife's younger brother.

After many days on top of the cliff, the abandoned boy was forced to eat his own excrement to satisfy his hunger. Finally, one day a jaguar, carrying a bow and arrow, passed by below and saw the boy's shadow. Looking up, the wild cat invited the boy to accompany him home and offered to help him descend the cliff. At first fearful, the hungry boy finally accepted and rode on the jaguar's back all the way to the wild cat's den. There for the first time he saw fire in a rock oven, roasted meat, and manioc pies. The jaguar's wife was none too happy with the Indian boy, but her feline husband insisted she treat him well.

Several times the jaguar's wife threatened her adopted son, but her husband always protected the boy, even giving him a bow and arrow, and lessons in how to shoot, should his wife threaten again. One day, when the jaguar's wicked wife attacked her adopted son, the Indian boy killed her and then fled to his native village, carrying roasted meat, cotton, and yams stolen from the jaguar's home. Delighted with the new foods, the Indians resolved to go off to the jaguar's lair and rob the wild cat of its fire. It is because of this incident that people now cook all their food, while jaguars roam alone in the jungle and eat only raw meat.

Some storytellers have a better sense of drama than others and go into more details, but no matter who recounts the story, everyone still enjoys hearing it again. Using nearby objects as props, the narrators act out all the parts—the angry brother-in-law, the fearful boy on top of the rock cliff, and the jaguar's jealous wife. The gestures are grand and completely unselfconscious. Even the jaguar's walk is imitated with precision.

Jaguars frighten the Mekranoti. This one in the men's house was killed only a few hundred yards from the village plaza, and might have harmed some of the children or killed people's pets; it might even have attacked an adult. Sometimes you can hear the jaguar's low coughlike barks as you pass through the forest, barks that according to the Mekranoti place the animal in the same family as dogs, and send fear tingling down the spines of the unarmed. Then you must be careful, for jaguars are not only strong, they're also smart, an Indian once explained to me, protectively. "They lie in wait for you on tree limbs. And then when they attack, the first thing they do is grab your bows and break your arrows, so you can't fight back. To get away from them, run behind a tree. Then the jaguar will attack the tree trunk and forget you. Or else climb into the branches; the jaguar won't come after you. It'll just wait below for you to come down."

Today, the jaguar is important for another reason. To protect the endangered species, Brazilian law permits its killing only in self-defense or by Indians. Outsiders like to buy the pelts in the form of native ornaments, and the Mekranoti have no qualms about selling the skins to Brazilians who happen to pass through their village. Although they never kill jaguars except for food, or in case of attack, the Mekranoti appreciate the profits from the skins. Self-sufficient in food and other needs, they like to have a few extra cruzeiros around to buy things like shotguns, ammunition, and cooking pots.

To the casual visitor, Mekranoti life appears easygoing. After a night of sleep interrupted now and then by a stoking of the bedside fire, people begin to wake up between 6:00 and 6:30 A.M. Unless there is a ceremony going on, no one is forced out of bed, and some people linger on their sleeping platforms until much later. On rainy days no one gets up so early. The dark gloomy skies delay the dawn, and it's no fun hunting or gardening in the rain anyway. Only the children sometimes like to frolic in a quick downpour if it's not too cold.

After eating a breakfast of the previous day's leftovers while huddled around the fire in the brisk morning air, the men like to wander off to the men's house or chat with their families before going out hunting or fishing. But if he feels like it, a man can stay home and do something else—weave a basket, repair a roof, or go out collecting Brazil nuts with his wife. In the late afternoon the men usually come together to relax in the men's house. There they exchange stories about the day's events, especially hunting tales in which the men dramatize a fast pursuit or imitate an animal's feeding or mating habits. Other men joke about the tales or laugh at an unfortunate animal's futile attempts to escape. Work seems more like sport than hard labor.

From the village, it might appear as if the women work a bit harder than the men. In the morning they have the children to feed and bathe. This means trips to the river to get water for cooking, drinking, and cleaning. The women also have to sweep out the garbage on the dirt floor, and make sure the family has vegetable food and firewood. A walk to the gardens where they harvest produce can take up to an hour, and the river is ten minutes away. Every day I saw small groups of women and children walk single file into the central plaza, their heads bowed low as they carried loads of manioc, bananas, or sweet potatoes stacked high in the baskets hung from straps across their foreheads. Other women made shorter trips to chop enormous loads of firewood, carrying the heavy cargo in the same sturdy baskets back to the village. No wonder they sometimes complained about pains in the neck.

But even the women found time to sit outside their houses in the late afternoon and evening to chat with their neighbors. Sometimes they spent hours painting each other's bodies with genipap dye in dramatic, but delicate, striped designs that would make the fashion industry take note. One art historian has labeled these paintings the Michelangelos of the primitive world. Just before daybreak, and again just before nightfall, the women also joined together in the central plaza to sit on palm leaves and sing one tune after another, their arms rocking to and fro to the steady rhythms. This was part of the women's *bijok* ceremony, I was told. The singing would continue without change for several months, before preparations began for the ceremonial finale.

Even during the day not all of the men and women went out to work. Sometimes I caught people just sitting by themselves in the corners of their houses, staring into space. Perhaps the closest thing we have to this quiet meditation is television.

Before leaving New York I had decided to measure the amount of time people spent on different activities. Some important debates had sprung up in anthropology about whether primitive people worked harder than those of us living in "civilized" societies, and despite thousands of accounts of life in different cultures around the world, almost no one had reliable information. My own casual impressions of Mekranoti leisure were fairly rosy, but I saw people mostly in the village, not in the garden plots or out hunting, so I could not be sure my judgments were accurate.

To get a more representative picture of Mekranoti work, I used a technique anthropologists had worked out for other areas of South America. At the beginning of each week, throughout the whole year I was in the field, I sat down with a table of random numbers and selected twelve households to visit at random hours during the week. When the time came for a visit, I simply walked into the house and looked around. I then wrote down everything everyone was doing at the moment I entered, and asked about those who were absent. By the end of the year I had almost seven thousand observations and could figure out the percentage of their time people devoted to different chores.

I decided to begin measuring work a few weeks after arriving in the Mekranoti village. Kentỳxti helped me learn words for the different things people do and the different places they might be. Just for practice, I spent two weeks walking into people's houses several times a day and trying out the new vocabulary. No one seemed to mind my barging in on them—they did the same with me and with each other. At first everyone assumed I wanted meat or other food—especially if one of the household men was out hunting and I came back later to confirm the report. The Indians often sent their children to scrounge off their neighbors in similar circumstances, so it was no wonder they should think I wanted meat.

Just so people wouldn't feel they had to lie to protect their meat supply, I decided never to accept food on these visits. Kentỳxti's vocabulary lessons paid off well. I had little trouble understanding where missing household members were. But for a long time I still didn't recognize everyone's face, and sometimes asked where someone had gone, only to have my informant tell me in a rather unpleasant tone that he or she was talking to me.

The time allocation studies gave a sense of order to my fieldwork. Other kinds of information were haphazard. Births, deaths, marriages, divorces, ceremonies, and political fights could occur at any time. Even planned interviews might yield nothing of interest for weeks, and then suddenly give a breakthrough. A linguistic rule would become obvious upon hearing the right sentence, or a confusing historical event would fall into place on learning about a hidden motive of one of the protagonists. There was no way of telling when these breakthroughs would occur.

The time allocation studies were guaranteed to give results. Sometimes they were tedious or annoying, but great things can come from the patient buildup of trivial information. On days when I felt I was getting nowhere with other information I wanted, I could always count on a random household visit to make me feel that I was accomplishing something.

While still experimenting with barging into people's houses, I decided to start gathering genealogies. Family ties are important in most societies, especially small ones where everyone is related to practically everyone else. Besides, no self-respecting anthropologist could possibly come back from the field without elaborate and messy diagrams of triangles and circles representing males and females with connecting lines between kinsmen.

The language requirements were minimal. I needed to learn only the words for father, mother, brother, sister, son, and daughter. There were a few ambiguities to clear up though. In Kayapo the word for "father" also includes father's brothers, and the word for "mother" includes mother's sisters, and even mother's brother's daughter, who would simply be a cousin for us. So I had to be careful about which "mother" I was asking for. Also, "brother" and "sister" could include the children of any "mother" or "father," including mother's brother's daughter's children. To confuse things even further, the Mekranoti also called some non-relatives by kinship terms if they were particularly friendly with them. To make sure I got the true biological parents when asking about ancestors, I had to ask, "Whose vagina did so-and-so come out of?" and "Who put the fetus in the vagina?"

Before I left New York, some anthropologist friends gave me some informal advice about genealogies: "Your best bet is to ask old women. They know all about dead people and like to talk about them." I decided to take this counsel to heart by asking Teptykti to help me gather the names of recent ancestors. More than sixty years old, Teptykti was a great-grandmother several times over, and in a few years she would probably be a great-great-grandmother. The matron of a huge household, Teptykti lived with her three daughters and their husbands and numerous children. Another daughter had died a year before I arrived in the village, but left Teptykti with an adult granddaughter, who also lived in the house with her husband and children. Also, one of her daughters' husbands had a son by a previous wife. This young man ate his meals here, although as a *norny*, he slept most nights in the men's house. All told, Teptykti's small home housed twenty-three people.

Teptykti's father died many years ago (in the 1930s by my estimates) and her mother was killed by Kenti some ten years later. By this time Teptykti, betrothed as a child, had already remarried and given birth to five or six children. Her first two babies had died a few years after birth, but the others were still alive, and already approaching adulthood themselves, when their grandparents died. Teptykti went on to bear a total of ten children to her husband, who died soon after the last child was born. Today she has three living daughters who reside with her, and two sons who live with their wives in other Mekranoti households.

Teptykti was a kindly old lady and a delight to be around. According to the Mekranoti no one can live very long without being gentle to people. Those who get angry easily or treat others badly usually get sick in the stomach, and give headaches to everybody including themselves. Inevitably they die young. Teptykti's advanced age and her easygoing personality provided living proof of this native theory of longevity.

Unfortunately, Teptykti's talents at unraveling genealogical connections were less impressive. I decided to start by asking Teptykti about her own family. I asked for the names of her mother and her father and her grandparents. These were easy enough. But when I got to her mother's brothers, Teptykti started giving strange answers. I realized she was not very sure about who her biological relatives really were. At first I thought I had a language problem, but when Kentyxti could not get consistent answers, I realized Teptykti herself was unsure about these people. After all, her mother's brothers did not live in the house where she grew up, and were not the only people she called "uncle."

Poor, dizzy Teptykti. A gentle and charming old woman, but verging on senility, she just couldn't keep things straight. When Kentỳxti pointed out some of her inconsistencies Teptykti simply answered quietly, "Oh dear, I guess that's true, isn't it." Teptykti had a marvelously comic tolerance for her own shortcomings.

After the confusion created by Teptykti's responses, I decided to turn to more reliable sources for information. I would have liked to interview another woman, but the Indians, including the females, advised differently. Men knew more about the subjects that interested me, they pointed out. Besides, women had to be near their children, making it difficult for them to sit for long interviews. I realized firsthand why anthropologists usually gathered most of their information from men.

According to the Indians, Bokrã, the old man who gave me my Indian name, was one of the best at recalling the ancestors. One of the village's haranguers, Bokrã looked much older than Tàkàkrorok even though he was at least five years younger. Much shorter and frailer, Bokrã nevertheless enjoyed a greater reputation as a warrior. After talking to him, I found it hard to believe that such a sweet little man could have been such a vicious killer, but when he gave his speeches around the village plaza at night, and recalled past battles with the Kreen Akrore Indians to the south, some of his warrior's fervor came back. Then his voice became tense in the narration and he bellowed out threats to the enemy and stomped his talking club into the ground. He continued with this tone of voice even when talking about current affairs, as when he scolded the young men for not bringing in enough meat for the elders. Before talking to him in the privacy of my house I was a bit afraid of him.

Perhaps his fierceness explains why Bokrã had so much trouble with his family. The old man had numerous kinsmen, but they were spread throughout the village. He lived with his wife and one of their two daughters and sons-in-law. The other daughter had moved off with her husband to live alone in another house. The couple also had a son, who, as usual among the Mekranoti, lived in his wife's house, and two daughters by a previous wife who both lived elsewhere. One of the daughters was a *kupry* with three sons to support. Normally she would have lived with her sister, but the two did not get along well enough to live together, so she stayed instead with an elderly couple next door. Bokrã may have been a good warrior, but he was not much at keeping his family together.

Bokrã and a few other elders helped me put together the genealogies. In order to get a better picture of the changes taking place among the Mekranoti I wanted to know what people died of in different historical periods. I tried to estimate the death dates, ages, and causes of death for all of the ancestors. In a society without calendars this was no easy task. First, I had to come up with an event calendar that would allow me to estimate dates for famous moments in Mekranoti history. Then I had to connect people's births, initiations, or deaths with famous historical events. Only then could I estimate when people died and how old they were when they died. Since much of the historical information would come bit by bit as my Kayapo improved, I would have to review the genealogical data several times during my stay.

Because I failed to notice that people sometimes appeared twice on my data sheets—once as someone's husband, and again as someone's brother, for example—I sometimes asked for the same information twice. This bored and irritated my elderly informants no end. Tàkàkrorok finally told me point blank that he would not talk to me any more unless I remembered what he had already said. To make sure I understood the seriousness of his point he got up and walked out. Forced to put my data in order, I finally made up an index showing the pages on which different ancestors appeared. It took a little convincing, but Tàkàkrorok and the others finally came back to help me finish the job.

As my work gradually became routine, the high point of my days became an afternoon swim and bath in the small stream that passed through the Mekranoti village. During most of the year the water was dark, almost black, and moved quietly around a bend the Mekranoti used as their beach. Now, at the beginning of June, it was particularly pleasant, for the wet-season floods had receded, leaving plentiful clean water behind. The forest canopy covered the river for most of its length, but in the bathing spot a small clearing allowed the sun to pass through. Surrounded by tall forest trees, the river appeared to emerge mysteriously from the dark still tunnel created by the overhanging branches and lianas. An old crooked tree grew out of the black water at the concave side of the bend and served as a diving platform for the children. It was a noisy focal point for this otherwise peaceful retreat.

Modesty prevented Mekranoti men and women from bathing at the same time. The men would join together in the men's house and agree to descend on the river en masse. With loud falsetto barks they warned the women of their arrival, causing a flurry of activity as the women and children scurried about filling their water cans and gathering up their belongings. On arrival, the younger men who wore swimming trunks during the day took them off, revealing penises tied tightly against their abdomens with strings around their waists. It was shameful to expose the glans penis even in front of other men, and modesty required tying up the foreskin even when wearing shorts. Restricting their playfulness, which is unbecoming to adult warriors, they walked gingerly waist-deep into the water, and then splashed water onto their backs and over their heads. The men's caution may have been justified. Although this stream was free of the stingrays and piranha fish that plagued larger Amazonian rivers, no one could ever be sure that the water was clear of snakes, or *tep kaàk,* those tiny, invisible fish that cause infections when people spend too much time in the water. Once we saw a crocodile swim up this isolated stream.

When the men left, the women returned to the river to finish their bathing. Most mothers simply sat on the sandy stream bottom, waist-deep in water, holding on to the toddlers as they dipped calabashes into the river and poured the water over the crying infants' heads. They also filled their mouths with the dark water and squirted it into the children's eyes to remove the mucus caused by the eye infections most children suffered. Only the older children played in the river, diving off a high bank, or swinging from a liana slung over the crooked tree. Sometimes I joined them, although some of the Indians said it was too dangerous. To the Indians I was virtually sexless and so could bathe with whomever I liked. During the dry season both men and women liked to go to the river to dip roasted sweet potatoes into the water. Cooked in earth ovens, the unpeeled tubers were covered with dirt and the Mekranoti liked to clean them in the water and have a drink at the same time. They were a curious sight, squatting at the river's edge munching on the tubers while laughing with their neighbors.

A fallen tree served as a bridge to cross the river near the bathing spot. It was an adequate bridge when the river was low and no water ran over it. But at flood time, which was most of the year, traveling over it was a risky operation Most people never used the foot passage at all, for the area on the far side of the river had little to offer. An almost continuously flooded swamp, this area had neither gardens nor hunting spots. Occasionally someone would cross the bridge to bring back firewood. One day, while bathing at the river, I watched as Amakkry, Teptykti's son-in-law, tried to carry ten-foot logs across the bridge. On top of the formidable task of lifting the heavy cargo, Amakkry had to perform a balancing act on the bridge. He almost lost his footing several times, but did manage to transport one of the logs to the village side. While he was resting before attempting a second log, I went over to offer help. I suggested we float the logs across the river. Some of the children agreed to push them along with me. A bit skeptical of the whole thing, but tired of maneuvering the bridge, Amakkry agreed.

When Amakkry dropped the first log into the river, the boys and I tried to keep it moving straight to the other side. But the current was too strong, and all our efforts failed. The log jammed up against the bridge and eventually washed over it to disappear down the river. Disappointed and embarrassed, I climbed on the bridge. I was afraid to look at Amakkry, and concentrated instead on my hand, where I had what I thought was a bad splinter from the log. I was contemplating going to Ronaldo to have it removed since it seemed so deep, when Amakkry came up to me wanting to see my hand. He looked at it a bit and then said, "*Mak*." In a fatherly voice he added that I ought to go to FUNAI headquarters to have Ronaldo look at it. I had no idea what *mak* meant, but suspected that Amakkry simply wanted me to leave so he could transport his logs in peace. When I hesitated too long he asked some of the boys to take me to FUNAI. I agreed reluctantly.

When we got to FUNAI headquarters I discovered that Ronaldo was asleep. Another FUNAI attendant, Mateu, had also recently arrived in the village, but had gone out hunting for the day. I did not want to wake Ronaldo simply to remove a splinter. But the boys were insistent. When they finally saw that I refused to wake up Ronaldo, they decided to drag me to a missionary who had also recently entered the village. Esther was working at her desk when we arrived.

Esther had already spent some six years with the Mekranoti, and complained whenever her superiors forced her away from the Indian community. The Indians were fond of her, and always greeted her arrival with excited shouts of "Birbir," her Mekranoti name, and an unusual amount of attention. Along with another missionary, Esther had published several articles on the Kayapo language and could speak it as well as anyone.

For three years Esther had been the major source of medicine for the Mekranoti. Even after the arrival of FUNAI's medical attendant she continued to help the Indians when they went out on trek. Esther seemed to thrive in the forest. She accompanied the Indians on long expeditions into the jungle, taking almost nothing with her. Like the Indians, she traveled barefoot, and she helped them set up her temporary trekking house and gather wild foods. She even went out hunting with the men at times, a habit which caused some Mekranoti to suspect that she might be part male.

Esther's partner, Mary, was less experienced and spent less time in the village. A bit timid at first, Mary became quickly acclimated to Mekranoti life.

A few days after her arrival, the Indians decided to go on a trek into the forest. Not knowing what to expect, Mary asked Esther what was going on. Esther simply informed her that they were going on an "overnight." She gave Mary a Mekranoti basket to hang from her forehead, and suggested she take along a few small items. The "overnight" lasted several months, but by the end of it Mary had become well adjusted to life in the Amazon.

After the boys explained why they had brought me to her hut, Esther turned to me and asked if my hand hurt much. When I said no, she replied calmly, "It will later. They say you were stung by a scorpion." I realized now why Amakkry had been so insistent in my seeing FUNAI.

Scorpions, like jaguars, play an important role in Kayapo mythology. They are closely associated with night. A long time ago the Kayapo did not have night, elders like to point out; they had only the bright sun. Night belonged to Brazilians. It was brought to the Kayapo in a calabash tightly covered to prevent its escape. But a young man brashly opened the package and let the darkness free. As happens today with people who are too curious about the night, a scorpion stung the man, and he cried out in pain, "Ngua, ngua." His companions grabbed him by the arm and threw him in the air, where he turned into an owl, which to this day continues to make the same cries at night.

Since neither I nor Esther had any medicine for scorpion stings, Esther gave me some snake antivenin she thought might help, and insisted I see Ronaldo. Ronaldo jumped to his feet when he heard the word scorpion. Some time before, one of his patients, a young girl, had died from a scorpion bite. He gave me some medicine, although he had nothing for scorpions either. Scorpion medicine is expensive, and there are so many different species of the insect that you can never be sure whether a given antivenin will work or not. I still felt okay, but Ronaldo wanted me to sit in the infirmary for a while.

After about half an hour I began to feel dizzy and moved to a hammock. Then the contractions began. My whole body felt numb, like a leg whose circulation has been cut off. Anything that touched me sent me into violent muscle spasms, as in lockjaw, jerking my spinal column into a bend either forward or backwards. Soon, even my breathing caused contractions, and I began to worry about suffocating. I kept telling myself that scorpions don't kill normal, healthy adults, even though I knew they could kill small children.

Even though I couldn't talk, I could hear everything perfectly and I understood what was going on with the crowd of people surrounding me. Some of the Indians were sympathetic to my plight. Kentỳxti came by to offer help. He grabbed my hand and started spitting tobacco on it. But the touch caused spasms even more violent than the ones I was already experiencing. He walked away with the comment that my case must be serious if his remedies failed so badly. Other Indians were less compassionate. I could hear some of the children imitating my spasms, as they laughed uproariously at the sight. Even some of the adults joined in on this play.

The village's outsiders were put off by the conduct of some of the Indians, and asked that the room be emptied. Esther tried to call for a missionary plane to take me out of the village, but was told that it was too late in the day. Ronaldo then got on the FUNAI radio to ask about FUNAI planes, one of which just happened to be nearby in a neighboring community. Arrangements were all set for a flight into the Mekranoti village when the FUNAI attendant at the other end of the radio asked for the name of the Indian who was stung. Ronaldo replied that it was not an Indian but an anthropologist. The response was quick, but final. "This changes everything," the voice at the other end of the radio explained. "Anthropologists are supposed to take care of themselves. They cannot expect to use FUNAI services." The plane would not come in.

Gustaaf, Esther, Ronaldo, and Mateu watched me through the night as the spasms gradually diminished. I was grateful for all of the attention. As with most anthropologists, I felt ambiguous about the presence of other observers among the Indians I was studying. I would have preferred to be "alone" with the Indians to see them more isolated from "civilized" contact. On the other hand, I felt more protected, knowing there were others of my own culture around. I imagine the missionaries and FUNAI people felt much the same, for we rarely crossed paths. The missionaries were cautious with me and downright fearful of FUNAI, which sometimes refused to grant them authorization to enter the village. But now, in an emergency situation, everyone seemed to get along fine. I was thankful there were people who understood Western medicine living close by.

By morning I could breathe easily again although I still couldn't move. I was getting better, but decided nonetheless to take the plane the missionaries had called. I could not continue to depend on FUNAI to take care of me, especially after the no-nonsense statements I had heard the day before. The young men carried me to the plane in my hammock, and Gustaaf accompanied me to a clinic in a Brazilian town some 500 miles away.

The scorpion incident was over quickly. I felt as good as new with only one day in the clinic. After buying a few more things to take back to the village—including scorpion antivenin—Gustaaf and I returned a few days later. But some things continued to remind me of the incident. A numbness remained in my fingers for several months. The boys teased me constantly, trying to convince me that scorpions were hiding nearby. They imitated well the high-pitched squeaks scorpions make in the morning. But most of all, I became an expert on scorpion stings. Like Mekranoti shamans who acquire power by suffering through the diseases they treat, I was now an authority on scorpions.

# 6

# DEATHS

Traveling to the Mekranoti village was much easier the second time around. Less nervous, I even managed to sleep on the bus to Miranorte. The dry season was in full swing so the road to Araguacema was good and the flight to the village, sure. Even the Indians seemed calmer when we arrived. Many had decided to go on a trek to a distant part of the forest, leaving the village half empty. The women's *bijok* ceremony would just have to be suspended until the trekkers' return later in the year.

The calm was interrupted one day by a loud scream from the other end of the village. Running outside, I saw some men carrying a large peccary carcass to the center of the plaza, where they began the job of butchering and distributing the meat to all of the villagers. One of the old women was wailing loudly because the men had just killed her pet. She had inherited the right to raise the animal, and had suckled it on her own breasts when it was still a piglet. It would follow her around the village, and sometimes nudge people to get petted. Peccaries have glands on their backs for leaving scents to mark their group territory, and periodically they rub each others' backs to verify this scent. The dirty, bristly hairs must have carried lice or worse, but the children and some of the adults stroked it just the same. The only problem was that like all wild animals it could never really be tamed. This one had just bitten a child so the Mekranoti decided it had to be killed.

Other pets were less bothersome. The macaws and parrots in the village had their wings clipped. They stayed out of the way most of the time, perched on shelves or crossbeams under the hut's roof. Some of the parrots learned to talk a little Kayapo. Pet birds were plucked now and then so their tail feathers could be stuck into headdresses and their body down pasted onto masks. They were a sad sight walking "nude" around the village. Another large black bird liked to follow its owner around everywhere she went. The Indians called it a *mỳrmỳr* because of the cooing sound it made. Several women also had small monkeys that would cry unless they could clutch onto their mistresses' hair. When they grew up, the monkeys learned to scurry down their mistresses' backs and legs to cause mischief. Other wild animals fared less well. Hunters handed over small paca or weasels to their children to play with. But the kids almost always killed their pets with rough play. The only jaguar kitten I saw was independent-minded and soon escaped to the forest.

The feeling of calm was also interrupted by an incident with Kaxre. Descending on my hut with a group of other Mekranoti, the chief's son claimed that he should be paid for helping to carry me to the airstrip after I was stung by the scorpion. Gustaaf and I managed to convince him that just as we expected no payment for giving medicine to sick Indians so they should expect no recompense for helping the ill. But the real problem behind this confrontation was unsolvable: the injustice of different health standards for "whites" and for "Indians." Why should I be able to get a plane immediately when I was sick, while they had to wait for weeks? Was my life really worth more than theirs? Later in the year the Indians, who knew of a toothache I had suffered, asked if I had had the tooth extracted when I visited the city. It was difficult to explain fillings and other dental care unavailable to them. The sting of social inequality would be hard to accept after centuries of egalitarian living.

Illness was on the minds of many Indians. Several people were suffering from malaria, and several more had gonorrhea. Ultimately, the Indians feel most illness comes from the sorcery brought to the world by a treacherous pet heron back in the mythological past. Swooping down on people while they were out poisoning fish, the heron scared most people to death and caused the others to fall in the water and become sick. Perhaps the present diseases came from Indians returning from the trekking group, people speculated. Before going off by themselves, the trekkers had visited another Kayapo village to the north to get manioc flour and other garden produce to take with them. Malaria was much more common among these people than at home.

Another "health" problem had also arisen. Iredjo gave birth to twin girls. There was something animal-like about having a "litter" rather than a child. Besides, Iredjo already had three sons to take care of and, as a *kupry*, she could not count on the support of a husband to help her. She often brought me heavy loads of firewood or garden produce to obtain the things other women could get from their husbands—who gave me meat. Her sons lacked the attention other children in the village enjoyed. They walked around dirty and rarely got painted with genipap dye or wore elaborate ornaments. The men who had fathered Iredjo's children were still in the village, but they had their own families to support.

Iredjo was married when her first child was born. But when it died soon after birth and her next pregnancy resulted in a miscarriage, her husband left her to marry a younger woman. Iredjo had to rely on other men—her father, Bokrã, and her brother, brother-in-law, and paramours. They gave her meat and things that men provided, such as woven baby slings.

Years ago Iredjo would simply have killed one, or both, of the twins as soon as they were born, but with *kuben* in the village this did not seem wise. Instead she waited almost two weeks. Then suddenly we were told that one of her babies had died during the night. Yet there was none of the traditional mourning associated with death—there was no wailing, and Iredjo did not cut her hair. Soon afterwards the entire story had changed. Iredjo had given birth to only one child in the first place, people said. The *kupry* firmly denied any knowledge of twins.

People could ignore Iredjo's problem, but the malaria was harder to explain away. One case of the mosquito-carried illness became particularly serious. Tep'i and Kokokamrek's seven-year-old daughter was now under the care of the FUNAI clinic. Kokokamrek, Iredjo's sister, had already lost five out of the nine children she had borne. One she killed soon after birth, another drowned accidentally, and the other three succumbed to illnesses, two of them during an epidemic. The sick girl was Kokokamrek's only live daughter. I volunteered to stay up a couple of nights to take her temperature every hour and wake up Ronaldo if she appeared worse.

Ronaldo felt the girl probably had malaria combined with a bad case of anemia from the worms and amoeba most Mekranoti carry around in their intestines. After treating her for several days with chloroquine and "soro," a mixture of vitamins given intravenously, Ronaldo felt she was getting better. But then the girl's parents decided to take her back, and refused any further treatment from FUNAI. One of the shamans had been pressuring the family to accept native remedies.

Almost one out of every four Mekranoti men is a shaman of some sort, and a couple of women are recognized curers as well. After learning about medicinal plants, mostly from their parents, shamans acquire extra prestige when they suffer through the illnesses they have learned to "cure." Most of them are old men by the time they gain sufficient renown to practice their craft. After mixing the leaves of different forest plants with water, shamans ask their patients to drink the concoction or they pour the mixture over their heads. Filling the area with tobacco smoke, they also chant over their patients' bodies, and sometimes suck out "evil sorcery" from the offending organs. Fortunately, only people in distant places work sorcery among the Mekranoti, so there was no problem with witchcraft accusations. Some parts of their cures were difficult to accept. I was often horrified at the sight of a shaman spitting tobacco into the boils the Mekranoti get on their buttocks or legs. The infections sometimes got so bad that Ronaldo had to lance the sores, a painful operation most people tried very hard to avoid.

Other shamanistic "cures" also seem to cause more trouble than good, but they may be beneficial at times. When suffering from a high fever, sick Mekranoti are thrown into the river to cool off. Normally this is unhealthy, but in an emergency it may act like aspirin to bring down a dangerously high temperature. In any case, the cures, like placebos, may help even if they don't really "work." Illness is one of those uncontrollable and unpredictable things that call for magic to relieve anxiety.

The Mekranoti feel unsure about Western medicine. They recognize its power and use it whenever they can see it is effective. Women bring their children every day to the FUNAI clinic for minor treatment of cuts and skin infections, but in more serious cases where cures are less certain, they lose confidence. Then they can be persuaded by the shamans that the illness is not a "civilized" disease, but an "Indian" one, and therefore deserving of "Indian" cures. The shamans, for their part, would like to do as much curing as possible. It enhances their prestige, and brings in extra income as well. FUNAI dispenses medicine free of charge, but the shamans ask for expensive gifts like hammocks or shotgun shells. When their daughter was still at the FUNAI clinic, several shamans made daily visits to Tep'i and Kokokamrek, demanding that the couple bring their daughter back home to receive native treatments.

At home the fevers and chills grew worse every day. Anxious over her deteriorating condition, the child's parents eventually decided to take the girl back to FUNAI. Ronaldo was not at all pleased with the decision. Several years earlier he had gone through a similar experience. The Indians waited too long to bring him a sick child who was already beyond help. The morning after the patient died, Ronaldo was awakened from his sleep by a man at the door. "Ronaldo, come out here," the Indian said softly. "I'm going to kill you, just as you killed this girl." It took some fancy talking for Ronaldo to get himself out of that situation, and he didn't want to risk it again. Still he agreed to take back the patient.

Calling every day for a FUNAI plane to take the girl to Belém or Altamira for treatment, Ronaldo tried for a week to keep his patient alive. But when it became obvious that their daughter could not possibly survive another day, her parents took her back home to die.

I was expecting the wails that night, but they were chilling just the same. When I timidly entered Tep'i's hut, it was crowded with people, most of them talking angrily about FUNAI and foreigners in general. A kerosene lamp, set in the middle of the floor, illuminated the dead girl lying on her platform bed, surrounded by people examining her body. "It's the worms that killed her," several people commented. When the body dies and oxygen is cut off, the worms crawl out through the mouth and anus to find air.

The Kayapo bury their dead in a cemetery in the weedy land surrounding the village. At night people avoid this area altogether if they can, but if they must pass through it they blow tobacco smoke to protect themselves from the spirits in the place. The *norny* dig the graves. The deceased's relatives or in-laws prepare the corpse, first painting it with genipap dye, and then adding other decorations used by the dead person while still alive. The body is lowered into the grave, and placed on a mat in a sitting position with knees doubled up against the chest.

So that the spirit of the deceased will not return to the village to get personal possessions, the deceased's beads, weapons, and feathers are placed nearby. At times one of the dead person's dogs is also killed and buried with its owner. There are even recorded cases in which the Kayapo have killed children to accompany adults to the grave, especially very young or crippled children who would have trouble surviving in any case. A grating of sticks covered with a mat goes over the body so that the dirt shoveled on top will not touch the corpse. People avoid stepping on the resulting mounds. It is because the moon once stomped on a grave, the Kayapo say, that humans no longer recover their bodies after they die. There is no reason to make matters worse by further violating burial grounds.

At the gravesite the mourners wail loudly. The women struggle to wrest machetes from one another's hands. To demonstrate their grief they hit themselves over their heads with the knives until the blood streams down in tiny rivulets over their faces. Fortunately, they never bring enough machetes to cause real damage before someone else grabs the knife from them.

The graveside mourning is intense but brief. The dirt is piled into a mound over the grave, and a personal possession belonging to the deceased is placed on a stick on top. When the dead person's spouse or parents shave the tops of their heads in mourning, they also sometimes place a few locks of hair above the grave.

The burial preparations help the dead get to their final home somewhere in the savanna regions to the east of the Mekranoti village, and discourage them from returning. Feeding on lizards and dirt, the spirits of the dead sleep in rocks and come at night to the forested areas of the Amazon, where they seek out their relatives and try to kill them. They want to bring these people with them to the village of the dead to alleviate their loneliness. Sometimes the spirits, who hide behind trees, appear as flashes of light in the dark forest and scare the living, who do not want to be killed by their dead relatives. I heard at least one Mekranoti say he killed a spirit when he saw it turn its head.

Mekranoti religion offers no comfort in death—no peaceful resting place, no legacy of good will for the living, no feeling of having pleased the supernatural. Their religion seems to offer little consolation for the living as well. All of the spirits are evil—the invisible fish that cause infections, the rocks that give people disease, and the ghosts of the dead, who try to kill their relatives. There were a few heroes in the mythological past, but they are no longer around to protect people from the malevolent spirits that still inhabit the forest and the waters. At most, people can seek help from the shamans, but they are no longer as powerful as they once were.

The spirits mistreat good and bad people equally. But this does not mean that evil deeds go unpunished. If people misbehave they simply estrange themselves from their fellows. Bad people give everybody headaches and stomach problems, and, because they ruin their appetites and do not eat as they should, they also die young. Still, the punishment for misbehavior is entirely secular. The spirits do not get involved. It is mostly in stratified societies with courts and lawyers to judge people that the gods, like the government, take on the job of moral custodian. In simpler societies religion generally has little to do with morality.

The plane that was to take the sick girl to the hospital arrived the day after the funeral. Too late to do any good, it only added to the frustration everyone felt. Having sent the child's soul off to the spirit world, most Mekranoti were reluctant to talk about the death. It is unwise to bring up the subject and taboo to mention the dead person's name. People turned their complaints to more secular matters.

The FUNAI plane was supposed to take several Indians to Belém to buy goods for the village. The trip had been promised as payment for the Brazil nuts the Mekranoti collect for FUNAI every year. The nut-collecting had taken place in January or February, and it was already July. The Indians were growing impatient. After finally landing, the pilot reported that he could not accommodate these Indians, since he was going to another village afterwards and would have too many things to carry. Instead, he brought in a black peasant with his wife and many children. The family was employed to check on using the Mekranoti River for navigation, although no one seriously believed boats could travel on the tree-cluttered and irregular waterway.

The Mekranoti were furious over the treatment they were getting. They increased their aggressive talk and threatened to go off by themselves to the forest to live with bows and arrows as they had done before contact. Unprepared for such hostility, Mateu, the neophyte FUNAI representative, unofficially boarded the FUNAI plane, citing "personal safety" as his reason.

Perhaps because of Mateu's desertion, the FUNAI plane returned to the Mekranoti village the next day. This time it brought back a Mundurucu Indian along with Mateu. The Indian had been a troublesome welfare case for FUNAI. Getting along poorly with other people, he refused to stay in any of the villages where FUNAI had sent him. Finally, to make sure he could not escape again, FUNAI decided to place him in the Mekranoti village, one of the most isolated spots in Pará. The Mekranoti were puzzled by all of this confusion but calmed down a bit after the pilot agreed to take Tàkàkrorok, Kentỳxti, and Kaxre to Belém.

With nerves a bit easier, I returned to my work. I was interrupted every now and then, though, by Tep'i and Kokokamrek. At first I didn't recognize them because of their newly shaved heads. They wanted to give them things. After their daughter's death people had come by their house and confiscated all of their belongings. "That's the way it is when someone dies," Tep'i explained, his voice almost a whisper. Because of his mourning he would not be permitted to talk loudly for months. "The people who aren't related to the dead one take everything," he lamented. "They took all our pots and machetes and shotguns, and left us with an empty house." I was shocked at the custom. As if the family hadn't suffered enough already, people had to make the mourners' lives even more difficult by robbing them of their property.

It took a bit of reflection to realize what was behind the custom. In the past the Mekranoti had few goods to give up on the death of a loved one, and it mattered little if they were lost. Most belongings were simply buried with the corpse. It is probably good to get rid of things strongly associated with a departed loved one. Free of constant reminders of the past, mourners can more easily adjust to a new way of living. Today it is more difficult to replace acquisitions, so people are less willing to bury them all. Letting other people take these goods from the mourning family may seem horrible at first, but it may actually help in the long run. For the family, the goods can only bring back sad memories, but they can still be used by others. Since the Mekranoti share their goods so extensively, Tep'i and Kokokamrek would easily be able to recoup their losses. Perhaps because of all the household goods the villagers took from her, Kokokamrek enjoyed a reputation during my stay for unusual generosity. Curiously, though, her husband did not share this esteem, perhaps because most of the goods taken were " women's" property, like pots.

Mekranoti exchanges are so fluid that it's difficult to distinguish gifts form thefts or loans. This was brought home to me one day when Nhàkngonhti, one of the women of Takakrorok's household, came into my hut to complain about her neighbor. While bathing her child, Nhàkngonhti saw another woman walk off with the beads she had left on the river bank. She called after the woman, insisting that the beads belonged to her child, but to no avail. The other woman would not give them back. The list of past exchanges between the two women went on and on, so there was no way of knowing if the "theft" was justified or not. Nhàkngonhti wanted me to talk to the other woman, or else replace the beads from my own stock. I eventually agreed to some interviews and some gifts of food from Nhàkngonhti and replaced the beads she had lost.

To get away from their problems, Tep'i and Kokokamrek often left the village for a couple of days to hunt or fish in more distant parts of the forest. Their leaving gave me a respite from the constant haranguing about giving them things. At these times they took along Iredjo, Kokokamrek's sister, as well as Kokokamrek's brother and his wife, or Tep'i's sister and her husband. These trips were good opportunities for Iredjo to obtain the meat and fish that are difficult for *kupry* to get. Several times during my fieldwork Iredjo went out hunting herself. Although she did not own a shotgun, she managed to club peccaries to death and to dig up armadillos. She laughed when reminded of these masculine exploits and insisted that she enjoyed the hunting. She even mentioned a few other women in the village who did the same thing at times, and seemed to feel a certain pride in her masculine accomplishments.

The rest of the village quickly got over the death of Tep'i's daughter, and turned their attention to other matters, like the new strangers in the village. The Mundurucú Indian had already begun to anger many of the Mekranoti. Much shorter and darker than the Kayapo, he stood out as very different physically. He also wore long pants and a collared shirt. He usually walked around with his nose buried in his collar, complaining that everyone smelled bad, and trying his best to filter the air that reached his nostrils. He also begged for food from everyone, and sometimes just took things. He even insisted that he was a great Mundurucú chief who was being persecuted by FUNAI. The Mekranoti laughed about such pretensions, and they managed to imitate the Mundurucú's mannerisms perfectly. Things finally came to a head, though, when some children playing on the airstrip picked up some rocks and began throwing them at him. It became obvious that the Mundurucú could not continue with the Mekranoti.

The new Brazilian family was more welcome. Some of the Indians already knew the household head, a husky dark-skinned man, some fifty years old. He had been around when Meirelles first contacted Angme'ê's group, and he helped mediate between FUNAI and the Indians during Brazil-nut-collecting. Illiterate, Pedro identified more with the Indians than with the rest of us *kuben*. He had a passable command of Kayapo and enjoyed going out hunting. He knew the plants in the forest, and had his own mythology about them—his stories coming from a combination of Indian lore and backwoods Brazilian Catholicism. Traveling around barefoot, he had a reputation for strength that the Mekranoti extended to all black Brazilians. "Blacks are strong like Indians, and they work hard," the Mekranoti sometimes commented. "Whites are weak and lazy."

Even though they got along well with Pedro, the Mekranoti were still a bit put off by the arbitrariness of FUNAI in bringing in so many new people. To clear their minds of all the confusion that accompanied the importation of so many strangers, many of the Indians thought that now would be a good time to make a long trip to a distant river to hunt and fish. Ronaldo objected to the trip because FUNAI's traveling medical team would be coming soon to the village to give vaccinations, pull teeth, and clear up parasites. The team would remain only a few days and would be able to do very little if no one was around. Already half the village was away gathering palm oil. If the remaining half decided to trek as well, there would be nothing for the medical team to do. But the Indians no longer believed FUNAI's promises and thought it useless to base their decisions on them.

In preparation for the trek, the women spent several days making extra trips to their gardens to bring back sweet potatoes, bananas, and bitter manioc roots. Then they worked hard at peeling and grating the manioc. Using the sides of kerosene cans punctured with nails and attached to a board, the women sat for hours in the open manioc shed near the FUNAI house, grating the tubers in the company of the other women. First putting the soggy mash into a large wooden tub they eventually transferred it to a press made of four poles stuck in the ground with sticks loosely criss-crossed up the sides and lined with banana leaves. The press was topped with a large sturdy pole used as a lever to squeeze the mash. Sometimes people hung from the pole to weight the press so that the poisonous prussic acid in the manioc water would drain out, but the press usually ended up with a rock on top. The side sticks were gradually removed as the drying pulp began to shrink. Unlike other Indians, the Mekranoti do not save the manioc water, whose residue is tapioca.

After the water all drained out, the pulp still had to be toasted. The Mekranoti now have a huge iron grill some six feet in diameter, lying atop a clay oven. Keeping a fire going underneath and stirring the manioc above requires at least two people working full time. When a group is preparing for a trek the grill is in high demand, so couples sometimes work overnight. It's cooler at night anyway, so the heat from the oven seems less oppressive. In the years before contact with whites, the Mekranoti did not use bitter manioc and did not know how to process it. It was other Brazilian Indians who discovered the secret of turning the poisonous root into a high-energy food. Some Kayapo made mistakes at first and were poisoned, but now the Mekranoti have made manioc their own. Women spend almost four hours a week processing the plant, and even the men help out for an hour and a half every week.

As the Indians busied themselves with trekking preparations, I tried to figure out what to do myself. None of the other outsiders in the village wanted to go with the Indians. Esther and Mary had already left the village, and Gustaaf planned to catch the next plane out. I would see little of him after this trek, for he would be studying other Kayapo groups in distant villages. Ronaldo and Mateu had to wait for the medical team and Pedro and his family were looking forward to a month or so of calm to set themselves up in the village. Besides, Pedro could provide meat for the visitors who stayed behind.

I finally arranged to go with Amakkry on trek. Because of his attention to my scorpion sting I felt secure with him. He was also a good hunter, and had provided Gustaaf and me with plenty of meat. I might have gone with Kentỳxti had he still been around, but Esther warned me that his wife, Kotjaka, was too lazy, which would make life difficult for me. I did not yet know Amakkry's wife, Kokokà, but Gustaaf assured me she was okay, although a bit loudmouthed.

When I asked Amakkry about my plans, he immediately agreed. He also called me his son, and told me I was to call him "father" and his wife "mother." Kokokà also liked the idea since she knew this would mean more gifts of beads and pots. I was happy with the arrangement, but still a bit apprehensive about spending a month or so wandering about in the forest. I would be alone with the Indians for the first time.

My nervousness increased when I thought about giving medicine. Ronaldo insisted I take along various articles from the FUNAI pharmacy, to which I added many of the drugs I brought along myself. I had never given medicine and knew nothing about it. Fortunately, I had an excellent medical guide prepared by S.I.L. missionaries. Since it was organized according to symptoms, I could look up the problems people described to me. The guide recommended the best remedies, along with alternatives in case I was short of a given medicine—including a few rather unusual folk remedies for problems like snake bite.

After half a day of gathering my things together, I finally trudged over to Amakkry and Kokokà's hut and joined them as they made the final preparations for the trip. Amakkry agreed to carry the medicine, and I was left with my backpack, my hammock, and my machete. We departed without a word to the others left behind.

# 7

# ON TREK TO THE SABUJÍ

The path went past the river behind my house. I had traveled it before but only as far as the gardens on top of the hill. Amakkry walked at a fast clip in front and soon left the rest of us behind. Kokokà slung a huge basket from her forehead. Filled with sweet potatoes and bananas, the heavy container also supported pots and sleeping mats hung on its sides. Above the basket, Kokokà balanced a kerosene can full of toasted manioc flour. Her one-year-old daughter, 'Okàre, rode on top. It was a wonder Kokokà could even lift the load, let alone carry it along the narrow path. Tàkàk'y, her energetic ten-year-old son, ran ahead, scrambling up thick lianas and shouting to us from the tops. Irekĩ, her six-year-old daughter, was quieter and simply walked alongside her mother, every now and then blowing the firebrand she carried to keep it glowing.

The path was narrow. To keep from slipping on the edges of the gullied footway, I had to walk pigeon-toed like the Indians. The forest was cool and, except for the rocky hillside, traveling was easy. Expecting a long hike that first day, I was surprised when Kokokà stopped after only an hour of travel. The sundappled glade was bustling with over a hundred Indians who had dropped their cargos and were cutting down the saplings around them to make small clearings. We had just passed the hill gardens so I assumed people wanted to rest awhile and perhaps harvest more produce. But no, I was told. This was our first campsite. We would travel more the next day. I was disappointed. It hardly seemed worth the bother if we moved no farther than an hour from the main village.

Kokokà cleared away a few trees near where she had plopped her heavy baggage, and then smoothed the earth underneath to remove all of the roots and stones that could make sitting uncomfortable. "This is the family's sleeping place," she explained. "I'll put some leaves on the ground and then put the mats on top."

"What if it rains?" I asked, trying to catch a glimpse of the sky through the thick forest foliage.

"It won't," she answered, looking back as she bounced off to collect her leaves. "It's the dry season already." I slung my hammock between two trees nearby and cleared the ground underneath. I hoped she was right about the rain.

The campsite began to look a little less hectic as the men dashed off on the forest trail to spend the day hunting. Their dogs, confused by the new surroundings, reluctantly trotted along behind. A few of the curs, totally disoriented by the new surroundings, had to be carried out of the encampment, much to the chagrin of their owners, who normally took great pride in their hunting pets.

Gradually the women returned to arrange their leaves on the ground. But they were quickly off again, chopping firewood or returning to the village or the nearby garden to haul more produce to tomorrow's campsite. On trek the Mekranoti average almost two hours a day simply carrying around bundles, each weighing seventy pounds or more.

During the morning, the boys of Tàkàk'y's age-grade, known as the *'okre*, had to clear a special area in the center of the campsite, and cover it with leaves. This was the "men's house" while on trek. At night while women and children passed by all around, the men gathered here and exchanged stories of the day's hunting, or perhaps wove a baby carrying-sling or arranged feathers for a ceremonial headdress. The boys had no trouble with this simple task, and soon ran off to go fishing or to shoot birds with their tiny bows and arrows while hiding in the leafy blinds they built near the birds' feeding places. They plucked, cooked, and ate whatever they caught, even though the birds rarely had much flesh on them.

The bustle of that morning contrasted sharply with the lazy afternoon. By noon Kokokà had already settled down to play with 'Okàre, nursing her for a time and occasionally giving the infant some pre-masticated banana pulp to eat. Whenever 'Okàre defecated, Kokokà simply called the dogs. They rushed to her summons, lapping up the mess and licking the baby's behind. Finally, in a minimalist lullaby, Kokokà hummed a repeated single note to put 'Okàre to sleep. The other mothers did much the same with their own infants, so at times the campsite buzzed with the quiet purrs of several mothers at once.

"It is much easier to paint children when they're asleep," Kokokà pointed out, as she prepared her body-painting dye. The black coloring is made from the juice of the wild genipap fruit mixed with the ashes from inner bark and saliva. Keeping one hand clean, Kokokà used the other to coat the stem of a palm leaf that served as a palette knife for laying on the delicate stripe-line designs. Some of the body paintings are original creations of the mother. Others represent fish or jaguars or armadillo shells. The Kayapo claim that one of their striking hexagonal patterns was taken over by tortoises.

According to legend, there was once a man who asked his wife to wait for him at the bottom of a tree while he collected fruit from the top. Newly painted for the birth of her nephew, the attractive woman was approached by a shaman who tried to seduce her, without success. Angry at this rejection, the sorcerer turned the woman into a tortoise, which her husband took home to eat. It was the tortoise's singing and its painted back that allowed the man to recognize his wife and return her to human form. But the body-painting remained on all later tortoises, which to this day still have Kayapo designs on their backs.

When Tàkàk'y returned to camp at one in the afternoon, he brought some small fish that he boiled and served over manioc flour. He gave some of the food to his little sister, Irekī, although there was very little fish to share. Amakkry returned at two o'clock carrying on his back a small foxlike animal the Mekranoti called simply "red animal." Like his son, Amakkry also shared his catch with his sister, who had set up camp nearby. But we all got some of the meat.

The rest of the afternoon was quiet and peaceful. For an hour or so Kokokà deloused Amakkry. Sitting behind her husband, she slapped his head to stun the lice, and then searched through his hairs and bit to death any insects she found. Delousing was one of the most intimate acts between a man and his wife. It was practically the only time they ever touched each other in public. Couples usually ate separately as well. Instead of set meals, the Mekranoti simply indulged themselves whenever they were hungry. The men often ate in the men's house. Women ate snacks when out in the garden, or whenever a particularly tempting food came into the house. Sometimes couples did not even sleep together. For two years or more after the birth of a child, sex is taboo for the new mother. At this time men must spend most nights in the men's house.

The day ended with a festive picnic. The *norny* returned from hunting with six macaws. The birds were especially prized for their long red tail feathers, which the Mekranoti use for ornaments. If possible, the Indians like to catch them live to bring home as pets. But the young men had already killed these birds so they gave them to the women to cook. Since this was the first night on trek, the women decided to roast the birds in a community oven.

During the day the women had already collected firewood and the large round stones they would heat for the earth oven. Now they arranged the split logs in what looked like a confusing heap, but was probably the best arrangement to get a good fire. After placing the rocks on top, they ignited the pile. While waiting for the wood to burn, the women busily began preparing the macaw pies. Pies are the most traditional kayapo food. Before metal pots made boiling possible, roasting was the only kind of cooking the Kayapo knew, for they had no pottery of their own.

To make the meat pies, the women first grated sweet manioc root and wrung out the juice with a small straw squeezer. Then they arranged banana leaves in a star shape on the ground and placed the squeezed manioc inside with tidbits of meat on top. After wrapping up the leaves, the unbaked pies were ready for the oven. If all went well they could be very good. But usually they were made without salt and unbearably bland.

When the fire finally burned out, the women gingerly rolled away the hot stones and carefully placed sweet potatoes and meat pies in the oven's center with the heated rocks on top and a layer of leaves over this. A heavy pile of dirt over the leaves insulated the oven while everyone waited for the pies to cook. The roasting banana leaves sent cardamom-scented smoke wafting through the campsite. The delicious aroma made stomachs growl. Sometimes people grew impatient and took the oven apart too soon. Then the meat was raw and had to be roasted on another day. But this time everyone waited stoically until they were sure the birds would be thoroughly cooked.

The women carried the meat pies, one by one, to the men's house, where the men hastily opened them and checked to make sure the meat was done. Three or four men normally shared a pie, lustily sticking their fingers into the doughy mess and wiping their hands on the floor leaves. They passed the pies around to make sure all of the men would get some. The women and children often had to content themselves with mostly boiled food back in the houses.

The first night on trek ended quietly. A few children had minor cuts and scratches to treat, but I spent most of my time with the men, as they talked excitedly about arriving at the Sabují River where fishing was sure to be good. Exhausted from the change in life style, people went to bed early—about nine o'clock. Tàkàk'y stayed with his parents until the last minute, when he retired to the men's house to sleep.

From my hammock I could hear the quiet household conversations at the other end of the campsite. Unlike the more closed and formal life of the village, there was a gentler, more intimate feel to trekking life. I could understand why the Mekranoti enjoyed the trips so much. The night remained peaceful. The dogs occasionally wandered off around the camp periphery to bark at unknown creatures, with none of the mad attacking en masse that occurred every night in the main village. Perhaps the animals were just tired from the day's hunting.

The next morning we were up by six, slightly earlier than back in the main village. The open-air sleeping meant that light appeared sooner and woke people up. After a quick snack of sweet potatoes from the previous night, we packed our things and set off again. After several days of trekking I learned to tie up my hammock so I could take it down right away, but at first I was slow, and ended up leaving after most of the village had already departed. Usually the next day's camp was only forty-five minutes to an hour away.

Although we followed the same basic schedule every day, trekking never became monotonous. One night a small flock of birds settled on some trees only a few feet from the campgrounds. I tried in vain to see the colorful feathers hidden in the upper branches, but no one else seemed to have any trouble at all. The villagers were excited but controlled themselves enough to allow all of the men to get their guns ready before anyone began shooting. Amakkry got one bird, weighing about ten pounds. I saw it only when it fell. Other men downed three more.

In the main village people almost never found game so close to home. The Indians remembered only one instance in the past twenty-five years, when a herd of peccaries stomped by within a few yards of their main village. On trek such experiences were much more common, and almost expected. It was no wonder that the Mekranoti ate game on nine days out of ten while on trek, but only six out of ten while at home.

Another night Amakkry spotted a tree near camp that, from underneath, appeared full of fruits people considered a delicacy. As he began chopping through the two-foot-diameter trunk, the other villagers took note. The women rushed to get their baskets to join in the scramble that was sure to take place when the tree finally fell. As Amakkry and the other men took turns chopping through the hard wood, the noisy crowd looked on. Mothers screamed at their children and ran after them to keep them clear of the area where the tree would finally fall.

Slightly off target, the heavy trunk crashed through the forest canopy, and people ran for safety. But they quickly rushed back to pick the fruit before others beat them to it. There was a loud sigh and a sudden pause in the scramble as the first women reached the fallen treetop—the tree was the wrong species and had nothing edible on it! Everyone had mistakenly identified its leaves. My faith in the Mekranoti's knowledge of their environment was shaken. But then it was nice to know that the Indians were only human.

Because of the more intimate atmosphere of trekking life, I began to learn much more about the Indians—their work habits, how they joked with each other, and the ways they helped each other out. Kokokà sometimes had me ask her *krabdjwỳ*, Beptu, for meat, telling me the proper way to request things from these special ceremonial friends enlisted to dance with one's child during the final days of Kayapo ceremonies. When Beptu responded in surprise at my brazenness, Kokokà simply laughed and attributed the gaffe to my ignorance of Mekranoti custom. She was using me much as any mother would use her children. So, as the days wore on, faces and names finally became clear and I began to recognize individual personalities. I had been in the village for more than two months, so it was about time I learned everyone's name. I felt at home with Kokokà and Amakkry, my adopted family.

A fat, young, carefree woman, Kokokà was a curious mixture of fun and business. Like any mother with her child, she yelled at me whenever I grossly breached Kayapo etiquette by not responding properly to things the others said or did. I learned the kin terms I was to use with others, and the proper way of handling the ribald jokes the relatives of ceremonial friends played with each other and with me. Sometimes I grew annoyed with Kokokà's scolding. But whenever she noticed that I was peeved she simply rolled back on her sleeping mat and laughed loudly, her large belly contracting with the guffaws. This was her way of letting me and the others know that the scolding was in fun.

After Kokokà's infant betrothal, Amakkry was her first real husband. So far she had given him five children, but two of them had died—one during a measles epidemic that killed off almost a third of the village. As Teptykti's oldest living daughter, Kokokà, along with Amakkry, held an important position in the household. After Teptykti died people would probably speak of the household as Kokokà's unless one of her sisters managed to have more daughters to bring husbands home.

Amakkry was very different from Kokokà. Much more serious, he rarely joked with his wife or with anyone else for that matter. His high cheekbones and long face made me think of the Apache Indians I associated with American cowboy movies. He once wore a large wooden disk through his perforated lower lip, but after contact he had the lip sewn together. The hole was too large to close properly, and Amakkry was left with a scar that made him look much older and even more serious than he really was. His long straight black hair set off the sternness of his countenance.

Amakkry's father had died when he was a child but not before leaving him several siblings. His mother raised the children through adulthood, but succumbed to the epidemics that followed the first contact with whites. By that time Amakkry, as well as his two brothers and his sister, had established his own household. Amakkry's first marriage did not last, though. Some people claimed it was only an "affair" in any case. The woman still lived in the village with one of Amakkry's daughters, and Amakkry visited them on rare occasions, but there was otherwise little communication between them. Amakkry's second wife gave him a son, Bekwỳnh'i, before she died. When Amakkry took Kokokà as his third wife, he brought Bekwỳnh'i along and the two of them moved into Kokokà's large household.

During the quiet afternoons, while Amakkry hunted or napped and while Kokokà chatted with her neighbors or went to a nearby stream to bathe and fetch water, I busied myself weighing the food my adopted family carried around, and trying to record all of the items that were traded into and out of the household. I wanted to know who traded with whom in order to figure out how important different social ties were in everyday situations.

Nothing seemed to stay only within our family. Amakkry's hunting had been good, and he usually managed to bring back a ten-pound armadillo, a monkey, or some other game which he gave to others to butcher. Some of this meat, usually the less desirable parts like the back or tail, almost always went to his sister, Bekwỳnhry. Other pieces went to Kokokà's niece, Ngrenhkangro, or to her sister, Kokopa. But the "good" meat stayed with us. In return, we got sweet potatoes, bananas, and manioc flour from these women. Occasionally one of Kokokà's brothers also brought us some meat while Kokokà gave produce to them.

The same social ties showed up in the campsite layouts, although not as strongly. Originally I had expected one camp to look much like another, but every day arrangements were slightly different. I began mapping the daily encampments. People seemed to set up their sleeping mats anywhere they chose. Large trees, small hills, ants, and wet ground sometimes forced people to move into different spots. It seemed we were next to a different set of people each day. Only Kokokà's niece, Ngrenhkangro, stuck close by us throughout the trek.

As the days went by I got to know my adopted parents' families. Ngrenhkangro and her husband, Ropti, seemed to be busy all the time. A short, husky woman, Ngrenhkangro had to take over the raising of her two younger sisters as well as her own three children when her mother died a year before. Although younger than Kokokà, she seemed older, perhaps because of her heavier responsibilities and her more serious personality. Ropti spent most of his free time gathering leaves to make a baby sling, and twisting the fibers into cord for weaving. His reputation for hard work seemed well deserved.

I saw less of Kokokà's sister, Kokopa. Enormously fat, Kokopa had a curious reputation for her good looks. I conceded that her face was pretty, with smooth skin and fine features, and her personality was as gentle as her mother's. But I found it hard to understand why the Mekranoti praised her enormous body. Perhaps a taste for fat women has something to do with wanting babies. Mekranoti men say they want as many children as possible, and recent research shows that fatter women are generally more fertile than thin ones. Later I discovered that the Mekranoti generally rate the more fertile women as prettier than the less fertile ones. Kokopa was no exception to the rule. Although younger than Kokokà, she had already borne seven children, five of whom were still alive. Kokopa's husband, by contrast, was tall and lean. They made a curious couple.

Kokokà's brothers also dropped by a couple of times to give meat. Kamti was as big and burly as his sisters, but Wakõte bore no resemblance to the rest of the family. A short, thin man with a friendly smile, he brought tortoises and deer meat to Kokokà. She sent him bananas and sweet potatoes in return. The brothers never stayed long with their sisters, though. It was "embarrassing" for them to be around when their sisters' husbands were close by.

Bekwỳnhry, Amakkry's sister, came around every now and then as well. A few years older than Amakkry, Bekwynhry was already an old woman. She had been married several times, but spent twelve years of her life as a *kupry*. In the village she lived with her two married daughters. The oldest was fathered by her first husband, but the second was born during her *kupry* years. Bekwỳnhry had a reputation for disliking children. She had sent her young son, by her present husband, to live in her husband's sister's house.

These were the people who most often traded food with us. The exchanges looked like simple gift-giving, but probably evened out over a fairly short space of time. Still, they set up important ties—especially between brothers and sisters. I realized the importance of gifts—rather than trade—

when young Tàkàk'y, as he handed some meat to a neighbor, jokingly imitated me by saying the food was "in payment" for a previous gift. Kokokà was appalled and struck the boy soundly on his arm.

As the days wore on, I had to spend more time on medicine. I eventually set up evening "clinic" hours. At the beginning only a few mothers brought me their children to treat for minor cuts and eye infections, but more and more people showed up every day. They seemed to grow careless as trekking became more routine, and their problems grew more serious. I had to send a couple of them back to the main village.

One night, when the campsite was split in two because of a colony of ants, I was called to give medicine in the more distant site. Ryti was having trouble giving birth. Although I had nothing to give her, I went anyway. As is customary, the expectant mother had gone into the forest as soon as labor began. Usually men are not allowed to witness the actual birth. But since Ryti was having trouble, I was called in. Wore, her brother, also watched from a distance. Surrounded by five or six old women, Ryti grasped a tree limb to give her support as she half hung and half squatted in the dark clearing. Arching backwards in agony, she screamed every now and then when the labor pains grew too intense.

I would have been more nervous about my medical responsibilities except that the old women sounded confident. They mocked Ryti's screaming. "What's all the noise? You're a big girl now. You've already had one baby." One woman sat in front between Ryti's legs. She reached inside the vagina during the contractions and tried to feel the baby's head. Finally, amidst a final scream, the newborn slid into the old woman's hands. The onlookers quietly passed the news to each other—"It's alive, a boy."

Ryti remained hanging from the branch as the midwife passed the child to the woman standing at her side. Cradling it gently in her arms, the woman cleaned the baby's mouth and nose, and waited for it to begin breathing. There was no spanking and no hanging it by its feet. After pressing shut the umbilical cord about two feet from the navel, she took a razor blade and cut the cord. Meanwhile, the midwife attended to Ryti to make sure the afterbirth came out as it should.

Tying a rope made of inner bark around her waist to relieve the pain, Ryti finally sat down and took the baby herself. As it nursed quietly, the onlookers began to depart. Ryti's brother, Wore, the only Mekranoti male present, was the first to leave. Now that the danger had passed, he really had no business being there. I gave Ryti some vitamin K in case there was any internal hemorrhaging, and was relieved that no one seemed to think my services necessary or important.

Ryti remained behind when the group traveled the next day. But one day's rest was enough, and she was soon carrying her baskets and her new baby from one camp to the next. She also chopped firewood and did all the other chores women need to do every day.

Ryti's husband had died the day before I arrived in the Mekranoti village, and like all the Mekranoti, Ryti mourned his death. But she was less concerned about it than were the man's sisters and other relatives. One can always get another husband, the Mekranoti explained, but a brother is irreplaceable. The food exchanges I had been observing confirmed the importance of the brother-sister ties. For the time being, at least, Ryti would remain a *kupry* like her mother's sister, and her aunt's two daughters who also lived in her house.

After a week of moving camp every day, we arrived at a garden. Bekwỳnhry and a few others had planted sweet potatoes, manioc, and bananas in this out-of-the-way place for just such occasions as this, when people would need produce far from home. In the past the Mekranoti traveled hundreds of miles on trek and planted gardens throughout the tropical forest.

We waited two days at the garden while everyone refreshed supplies, and then moved on. I cajoled Amakkry into letting me accompany him on a couple of hunting trips. I wanted to know exactly what the men did when they went off to the forest—partly so that I could judge reports of hunting for the time allocation studies I was doing, and partly because I was simply curious. Amakkry was not very enthusiastic about having a clumsy foreigner follow him around, but since I insisted he let me go.

On our first trip Amakkry decided not to take the dogs. He was looking for birds and monkeys, and dogs simply scare them off. We loaded ourselves with bananas to drop off at the next day's campsite and then continued from there. Amakkry walked at a fast clip, but stopped every now and then to listen. He also showed me markings on the forest floor that he said indicated different animals had passed by—old footprints, animal spoors, broken leaves, and the remains of partially eaten berries. Sometimes we could hear the sharp falsetto hoots the men make to keep track of one another's whereabouts, and a couple of times a shot rang off in the distance. Amakkry would then tell me who he thought was doing the shooting and what animal he was after.

At one point Amakkry lost his pipe and we had to backtrack to find it. Funnel-shaped tubes carved out of hard wood, the pipes are smoked by both men and women. The tobacco often falls out the end and is difficult to keep lit, but the Indians hold the pipes in great esteem, especially if they are old and smelly, and properly worn in. He wasted a lot of time looking for the pipe. But the day had not been very successful in any case. Amakkry spotted some birds in a thicket he claimed was a former garden. He fired only one shot, and missed. We returned to camp empty-handed except for some medicinal herbs Amakkry managed to find along the way.

The next morning Amakkry decided to take his three dogs along. Hunting with dogs was a very different experience from the day before. The dogs dashed from one ravine to another, and we chased after them. I lost my shoes in the mud a couple of times and ran into bushes covered with stinging ants. I realized the Indians were right to walk barefoot and virtually nude, as I tried to keep up while pulling off my shirt and brushing away the biting insects. I finally got some rest when the dogs found a tortoise and Amakkry spent a minute or so making carrying rope from bark he tore off a nearby tree. Once the tortoise was fastened to his back we were off running again.

After the dogs sniffed out a paca, we chased the large rodent for half an hour, but eventually gave up. Meanwhile, the dogs had spotted some monkeys. Amakkry managed to shoot a large one which fell to the ground. Still alive, it badly bit one of the dogs. Amakkry finished off his prey by clubbing it to death. We walked around a bit, looking for leaves to make a carrying basket for the monkey, but continued hunting soon after. Amakkry was still not satisfied with the day's catch.

At one point we came over a hill to find a huge pile of red dirt towering above Wore, who, sweaty and dirty, was standing shoulder deep in a hole he had been digging all morning. "The armadillo just keeps burrowing deeper and deeper," he complained. But Wore persisted because he was sure he would eventually get his quarry.

We did not stay to watch Wore eventually pull out his armadillo. But about one o'clock, before going home for the day, we finally rested for a few minutes to eat some unripe Brazil nuts that had fallen around the huge tree. Once Kukrytbam asked me if the skyscrapers in Belém were as tall as these forest giants. I couldn't answer.

On the return path we came across three more hunters and the men exchanged stories. Amakkry told the others about the paca his dogs had scared up, so two of the men ran off to the spot, hoping to find the animal. I realized that although the land far from the village had more game on it, hunters on trek had other problems. They kept getting into one another's way, and had to be careful about where they were searching for game, and what they were shooting at.

By the time I got to the village I was exhausted, but I had a greater admiration for Mekranoti hunting skills, and a greater appreciation of their dogs, which, after all, did scare up a fair amount of game. I now understood the protectiveness the Mekranoti felt for these psychotic pets that barked at nothing in the night and attacked people without reason.

As the village animal shaman, Amakkry had the job of curing sick dogs. He now had to help his own injured pet. After mixing herbs with water, he poured the concoction over the animal's body, and then covered it with red achiote dye. This time his patient got better. But on other occasions he was less successful. Once a peccary broke the lower jaw of a neighbor's dog and Amakkry tried to make a cast. The dog could not eat and eventually starved to death.

I tried taking notes on a few more hunting trips but eventually decided I could learn more in the campsite. I was expecting the trek to continue for a month or more, but after about two and a half weeks the Mekranoti heard a plane pass overhead. They assumed it was the FUNAI medical team and prepared to return home. I was surprised at their enthusiasm for the medicine after all of the terrible things they had said before. But I guess, having passed through epidemics that decimated their village, they were determined to do anything to avoid repeats. The men would go to the Sabují River the next day, they decided, and then all would return.

As we walked to the Sabují, several men told me they would never have actually set up camp on the river in any case. The children might be tempted to go swimming, and would be careless about the stingrays, piranha fish, and crocodiles. People would simply have camped nearby. So there was no need for me to feel I had missed anything special because of the early return.

There was an old garden at the point where the small river that passes in front of the Mekranoti village joins the Sabují. It still produced some bananas and sugar cane. I welcomed the sweets because we had run out several days earlier. But the fishing itself was not very successful. A few men brought back decent catches, but the people I traveled with caught hardly enough fish for themselves, let alone to take back to the main village. The desire to trek to the river seemed more symbolic than anything else. It was the hunting along the way that was really important.

It had taken us two and a half weeks to get where we were in the forest. Returning on the same trail, we made the trip back in just two days. Still, after walking from morning till dusk to arrive in an old campsite, I was impressed with how far we had actually traveled. I understood now how the Kayapo could go on for months and even years wandering in the forest.

After weeks in the dark forest, the sunny village seemed hot. It was the end of July and the dry season was well upon us. Tàkàkrorok cajoled the villagers into cleaning out all the plants that had grown up in the central plaza. For a couple of days people busied themselves with hoes and wheelbarrows until not a blade of grass could be found within the first ring of houses. Some of the residents in the outer ring also cleared their home fronts, and a few young men cut a wide dirt path to the river. The weeds would not grow back again until the rains began in September.

The children exulted in the unaccustomed spaciousness. Dancing and running from one house to another, they tried out new muscles and body movements that their earlier confinement had made impossible. Rollicking behind my house, one group of children forced a dog into their play. A boy playfully hit the animal with a stick. The others, drunk with the novelty of their environment, joined in until a few minutes later the dog was a bloody, lifeless heap. The adults simply carried off the carcass without a word to the children, who continued their play. In the past the Kayapo sometimes gave their children dogs to kill, just to get them used to warfare. Sometimes they even gave them a sickly child to assassinate.

The newly cleared plaza was soon the scene of a short ceremony. While out on trek, Nhàkmroti gave birth to her first baby. One of the *norny,* Nokinh, claimed the child as his and so would join the age-grade of the *mẽ krare,* the parents. There would have to be a *pytê* ceremony to mark the event. Nhàkmroti was excited about this confirmation of her marriage to Nokinh. Her mother had died some years before, and, unlike many other motherless girls, Nhàkmroti could avoid becoming a *kupry.*

Many people thought the birth and the coming ceremony were mistakes. Nhàkmroti had no milk. She had to carry the baby several times a day to another woman at the other end of the village to nurse. Tàkàkrorok mocked the baby's tiny size, and several villagers commented openly that Nokinh was not really ready to become a father. Still too interested in sex with different women, Nokinh was almost as promiscuous as Kentỳxti and Kaxre. Worst of all, he was not a very hard worker, and had yet to prove his hunting skills.

Nokinh himself was unsure about what he wanted. He was reluctant to give up his friends in the *norny* age-grade. Now he would have to choose one of the men's societies to enter. These civic political "clubs" are at the heart of Mekranoti social life. All fathers must belong to one society or the other, and a young man's choice about which society to enter is a major decision. Nokinh's friends would come from the men of his chosen society. Evenings in the men's house, he would sit and chat with this group of people. He would go off with them for community hunts and work with them whenever a house needed to be built or a special men's society garden planted. In the past he would have gone off to war with these men as well. Often men joined the society of their future fathers-in-law, in whose house they would begin to sleep. As a result, most of the men in a given household belonged to the same society. The wives usually joined the women's society associated with their husbands' men's society. The women's societies were less prominent than the men's. Usually they were noticeable only during ceremonies when the women had to harvest food from the gardens of their husbands' men's societies. Nokinh must have felt anxious about the coming ceremony for he commented several times that he really wasn't married to Nhàkmroti. He changed the subject whenever anyone brought up his imminent rite of passage.

To complete the *pytê* ceremony, Nokinh's "brothers," including a few unrelated men he merely called "brother," went to work. They gathered long poles of buriti palm and painted them red with achiote, a dye made from the annatto seed, which the Mekranoti grow in their gardens. After shaving the tops of their heads and painting their faces black, they walked one by one to the front of the men's house, each carrying a long pole across his shoulder. When all had arrived they sat down together in silence, with the poles across their laps. The entire village remained quiet for a few somber minutes that were a surprising contrast to the bustle of everyday life. Then suddenly the men got up and walked over to Nhàkmroti's hut where they quickly stacked the poles against the outer wall. The ceremony had ended. As with most Mekranoti rituals, the simple marking of the passage from one age-grade to another was more important than any supernatural beliefs surrounding it.

Several of the men dropped by my hut later in the day. I was sure that I had never met one of them before. But fortunately, he spoke to me before I had a chance to ask who he was. It was Kentỳxti! With a shaved head and his face and body painted totally black, he looked nothing like my informant of more than two months. Nokinh was in a bit of a daze, and wanted to avoid thinking about his new position in society. He left only late at night, when everyone else had already gone home.

In the weeks following Nokinh's ceremony, I busied myself trying to unravel the Mekranoti recent past. I needed to do history now because other parts of my research depended on it. I could not estimate people's ages, for example, until I could put dates on past Mekranoti events. With a few well-known historical incidents to use as reference points I could ask informants to tell me whether so-and-so was born before or after such and such an event. Or I could ask how big someone was when a given event took place.

Because he liked to talk about the past and because he was always around, Tedjware became my first historical informant. Red-haired and freckled, he was born more than sixty years earlier, of a Brazilian peasant family that tried to plant gardens near Mekranoti lands. The Indians killed his parents and stole Tedjware along with a few other children. The only white child to survive, Tedjware grew up as an ordinary Mekranoti, eventually marrying a Mekronoti woman and fathering several children. He spoke only Kayapo and knew even less than most other Indians about the customs of civilized people. He never understood what money was all about. Seeing a picture of trees from a Canadian autumn, he once asked a missionary if these were the plants money grew on.

Once, a FUNAI official found a woman in an Amazonian town who was probably Tedjware's sister. She was about Tedjware's age and had been found as a child after the Kayapo raided her house. Tedjware was not the least bit interested in meeting her, and I imagine the sister felt much the same way about her Indian brother. Tedjware merely requested that we ask the woman if she would send him a hammock, some pots, and other manufactured goods. He knew the two could not communicate and were culturally worlds apart. As Tedjware puts it today, "I was nursed on Mekranoti milk, so my blood is Indian, and my saliva, and my semen."

Tedjware must have worn a large lip disk at one time because the scar left after FUNAI surgeons sewed his lower lip together is huge. It takes over his entire chin. Saliva drips from the hole that still remains and Tedjware is constantly wiping his mouth. Like other Mekranoti, Tedjware tries to improve his looks by plucking out his body hair, but the result is hardly flattering. His lack of eyebrows only accents the boniness of his face and makes his indented cheeks look even more hollow than they really are. To make matters worse, his freckles set off his pale skin, and his bushy red hair accents his narrow shoulders and skinny frame.

Part of Tedjware's frailty may come from the tuberculosis he contracted a few years before my fieldwork. He never quite recovered from the disease's weakening effects. Tedjware also suffered other illnesses in his past. Once his foot got badly infected, and if a missionary had not been around the Mekranoti would have killed him. "It smelled terrible," Tedjware explained, "and they didn't like it." He recounted the incident without bitterness. He was being treated no differently from anyone else.

Tedjware rarely went hunting or did much other work. He preferred to spend most of his time in the men's house chatting with anyone who would listen. His laziness did not earn him much respect in the community, but Tedjware still had great pretensions. He imagined himself a Mekranoti "chief" and claimed that a well-known leader a long time ago had named him as a successor. The Indians humored his delusions of grandeur and agreed that he was, indeed, a "chief." Sometimes they even half listened as Tedjware harangued the villagers in an evening speech around the men's house, but the children's laughter and mockery bespoke Tedjware's true status in the community.

Tedjware liked to talk most about past war adventures. The Mekranoti's enemies included practically anyone else near them—the Kreen Akrore Indians to the south and west, the Juruna Indians to the south, and other Kayapo groups to the east. The Mekranoti also fought constantly with Brazilians who ventured too close to their homelands.

Tedjware attributed most murders of other Kayapo to the need to avenge past Mekranoti deaths. He delighted in listing the names of all the Mekranoti killed in battle and all the enemies killed as well. In "payment" for the death of his relative, Ngoryti, Nokamenh (a Mekranoti) killed Tàkàkpe (from another Kayapo village). Then, Tàkàkpe's relatives had to avenge this death with the murder of Pãxmy and Krepny. The feuding—and the name list—went on and on.

Battles sometimes took curious turns. Once a faction from a neighboring Kayapo village tried to join the Mekranoti. From afar, they yelled out the names of their relatives and ceremonial friends and insisted they wanted peace. The Mekranoti took them in, only to have the newcomers steal food from their gardens and kill a dog of one of the chiefs. This was the beginning of a long series of killings in which each group pursued the other for miles into the forest, hoping to avenge lost relatives.

The Mekranoti's most feared enemies were the Kreen Akrore, who usually stayed at least two hundred miles to the southwest, although the two nomadic groups often crossed paths. Tedjware remembers a Kreen Akrore attack when he was a young boy. It was during the dry season that the enemy warriors attacked, about noon. They were surprised that so many Mekranoti men were still in the village. Having only bows and arrows themselves, they were no match for the Mekranoti guns. After killing a few Kayapo, the attackers retreated, but returned only four days later to finish their raid.

When the Mekranoti men returned from their day's hunting, they saw the bodies of their kinsmen and angrily vowed revenge. That same afternoon they set off in pursuit of their enemies. It was months before they finally caught up with the Kreen Akrore. After killing several men, they captured some children and brought them back to raise as Mekranoti. The pursuit undertaken on an afternoon's notice took almost a year to complete.

# 8

# SUMMER DOLDRUMS

The FUNAI medical team did not arrive until a week after the trekkers returned to the village. The plane the men heard earlier was probably a military jet on its way to Manaus—no one else ever passed through the area. Most Mekranoti waited around for the vaccinations and dental care the medical crew provided, but a few grew impatient and returned to the Sabují River to continue trekking. When it finally arrived, the medical plane brought in Tàkàkrorok, Kentỳxti, and Kaxre—and a cold.

It took only a few days for the sickness to spread to the entire village. The Indians had little resistance to the disease, and that was one reason for the rapid spread. But I soon discovered another reason. Kamerti, Tàkàkrorok's wife, came into my hut one day, sniffling loudly. I asked her if she had a cold. She answered, "Yes," and to demonstrate lifted her head, pushed a finger against one nostril and sprayed the room with mucus from the other. Unaccustomed to epidemics and always free to move away from their garbage or sickness, the Mekranoti never learned sanitary methods to control disease. Because I knew colds had killed many Indians in different parts of Brazil, I had always been careful to make sure I was healthy before going into the village. I was surprised at the FUNAI medical team.

I was reminded of a Kayapo fable, very similar to one of our own. It extolled the virtues of patient endurance over brute force. The jaguar had always disdained the tortoise for its slowness and its weak voice, but one day the tortoise challenged the arrogant wildcat to a contest of strength and resistance. The tortoise went first, living for weeks in a covered hole without food or water. The jaguar returned several times to the hole to see if the tortoise continued to survive. With the same even voice, the tortoise always informed the jaguar that the endurance trial was easy. Finally, it was the jaguar's turn to show its strength. At first the holed-up cat responded with a strong voice to the tortoise's queries about its well-being. But on the tortoise's second visit to the hole, the jaguar's voice had grown weak, and on the third visit, the jaguar no longer responded. Flies surrounded the hole where the wildcat had perished.

During the finale of the *kôkô* festival, villagers pause to listen to an elder's lecture.

Tàkàkrôrôk, the village's main chief.

Women spend hours practicing their bodypainting talents on their children. Decorations on this boy are made from shells, feathers, woody plants, and Czechoslovakian glass beads. Shell ear plugs are inserted into holes made shortly after birth, and steadily enlarged by the insertion of ever thicker earplugs.

The Mekranoti have numerous words for techniques of carrying things. This woman illustrates several of these techniques.

When there is little threat of rain, women on trek do not need to hurry in order to finish their shelters.

In preparation for a "samba" ceremony, the men divided into their different men's societies for a day's hunting. Here, one society brings back the spoils of their labor.

These girls wear downy feathers and crushed blue eggshells during the finale of the women's *bijôk* ceremony.

Other days I played an alto recorder a friend had given me the day before I left New York. When my breathing was good and I paid attention to what I was doing, the children sometimes came in to listen or to request certain pieces. I was impressed with how quickly they noticed poor phrasing or poor intonation. I had never had such good music critics. Perhaps they simply had more experience with flutes than most other people.

Mekranoti flutes were much simpler than my recorder. The men played them only for fun in their idle hours. No one ever thought of using them for ceremonies or in combination with singing. With only four notes in a simple tune characterized by a diminished fifth, these instruments demanded excellent phrasing and just the right amount of vibrato.

I began to hunger for literature about the outside world. I found myself reading over and over again the labels on medicines and canned goods. One day I borrowed some "foto-novels" from FUNAI and spent the whole afternoon reading the saccharine romances.

My boredom was broken now and then by visits from the *norny*. Traveling in groups, they walked in and sat around the table Kukrytbam had built me. They joked with each other and with me about their various "wives" or girlfriends. If any of them had scratch marks on his shoulder, the others commented about the sexual skills of the girl who gave them to him during their lovemaking. The scratched young man tried to invent stories to explain away the marks—he got cut on a sharp leaf while out hunting, or bruised himself on the house beams while trying to fix the roof. The *norny* also joked about the "weak" and "smelly" vaginas of the friends' wives.

Sometimes the men compared notes on the best way to stimulate their lovers. Almost all of them pulled lightly on their sex partner's clitoris during foreplay. Some men had sex while their lovers lay on their backs on the ground. Others remained seated and had their girlfriends straddle their waists. No one ever kissed his girlfriend, and no one ever had oral-genital sex. In the past, their enormous lip disks would have prevented Mekranoti men from any kind of oral sex. But even today they consider it disgusting. On one of his trips to Belém, Kentỳxti once saw some pornography depicting oral-genital sex. Spitting in disgust, he commented that perhaps this kind of sex was okay for people who had soap, but it was out of the question for the Mekranoti.

The men also had forest products to help them in their lovemaking. While describing the uses of different leaves to me, one man pointed out a leaf he said would excite women if he put it on his forehead. As he demonstrated how to use the plant, he laughed and pointed to his erection. "I get excited just thinking about the women's reactions," he said. Kentỳxti once began. With heads slightly bowed in respect, the young men listened to the elders' haranguing. Tàkàkrorok urged the youths to go out hunting more often and then went into a long speech about the changes taking place in Mekranoti society. "We had problems in the past," he commented. "But now things are going better. There is less illness, and we have *kuben* living with us to give us medicine and shotguns and pots. Our women are having children. This is all very good. But we need even more children. You young men should be spending more time with your wives, making babies. So dance tonight and then go to your women." Tàkàkrorok ended this last comment with a sly smile and a sweep of his hands. Several young men could not help snickering. Pãxkê also gave a short speech after which some people, having heard of the curious foreign custom, decided to clap.

Using a tape recording of Brazilian music alternating with native songs, the Mekranoti danced the boy-girl waltzes common to Western societies, but unusual for the Mekranoti. The girls picked boys for dances as often as the boys chose girls. The teen-aged daughter of Pedro, the black man, often danced with the "best" boys, causing some of the jealous Mekranoti girls to ask if she didn't have a husband. The young men were supposed to continue dancing until dawn, but the older age-grades went to bed earlier. As the night wore on, many young men and women sat around the periphery of the dance ground and necked. Kentỳxti eventually asked me to put out my lantern to give people more privacy. Occasionally a couple disappeared into the nearby forest for sex. Yet someone had to remain dancing all night, and no one could go to bed. That would be a sign of weakness.

The next morning villagers gossiped about one of the *norny* who was caught *in flagrante* with the wife of one of the fathers, in her house. There had almost been a fight, but the *norny* ran from the house and the affair was quickly forgotten.

After the samba ceremony, the days became monotonous. The weather never changed—hot in the sun of the day, and very cold at night. I wasn't sure how to spend my time. My command of Kayapo was not yet good enough for most of the things I wanted to do. I caught myself brooding in my hut. I realized how low my morale had sunk when one day I returned from my afternoon swim thinking I had something pleasant to occupy my time for a while. Then I remembered that the "something pleasant" was removing an insect from my foot. The Mekranoti called the bugs "fish-eyes" because when the eggs hatched under the translucent skin, they formed dark spots that looked like glossy eyes. Every day the women asked me for needles to remove the bugs from their children's feet. I had just learned a little trick to get the egg sac out without breaking it and wanted to try it out on my own foot.

The men dressed as "monkeys" watch the dance of the "anteater."

This man has inherited the right to don the "howler-monkey" mask and make fun of everyone in the village.

told me that too much sex makes you fat, but that too little makes you weak and lazy.

No one ever admitted to homosexual sex. Men knew that some *kuben* did this, but they had never heard of a Mekranoti case. While out on trek, though, I once saw a *norny* calmly masturbate a ten-year-old boy. He continued while the boy got an erection, but after people started joking about it, the boy got up and left.

Probably they do not much approve of homosexual acts. There is a myth about a Kayapo man who stopped going hunting with the men, preferring instead to work in the gardens. He was approached one day by a man with the legs and wings of a bat, but with a human torso. The bat man liked the human and began caressing him, causing the young man to laugh—the very first laugh ever. He then carried the human off to his cave, where the other bats also began caressing the human until he was totally exhausted and fell to the cavern's feces-ridden floor. Angry at this ill treatment of one of their members, the Kayapo organized an expedition to kill the bats, but they were unsuccessful. Only the laughter, hardly worthy of a warrior, remained.

People also thought sex was improper between relatives and between ceremonial friends. "This is how dogs behave," one man commented. But the impropriety did not stop some Mekranoti. One man went so far as to marry his mother's brother's daughter, and another married his father's brother's son's daughter. People thought these marriages somewhat scandalous. With ceremonial friends, scandal was easier to avoid. Kentỳxti simply called off a ceremonial friendship when it interfered with one of his affairs.

The young men joked with the young women about sex. The girls would accuse the *norny* of having big penises, which the young men always denied. The *norny*, in turn, commented on the looseness of the young women's vaginas. Sometimes things went beyond comments. I once saw two *norny* grab one of the adolescent girls and carry her off screaming to rape her in the forest. Other villagers saw the abduction, but no one protested. This was an affair of young people and adults should not interfere.

The adolescent girls who had not yet had children formed an age-grade known as the *kurerêr*. The Mekranoti men always talked well of them, praising their appearances and sexual abilities. In the past the young girls sometimes accompanied the men as they went off to battle. The men's only complaint was that there was not enough of the *kurerêr* to go around—at least not as many as there had been in the past when male war deaths left fewer men to grab them up.

I thought the *kurerêr* were the most difficult people in the village. Accustomed to favors from the men, they were a spoiled lot. They often came into my house to joke with me, assuming I would find their flirtatiousness charming. To tease me they would sometimes walk off with some of the food people gave me.

Late one night some of the *kurerêr* came into my hut while I was reading in my hammock. As part of their joking they bent over to show their naked buttocks and farted in front of my face. The next day, after they stole some meat I was looking forward to eating, I started complaining about the *kurerêr* to everyone who walked into my hut. My complaints must have gotten back to the young women, for they stopped annoying me soon afterwards.

The *kurerêr* were not the only people to break rules of modesty. In anger, little boys sometimes pulled their buttocks apart to show their anuses as an insult. Older women often failed to keep the hair plucked from their genital areas, and sometimes sat with their legs too far apart so that the outer lips of the vagina were open. This would have been scandalous in a younger woman, but was more tolerated in the elderly.

The Mekranoti have different ideas from ours about what constitutes immodesty. Kokokà once commented on the embarrassment foreigners feel at seeing the nakedness of Indian women. Rubbing her breasts and swiveling her hips, she walked seductively toward her audience, and then broke into a loud laugh as she explained that she would greet the next plane that came into the village just like this. The audience roared.

On the other hand, the Mekranoti also had their own peculiar types of modesty. The men with lip plugs became very embarrassed if caught without their wooden disk. One man even blushed at my seeing a spare lip plug he kept in his bag of valuable ornaments. I felt as if I had just seen his false teeth. And then it was curious that men felt obligated to sit down to urinate, while women urinated standing up, often not very far from their houses.

The stories about sex and violence kept me entertained during these summer weeks, but I began to long for more activity. Fortunately, a few moments of excitement broke the August dry-season lull.

# 9

# AFTER PECCARIES AND FISH

"Peccaries! Peccaries!"

The shouts resounded throughout the village. One of the *norny* had just seen fresh peccary tracks. I grabbed a notebook and rushed out to join the frenzy. Men scurried into their houses to fetch guns and then trotted off on the path behind one of the village houses. I ran behind them panting, trying to keep up. The pace did not slacken until an hour and a half later when the men arrived at the peccary trails. The *norny* showed the others the tracks he had seen, and they all split up looking for further signs of the wild pigs.

As it was the dry season, tracks were hard to see. Men ran from one hill to another looking for any sign of a peccary. Occasionally a hunter stumbled upon something and shouted to the others. Then all ran to the spot, trying to confirm the discovery. The exhausting search continued for several hours, without much success. Eventually, the men realized they would have to spend the night and continue the search the next day.

I was in no mood to spend another day on a wild pig chase. While running after the men, I had cut my neck badly on one of the sharp, knifelike leaves that abound in the forest. The gash had already swollen into a painful red sore. In Kayapo mythology, a man once tried to bring the orphaned daughter of one of these leaves home to raise, but the ungrateful child slit his throat, killing him. The Indians had a healthy respect for these forest problems, and advised me to return home. Also I had brought neither blankets nor my camera to capture the next day's hunt on film. I decided to return to the village with a few older men who also wanted to give up the chase. I hoped to observe a peccary hunt at a later date.

It would have been improper, if not immoral, for the *norny* who first saw the peccary tracks to chase the wild pigs alone. Peccaries are the only tropical forest animals that travel in herds. When assailed, the pigs sometimes counterattack. Then the Indians try to club them to death. Sometimes the hunters have to climb trees to escape charges by several of the pigs at once, and sometimes the wild boars kill the dogs. For one man to hunt peccaries alone would not only have been slightly dangerous, it would also have been a loss of good meat. This was a chance to bring back more than one man could kill.

The peccary hunt was not very successful. Finally, the men split up to go hunting in different directions. Most of them never even saw peccary tracks, let alone the peccaries, but a few men did finally reach the game and brought three animals home.

Another peccary hunt later in the year was much more successful. That time practically everybody brought back at least one wild pig, and Kentỳxti claims he killed four. The pigs, each weighing almost fifty kilos, were roasted and reroasted until they dried enough to last several weeks.

According to Mekranoti mythology, the white-lipped peccaries that travel in herds have always been around. They are social beings, like humans. But the smaller, more solitary species originated when a man became angry about his sister's mistreatment of his son. Every day when the son went to fetch manioc dough from his aunt, she sent him out to hunt, refusing to give him the dough until he brought back some game. When the boy's father found out about this mistreatment, he vowed revenge. Going off that very night, he threw magical seeds over the sleeping family of his wicked sister, and blocked the door to the house so that no one could escape. When the sister's little daughter began to cry because she could no longer go outside to urinate, her sobs gradually turned into the grunts of a peccary. On awakening, the girl's father and the rest of the family also turned into peccaries. The brother returned on other days to kill the pigs, but never managed to kill the largest, his sister. This pig ran off to the forest. To stop the fugitive, the shaman brother erected mountains and the mighty Xingu River, but the pig got away, and gave origin to the antisocial collared peccary.

The Mekranoti are keen observers of animal behavior. So that they can find their prey, they have learned the favorite foods of all their game. Peccaries crave wild yams, and fruits such as *kamokti*, large, purplish, and sweet, with a peachlike texture. Jaguars like tapirs, turtles, peccaries, anteaters, sloths, and paca, but according to the Mekranoti will not touch deer. Black wildcats like deer and paca. Anteaters are choosy about the kinds of ants they lick up their long mouths. Armadillos eat scorpions, spiders, and worms. The weasel-like *wakõre* is especially impressive because it kills not only these dangerous insects but also snakes.

Only the sloth's diet remains a mystery. Some Indians speculate that perhaps they eat sticks since they spend so much time on tree limbs, but no one has bothered to observe the filthy creatures in detail. This close relative of the anteater never cleans itself, and its fur is full of insects that people prefer to avoid. Sloth meat is taboo. Eating it, or even touching the animal, would cause one's children to become lazy.

There are many other meat taboos as well. Women are forbidden to eat jaguar, black wildcats, a species of large monkey, and a species of large bird. Sick people can't eat jaguar or any other wild cats. Nor can they eat anteater, or certain monkeys. People with special ceremonial names are barred from eating deer. Young boys of the *bokti* age-grade and old men can eat almost anything. Fish is good for anyone, any time.

The taboos seemed to have different effects on these different classes of people. Dietary studies showed that women often ended up eating less game than others, while the boys got more meat than most. Old people, also free of taboos, often got stuck with the animals and body parts no one else wanted, like the skins or intestines. Those with special names seemed to eat as well as anyone. Sometimes when I asked what they had eaten the day before, couples told me they ate no meat at all because "their children were sick." But since others with sick children had no qualms breaking this cultural rule, I suspected they simply cited the taboos out of shame for having no meat in their house. This reflected poorly on the household's men.

With three adult men, none of whom were very good hunters, and eleven mouths to feed, Bekwỳnhpî's household often felt embarrassed about its poor meat supply. Finally one night Bekwỳnhpî decided to do something about the problem. During the day he had seen a patch of small white flowers on the ground, flowers that pacas liked to eat at night. Since the full moon would emerge only after ten, leaving the early evening dark, Bekwỳnhpî decided to try some night hunting. So that he could use my flashlight, he invited me along.

We followed one of the well-trodden paths out of the village. Every now and then Bekwỳnhpî, not wanting to exhaust the batteries, turned on the flashlight for a second to make sure there was nothing unexpected ahead. We had traveled only half an hour in the silence of the dark forest when the hunter whispered to me to be quiet. Stepping a few yards from the path, we made ourselves a small clearing near the flower patch Bekwỳnhpî had sighted earlier. We sat quietly in the darkness for almost two hours, unable to see even our hands in front of us, listening to the soft, mysterious sounds of the night forest, half in meditation and half in alert attentiveness to the hundreds of tiny movements around us.

Suddenly, Bekwỳnhpî whispered "Deer," and lifted his shotgun, the flashlight tight against the barrel. I had heard nothing special, but then there was a loud rustle and Bekwỳnhpî quickly turned on the light. It was enough for me to see the animal, its eyes bright and alter with fear, only a few yards away. But the agile deer quickly turned on its hind legs and dashed off to the forest. Bekwỳnhpî waited for a few minutes, hoping the animal would come back. But when the silence crept back into the dark night, he got up with a frustrated grunt and abruptly announced our return to the village.

It was easy to understand the Mekranoti love of night hunting. Instead of running an entire afternoon after dogs that chased up game, we were able to sit in meditation for two hours, and wait for the animals to come to us. True, tapirs did not yell out to us telling us they were there, as they once did in the past, according to Mekranoti myths, but the animals gave themselves away easily. Mekranoti men went out hunting an average of fourteen nights out of a hundred. Night hunting was easiest in the dry season, when the men did not have to wade through water, but the men attempted it whenever possible.

Perhaps because he gave up so easily, Bekwỳnhpî was thought lazy by most of the Mekranoti. He was born in another Kayapo village, and his mother died shortly after she brought him to the Mekranoti. Since she was a *kupry*, Bekwỳnhpî had no father to take care of him, so his grandmother "provided him food," as the Mekranoti put it. A short, wiry, soft-spoken man who appeared to daydream a good deal, he was thought fairly intelligent, but he was not a very good hunter. This was especially bad because he had five children to care for. Often when he brought meat home he would hide a good part of it in my house so that his wife and kids would not eat it all. It was no wonder the Indians thought him greedy and suspected he disliked children.

Bekwỳnhpî was probably the most henpecked man in the village. Ngrenhkà, his wife, was about the same height as her husband, but she had a boisterous laugh and bellowed out her thoughts, letting the entire village know everything that was on her mind. At the beginning of my fieldwork, when Gustaaf was still around, she liked to come into our hut and make ribald jokes which Gustaaf seemed to relish. Ngrenhkà shared Bekwỳnhpí's reputation for greed and for disliking children, and was not a very hard worker. She nagged her husband about his hunting responsibilities and sometimes suggested a few alternative ways to bring her family the animal proteins it needed.

Peccary chases and night hunts were not the only way for men to provide for their families this time of year. As the streams around the village gradually dried up, the Mekranoti also began to make more and more trips to distant creeks to go fish poisoning. Sometimes just a man and his wife went off with a neighbor or two, opportunities Ngrenhkà did not like to pass up. Other times only the men went out. In these cases, one men's society would go off in one direction, while the other society went elsewhere. Kentỳxti once invited me to go with his society on one of the overnight trips and I decided to go along.

We walked for several hours in the dry forest before coming to a curve in a small stream. We would camp here, Kentỳxti told me. Nestled inside the river bend, the tiny rise was sparsely covered by a few saplings growing up in a clearing where a large tree had once fallen. After resolving a disagreement about the best place to fish, the men dropped their gear on the tiny peninsula and went off to gather the timbo vines needed to make poison. Mrytàmti and a few other elders returned with leaves after a few minutes. They would remain at the campsite to make baskets for all of the fish the men would get. A few young boys who had also come along went off to gather palm fronds and wild banana leaves to make the night's sleeping place.

A couple of hours in the forest were enough for most of the men to return heavy laden with timbo vines wrapped like cables in large cylinders on their shoulders. Tàkàkngo also brought back a paca, which was butchered immediately. The animal was pregnant, so the butcher threw the fetus along with the liver on a small fire to provide a snack for the returning men. The mother he threw in the stream bed. "The dogs won't eat it there," he explained. The trick seemed strange, but it worked. Although the dogs waded up to sniff, they left the paca alone.

Later, as one of the elders heated balls of clay to make an oven for roasting the paca, the young men felled a small tree across the stream to start the dam, which the boys and elders finished. It consisted of only a few branches and leaves and it leaked badly, but the Indians hardly seemed to mind. After a short rest, the men then began the vigorous job of beating the timbo with sticks. The work must have been exhausting, especially as after every few minutes they carried the vines into the stream bed to "rinse," swishing the heavy bundles briskly in and out of the water. The river soon became sudsy and the fish, their oxygen supply cut off, became sluggish. Deep in concentration, the boys stood guard at the dam with their tiny bows and arrows, waiting for the stunned fish to swim into the trap.

At two in the afternoon, more than an hour after they began, the men finally quit beating the vines and grabbed their baskets. By this time the fish had begun floating on top of the water, and the men could simply pick them up at the surface. The dam where the boys were poised was no longer functioning well, but the men had constructed another one farther downstream. It also leaked badly, but this mattered little. The water was still sudsy, and the fish remained behind the makeshift obstruction. I joined in the fun, wading into the stream bed and grabbing any fish that floated by. At first we picked up the bigger prey, but eventually there were only tiny ones left. I threw my catch into the basket of whoever was around me. I had been doing this for several hours when I finally noticed that the boys were not picking up all of the catch. When I asked what was wrong, they simply told me matter-of-factly that some of the fish were no good. I had been putting junk in the men's baskets all afternoon and no one had protested, but I then got a quick lesson in which species to avoid, and my contributions were more appreciated.

Most of the afternoon was spent collecting fish. It was six o'clock and already dark before the men stopped for the day. After a supper of paca and manioc flour some of the men began weaving more baskets, but it was not long before they, too, lay down for the night to rest on the palm fronds. The polluted water was all around, giving the forest encampment a strange feeling of security, as the evils of nature seemed far away.

The small fires between every two men were not enough to keep them warm on these cold, dry-season nights, so the men slept wrapped in each others' arms. I brought along a blanket which I shared with Kentỳxti, who also lay with his legs over mine. Ropti was on the other side. The men's conversation continued long into the night. As usual, the topic eventually turned to sex. Several began to joke about each other's sexual habits. Ropti protested that he had no need of the *kupry* since he had his wife. Kentỳxti at one point got up and went off with his flashlight to "look for fish." The explanation seemed strange at this hour of the night, and Kentỳxti took no basket, knife, or gun with him. He did not return until an hour later. I never did find out what he was up to. It could not have been an affair with one of his girlfriends, since there were only men here.

The next morning the men ate their usual breakfast of the previous day's leftovers and then spent a final hour or so collecting the fish that remained still stunned in the stream. On the morning trip back to the village each carried a fifteen-pound basket full of mostly tiny fish.

In anticipation of their menfolk's return, the women in the village had gathered banana leaves and prepared manioc dough to make fish pies. The other men's society had already returned when we arrived. The day was one of general feasting.

Fishing trips and peccary hunts were not the only dry-season diversions. Sometimes, in the late afternoon, when they had nothing else to do, the men would divide into their two men's societies to form soccer teams. They were great fans of the sport, and pretty much forgot their indigenous games. But, when their only soccer ball burst after being kicked too hard one day, they reverted to a native version of hockey. The hockey game was much like soccer, except that the men used sticks to hit a piece of hard fruit around. They usually played the sport on the airstrip to avoid hitting one of the children with the hard "ball." But even so, young boys liked to watch along the sidelines. One day one of the young spectators was hit in the head and knocked unconscious. The men thought they had killed him, but the boy eventually revived and seemed to be all right. Still, the incident was enough to make them drop the sport.

Competition was never very fierce in these games. People admired a good play now and then by one of the men, and sometimes they shouted out "gol," after the fashion of Brazilian sportscasters. But in neither soccer nor hockey did anyone keep score. As in many of the world's simpler societies, the Mekranoti had no need of competitiveness. People knew each other so well that the sorting function of competition was unnecessary. The ill feeling that could result from too many invidious comparisons could interfere with the cooperation required for many Mekranoti activities. Even Mekranoti leaders showed little in the way of competitiveness, a trait so often found among leaders in more complex societies.

One of the most cooperative of Mekranoti tasks was house-building. Men's societies generally took responsibility for this job. Since a young man usually joined the society of his father-in-law after his first child was born, most households contained men of only one of the men's clubs, so it was easy to decide which society would build which house.

Rik'o had been providing extra meat for his society members for several weeks, when the group finally decided to go out and gather the leaves necessary to make the roof of the new house. Rik'o had already cleared the land for his home and was now ready to erect the structure. Bringing the leaves into the village did not take long—one or two afternoons did the job. But many weeks went by as Rik'o and his friends wove the flat ōpor'o leaves onto the stripped saplings that would make the roof's shingles.

Only when the shingles were piled high in Rik'o's clearing did the men's society go out again to bring back the trees that would form the two large center posts and the four smaller outer corners. Using inner-bark rope to measure off distances, the men dug holes in the ground for the posts. With a smaller tree laid horizontally to connect the tops of the tall center posts and lashed into their notches, the hardest part of the house-building was completed. The rest of the work was easy. Four saplings connected the tops of the corner posts. Other saplings, lashed between these side housebeams and the taller central beam, formed the base for the steep pitched roof. The house's skeleton was complete. Only the shingles needed to be laid atop, in alternating rows of woven ōpor'o and heavy palm fronds.

Placing the houseposts and the shingles required several days of work before the men's society had completed its duties. The house could be used for sleeping as it was, even though it had no walls. Walls were an individual concern, and so would take much longer to build. On some houses the roofing shingles continued down the sides, to make a completely thatched house. This was the simplest type of wall, and the style accepted by Rik'o, who was in a hurry to move out of the chief's overcrowded hut. Other houses, such as the men's house, used split saplings, standing vertically next to each other to shut off the outside.

Later in the year Beptu also built a house, much like Rik'o's, but Beptu opted for elegance. To make his walls, he placed horizontal rows of saplings over vertical rows, and then brought wheelbarrow after wheelbarrow of mud from the river bank to throw into the interstices of the wattled sides. The resulting wall looked like plaster and kept out the cold better than the other styles. Fortunately, the Mekranoti had no problem with the lethal and incurable chagas diseases found in other parts of Brazil. The roachlike insect is especially fond of mud walls.

Beptu was a likable man. He tended to agree with anything anyone told him, and had the habit of responding "bê!" (well!) to practically everything. His exaggerated interest made me think, at first, that he might be mentally deficient, but he turned out to be one of the more intelligent men in the village, according to Mekranoti standards. He was especially close to his mother, Bekwỳnhrax, one of the village's oldest kupry. Bekwỳnhrax had no other children, and lived alone in one of the village's central houses. Normally, Beptu followed Kayapo standards and lived with his wife's family, but when they were out on trek the couple and their two children moved in with Bekwỳnhrax.

Bekwỳnhrax liked to brag that Beptu was the son of one of the deceased Mekranoti chiefs. Since she was a *kupry*, it was difficult for her to back up her claims, but many people believed her. She was a particularly puckish old woman who liked to joke with people. At the beginning of my fieldwork, when I still had trouble recognizing people, she sometimes brought me things and told people to tell me she was someone else. Everyone laughed if I accepted the story, which was soon corrected. She complained, now and then, about living alone in such a big house, and was constantly after her son to move in with her. But Kayapo traditions won out over personal attachments and Beptu ended up living with his wife's family.

Most people found the dry season pleasant, but there were a few stressful moments for some of the people. Tàkàkdjamti, one of the *norny* and the oldest grandson of Tàkàkrorok, had been having a summer affair with the daughter of Pedro, the Brazilian peasant. The other *norny* teased him no end about his sexual adventures. The Brazilian girl had lived before with Kayapo Indians and spoke a little of the language, but not enough to understand the intricacies of amorous affairs. Mekranoti girls would understand subtle cues about trysting places and times. They also knew the forest well and could find their way about alone, but the Brazilian girl had to be told everything explicitly. This meant that Tàkàkdjamti could not very easily hide his activities from the others. Everything that happened between them was public.

Tàkàkdjamti always struck me as the epitome of the American "boy next door." Good-natured, active with his age-mates, and well-rounded in the kinds of things Kayapo young men are supposed to do and know, he was also considered one of the more handsome *norny*. The affair and the teasing must have gotten to him, though, because at one point he went amok, running off into the jungle shooting at anything that moved.

I was in the men's house when Tàkàkdjamti went on his rampage. It was night, and my lantern was aglow in the center of the structure. Several men suggested I return to my hut, for no one knew what Tàkàkdjamti would do. They also warned me to put out my lamp. "When people go crazy," they explained, "they're attracted to light and will shoot at it." The Mekranoti sometimes see spirits of the dead as bright flashes in the night. To avoid being killed by the ghosts who want company in their lonely homeland, the Indians sometimes shoot at them. I suspected the "attraction" Tàkàkdjamti and other insane people had toward lights in the dark was related to this fear of ghosts.

Tàkàkdjamti's father, Ajoba, came into my hut late that night, when everyone else had left. Ajoba was one of the six or seven most influential men of the village. He was known for his skill as a hunter and warrior and for his fierceness. As the village's major song leader, he was also known for his knowledge of ceremonies. Considered one of the village's elders, he, in fact, looked older than Tàkàkrorok, his father. His wife had borne him many children, but he lamented that only four were still alive. The youngest boy cried a lot, embarrassing Ajoba, who, like most Kayapo fathers, expected his sons to be fierce. Probably because he avoided the youngsters in his house and attempted to ignore his boy's tears, Ajoba was thought by many to dislike children.

I rarely talked to Ajoba, who lived at the other end of the village and spent much more time with the FUNAI personnel. I was surprised to see him in my hut. I suspect he probably wanted to correct all the gossip that had spread throughout the community, for when I asked him about his son's insanity, he argued that the boy was not insane. "He simply has a little fever," he argued.

The next day Tàkàkdjamti was apparently all right. He dropped by my hut to tell me personally that his "fever" had passed. Fortunately, he had harmed no one on the previous night's rampage, so there were no ill feelings in the village, and Tàkàkdjamti was readily reaccepted into the community.

These rampages do not always end so happily, however. Years before, Ireti had gone amok and shot one man dead. He also riddled his brother's chest with lead. The event was scandalous, but no one "blamed" Ireti. He was simply temporarily insane. Still, the Indians were ready to kill him to prevent further murders and would have done so if FUNAI had not intervened. Ireti still carries a large scar from this event on his face, and has a twitch in one eye. He had once been an extremely handsome *norny*, according to all reports, before his face was ruined. His brother, Kute'o, also has large scars on his chest, testifying to the shoot-out, but he carries no grudges against his brother. Having married two sisters, the two brothers even live in the same household, and get along quite well.

The first time I met Ireti was when he came into my hut nibbling on something that he held in his hand. As a polite gesture, he offered me some of his food. It turned out to be the grayish clay from the river banks. Other people denied eating clay, but Ireti insisted everyone did this. "It tastes good," he remarked. "You should try it." The dirt from termite mounds is especially appreciated. (There are many societies in the world where people eat dirt, including the United States. Research indicates that the habit may be related to iron deficiency.)

Ireti had once been a prestigious *norny*, but his rampage spoiled his chances for Mekranoti success. Still a fairly decent craftsman, he was thought relatively intelligent, but no one would hold him in the high regard his brother enjoyed. Otherwise he was not seriously handicapped. Since the event happened long ago, no one feared he would repeat his rampage. The Mekranoti classification of such behavior as temporary "fevers" allows people to view the problem as a curable illness, like any other physical infirmity. Reintegration back into society is then much easier. Ireti even enjoyed a reputation for "gentleness," which although not complimentary in this society, still indicated a high degree of acceptance by the others. Personally, I found him one of the most agreeable people in the village. He rarely complained about things, and worried little about status, a preoccupation that sometimes hindered open conversations with the others.

The men enjoyed the dry-season peccary chases and fishing expeditions, but there was also hard work to do. Garden lands needed to be cleared before the rains introduced the planting season.

# 10

## IN THE GARDENS

"Run for cover," Kaxti shouted, as he swung his ax a final time. He had been hacking away at trees all afternoon, but none had fallen. Now a large trunk finally gave way, crashing to the ground and carrying with it an entire grove of trees, tumbling like dominos. The trick is not always so successful, but this time Kaxti was lucky and saved himself a half day of work. By chopping only part way through the trunks, he depended on the weight of other falling trees to finish the job. This time the technique worked perfectly. The trees fell outside of the clearing so that their branches did not need to be trimmed before burning the area to make way for a garden.

Clearing was on the minds of all the men. Even a few of the trekkers who had been gone all summer returned to the village to make sure they would have garden food for the coming year. They had been checking the forest all year for the best sites to make gardens. They looked for places high enough to avoid the flooding that covers much of the land during the rains, but without the large, hardwood trees that would be difficult to chop down. Also they thought about their wives' work in carrying all the produce back to the village. Often they made arrangements with neighbors to plant gardens in the same area so that all could share the same path even though each man would prepare his own garden by himself.

The planting of a Mekranoti garden always follows the same sequence. First, men clear the forest and then burn the debris. In the ashes, both men and women plant sweet potatoes, manioc, bananas, corn, pumpkins, papaya, sugar cane, pineapple, cotton, tobacco, and annatto, whose seeds yield achiote, the red dye used for painting ornaments and people's bodies. Since the Mekranoti don't bother with weeding, the forest gradually invades the garden. After the second year, only manioc, sweet potatoes, and bananas remain. And after three years or so there is usually nothing left but bananas. Except for a few tree species that require hundreds of years to grow, the area will look like the original forest twenty-five or thirty years later.

This gardening technique, known as slash-and-burn agriculture, is one of the most common in the world. The early settlers in North America adopted the method from the surrounding Indians, although it had been used in an earlier period in Europe as well. At one time critics condemned the technique as wasteful and ecologically destructive, but today we know that, especially in the humid tropics, slash-and-burn agriculture may be one of the best gardening techniques possible.

Anthropologists were among the first to note the possibly disastrous consequences of U.S.-style agriculture in the tropics. Continuous high temperatures encourage the growth of the microorganisms that cause rot, so organic matter quickly breaks down into simple minerals. The heavy rains dissolve these valuable nutrients and carry them deep into the soils, out of the reach of plants. The tropical forest maintains its richness because the heavy foliage shades the earth, cooling it and inhibiting the growth of the decomposers. A good deal of the rain is captured by leaves before ever reaching the ground. When a tree falls in the forest, and begins to rot, other plants quickly absorb the nutrients that are released. With open-field agriculture, the sun heats the earth, the decomposers multiply, and the rains quickly leach the soils of their nutrients. In a few years a lush forest, if cleared for open one-crop agriculture, can be transformed into a barren wasteland.

Slash-and-burn agriculture is less of a problem than open-field agriculture. A few months after planting, banana and papaya trees shade the soil, just as the larger forest trees do. The mixing of different kinds of plants in the same area means that minerals can be absorbed as soon as they are released—corn picks up nutrients very fast, while manioc is slow. Also, the small and temporary clearings mean that the forest can quickly reinvade its lost territory.

Because decomposers need moisture as well as warmth, the long Mekranoti dry season could alter this whole picture of soil ecology. But soil samples from recently burned Mekranoti fields and the adjacent forest floor showed that, as in most of the humid tropics, the high fertility of the Indians' garden plots comes from the trees that are burned there, not from the soil, as in temperate climes.

The long dry season may not have much effect on Mekranoti soil ecology, but it influences greatly the rhythm of Mekranoti life. It is not just the time to clear gardens. It is also the time to eat papaya, to roast and peel sweet potatoes by the river bank, to collect wild yams, to hunt paca at night, and to look for monkeys that make their nests in gardens. Turtle eggs, too, are a delicate dry-season treat, and the Mekranoti go out of their way to hunt for them in the river sand. Because the waters dry up, the dry season is also the best time to look for tapirs near waterholes, or to use in shallow streams the poison that stuns fish.

As the season wore on, the river that ran near the village became a stagnant pool of clayish water, cluttered with sweet potato peels left by Indians who dipped the roasted tubers into the water to clean them before eating. Bathing became unpleasant, and getting drinking water was a chore. The women dug holes into the riverbed and waited for water to seep through the clay into their calabashes, but the water was never very clean even so. A deeper waterhole farther downstream was more pleasant, but it was hard to get to and few people used it. Ronaldo persuaded a few of the Indians to dig a well near the FUNAI building. It was simply a hole in the ground covered by a board, with a roof overhead. The Indians used this water whenever they could, but many times animals fell into the well. Unable to escape, they died and rotted there, polluting the water. At such times, the Indians preferred the waterhole, but FUNAI people continued to depend on the well.

At the beginning of the dry season people rejoiced to see the end of the torrential rains. But even the deep blue skies grew tiresome. The cold of the nights confined people to their household fires, and the intense heat of the breezeless afternoons made people lethargic. With no rain to wash it away, garbage began to accumulate on the edge of the village. The absence of half of the Mekranoti still on trek did nothing to allay the feeling of stagnation. I once tried to explain snow to the Mekranoti, but my efforts were in vain. Now, as the dry season wore on, I caught myself thinking up ways to explain rain.

After so many cloudless days, the first faint signs of white in the sky caught the attention of everyone in the village. Tàkàkrorok noted the flowering of a tree by the river and told me the rains would be coming in a few weeks. Occasionally clouds floated over the village and finally the first light rain promised a change of season. The patter on the thatched roof made me feel snug and comfortable, but the rain failed to wash away the accumulated garbage.

After the first downpour the frog eggs in the waterhole hatched into tadpoles. The water was black with them. We had to brush them aside to bathe, and gathering water practically required a sieve. The Mekranoti have a horror of touching frogs, but they accepted the tadpoles with a stoic indifference. This was a normal beginning for the rainy season.

One day, just as I returned, exhausted from an overnight fishing trip, one of the women called me outside to watch her husband set fire to his clearing. I assumed the decision to burn a garden plot was an individual one, like most Mekranoti decisions. Gardening seemed like a particularly personal affair. But when, after some cajoling, I finally stepped outside, I saw the village encircled by a ring of fires. Today was the day for everyone to burn gardens.

Getting a good burn is a tricky operation. Perhaps for this reason its timing wa left to the more experienced and knowledgable members of the community. If the burn is too early, the rains will leach out the minerals in the ash before planting time. If too late, the debris will be too wet to burn properly. Then, insects and weeds that could plague the plants will not die, and few minerals will be released into the soil. If the winds are too weak, the burn will not cover the entire plot. If they are too strong, the fire can get out of hand. In the past, the Mekranoti accidently burned down villages several times because of fires that spread too fast.

Ronaldo remembered an incident when a garden fire caught some of the houses in the village. Fearing the flames would spread from one rooftop to the next until the entire village circle was ablaze, the Indians ran inside their homes and gathered their belongings to set them in the center of the village plaza. In the past, this reaction made good sense. Constructions were simpler, and people had fewer belongings to lose. Since moves were frequent anyway, destroying a village in smoke was not very serious. A fire could even get rid of inspect pests that infest villages after many years. But this time people were more concerned. Ronaldo finally persuaded some of the Indians to chop down some of the houses next to the burning structures and the village was saved.

Kaxti was unable to burn his garden. While working alone one day, he accidently plunged his ax into his foot. Bleeding badly, he limped back to the village where FUNAI treated him. His life was saved, but he was slow in recovering. Others had to complete his job of clearing. Kaxti might have asked his sister's son-in-law to finish the job, since their gardens were next to each other; but Tàkàkngo was gone at the time, so he had to rely on people of his own household.

Since his wife had no relatives in the village, Kaxti lived with his father's sister's son's son, Kwỳrdjo. Kwỳrdjo was a good work companion. A likable young man, he never stopped smiling, and was known for his gentle manner. But, since the Kayapo respect fierceness, this gentleness was not very highly regarded. Indeed, like other gentle men, including his brother, Kwỳrdjo was also known for his stupidity. Despite these "faults" of character, he was a good person to ask for help, and Kaxti enlisted him to finish his garden, at least until Tàkàkngo returned.

Shortly after the burning of the garden plots and the clearing away of some of the charred debris, people began the long job of planting, which took up all of September and lasted into October. Tàkàkngo returned in time to help Kaxti and his wife with their garden. Although he could not walk well enough to work, Kaxti could accompany his wife, Nhàkkamro, to the garden and take care of their children, while she did most of the planting.

Usually seen smoking her pipe, Nhàkkamro was a plump woman and friendly if left alone, but every now and then she could go off on temper tantrums—a habit that earned her a reputation for fierceness. Orphaned while still in puberty she was adopted by her mother's sister, and married soon afterwards. Shortly after her first child was born, her first husband left her, so she quickly married Kaxti. Kaxti had already been married before, and had several children, but they remained with his first wife's relatives when Kaxti was widowed in the late fifties. The couple seemed to get along well. Kaxti was friendly and easygoing so he rarely raised Nhàkkamro's temper. Unlike other couples who were rarely seen together, Kaxti and Nhàkkamro were a close pair. They often worked together in their gardens. Because of Kaxti's foot, they had to get along particularly well this planting season. The food had to be planted before the heavy rains began, or weeds would quickly take over the site.

In the center of the circular garden plot the women dug holes and threw in a few pieces of sweet potatoes. After covering the tubers with dirt they usually asked a male—one of their husbands or anyone else who happened to be nearby—to stomp on the mound and make a ritual noise resembling a Bronx cheer. This magic would ensure a large crop, I was told. Forming a large ring around the sweet potatoes, the Indians rapidly thrust pieces of manioc stems into the ground, one after the other.

The Mekranoti distinguish between a red-stemmed sweet manioc, good for eating boiled, and a white-stemmed bitter manioc, which is poisonous unless processed properly and which gives much higher yields. The distinction is not always so clearcut, though. The same manioc stem placed in different soils can be either poisonous or non-poisonous, depending on where it grows. And some informants disagreed about whether certain manioc tubers were poisonous or not. I once received a tuber from a Mekranoti woman who told me it was good for roasting or boiling. But after giving it to a neighbor to cook, I was told it was poisonous. Probably, there are different degrees of poison, and reactions to it may depend partly on the person and partly on the kinds of processing the tuber goes through.

One of the simplest ways of processing manioc is simply to leave the peeled tubers overnight in a river. To do this, the Mekranoti construct crude cages that can be seen standing up like reeds at the river's edge. The running water washes away the poison—and also much of the starch—leaving a mushy product that looks like soggy potato salad, but with a blander taste. If the manioc was not too poisonous in the first place, it can now be eaten directly, a food that serves as a quick snack for children and mothers on the return path from gardens.

If the tuber is more poisonous, the pulp needs to be toasted first. The most poisonous varieties of manioc must be grated with either a board covered with fish teeth, or, nowadays, a piece of a kerosene can with holes nailed through it from the inside, resulting in jagged metal edges on its surface. After grating, the juice with the poisonous prussic acid must be squeezed out. The doughy result can be used to make meat pies, which are wrapped in banana leaves and baked. Or, since the Mekranoti have acquired a six-foot-diameter copper griddle from the Indian Protection Service, it can be toasted into the coarse manioc flour that now forms the staple of the Mekranoti diet.

When grown, the manioc stems form a dense barrier to the sweet potato patch, and some of the plants must be cut down to gain entrance. Outside of the ring of manioc, the women plant yams, cotton, sugar cane, and annatto. Banana stalks and papaya trees, planted by simply throwing the seeds on the ground, form the outermost circle. The Indians also plant corn, pumpkins, watermelons, and pineapple throughout the garden. These grow rapidly and are harvested long before the manioc matures. The garden appears to change magically from corn and pumpkins to sweet potatoes and manioc without replanting.

The Mekranoti did not always depend so heavily on bitter manioc. Before acquiring the copper griddle from Meirelles in 1966, they depended on the crops they consider native, including bananas, which arrived in Brazil from Africa during the slaving days. But even the newer crops are given a ritual. Sugar cane, planted only since 1970, must be placed in the ground with the same Bronx cheer that sweet potatoes require.

Besides the gardens everyone planted for personal use, the men also cleared special fields for their men's societies. Whereas the average garden was only half an acre in size, the chiefs' gardens measured a good two and a half acres. The men planted four of these fields a year—two for normal produce, and two for rice, a plant grown nowhere else. The food from these gardens was reserved for special occasions. When the Indians worked together to cut new paths, or when they spent the morning carrying baskets of gravel on their backs to construct a new airstrip at the request of FUNAI, the older women of the different societies cooked them rice and other foods from these gardens. Since it was a rare treat, rice was highly regarded. Unfortunately, it did not grow well in the Mekranoti environment.

Some of the men also pitched in to clear gardens for some of the *kupry*. A few of the hard-working young men of the smaller society cut gardens for Iredjo, the women who had killed one of her twins a few months earlier. They also cleared a plot for Karàrti, an old woman stolen from the Tapirapé Indians when still a child, and for Kaxtykre, another older *kupry*. Other women without husbands scrambled to get whomever they could to clear a garden for them—a son, a brother, a son-in-law, or a brother-in-law. Some of the *kupry* found no one to clear gardens for them, so they depended on sisters or other relatives for support.

A couple of women who could find no one else to do the job cleared the gardens themselves. Bekwỳnhnor, at sixty-eight the oldest woman in the village, cleared gardens for herself a couple of times in recent years. The work was heavy, requiring the felling of larger trees than the women normally chop for firewood. The old woman was proud of her accomplishments, and liked to boast that she not only cleared gardens, but also went hunting at times. She was known for her generosity and her gentle manner, to which people credited her survival into old age. She was also a great joker. During one of the ceremonial seasons, she screamed violent threats to the ceremonial sponsor every night, coupled with insults about his stinginess and his terrible hunting abilities. At first I thought there was a serious argument going on, but everyone assured me that this was simply the proper behavior for the relatives of ceremonial friends.

Except for the rice fields, Mekranoti gardens, like their villages, are arranged in circles. When I asked a few men why they planted this way, no one could give an answer, except to say that this was the way it was always done—at least in the forest regions. In the savanna areas the Mekranoti planted only by the river banks, and circular gardens were too difficult there.

I mentioned that maybe the dense ring of manioc kept peccaries away from the sweet potatoes in the center. Several of the men paused to think about my suggestion, and then, to my surprise, they agreed that it made a lot of sense. It was the first time they took any of my suggestions seriously. (I later discovered that peccaries can eat manioc roots, although I never heard the Mekranoti complain about this.)

I began to accompany people to the gardens more frequently. At first I went mostly with couples as they planted the fields, but little by little I began to spend more time with the women as they harvested the foods. When I first arrived in the Mekranoti village, I was a bit wary of going to the gardens alone with the women. The men would assume I had other motives, anthropologists had warned me, but as the Indians observed me taking notes, my motives became clearer. Besides, I had let my beard grow, and this, along with my ill-kept clothes, made most of the Indians assume I was too old to have much of a sexual life anyway. I tried in vain to convince them I was only as old as the *norny* age set, but no one believed me. Only old people had beards and were so shameless as to use ill-kept clothes.

At first, I simply watched the women dig up sweet potatoes, or pull on manioc stems until the tubers freed themselves of the earth. I recorded how much everything weighed and how big an area was harvested. When we were ready to return to the village I always ended up with a load of bananas or a basket of sweet potatoes hung on a tumpline from my forehead with the weight falling on my back. I never carried as much as the women, but they appreciated my efforts just the same. (Later, when I furnished an apartment in New York, I used tumplines to carry all kinds of bundles up and down Eighth Avenue. Backpacks are cumbersome to put on and take off in subways and buses, but tumplines work beautifully. The Indians were right about the easiest way to carry things, even though a few New Yorkers took time out to stare.)

Mekranoti gardens grew well. A few Indians complained now and then about a peccary that had eaten a watermelon they were looking forward to eating, or that had reduced their corn harvest. Capybara, large rodents usually found near the river banks, were known for their love of sugar cane, but in general the animals seemed to leave the crops alone. Even the leaf-cutting ants that are problems in other areas did not bother the Mekranoti. Occasionally a neighbor who had not planted a new garden would make off with a prized first-year crop, such as pumpkin, watermelon, or pineapple. But even these thefts were rare. In general, the Mekranoti could depend on harvesting whatever they planted.

Eventually, I wanted to calculate the productivity of Mekranoti gardens. Agronomists knew very little about slash-and-burn agriculture. They were accustomed to experiments in which a field was given over to one crop only, and in which the harvest happened all at once. Here, the plants were all mixed together, and people harvested piecemeal whenever they needed something. The manioc could stay in the ground, growing for several years before it was dug up.

I began measuring off areas of gardens to count how many manioc plants, ears of corn, or pumpkins were found there. The women thought it strange to see me struggling through the tangle of plants to measure off areas, 10 meters by 10 meters, placing string along the borders, and then counting what was inside. Sometimes I asked a woman to dig up all of the sweet potatoes within the marked-off area. The requests were bizarre, but the women cooperated just the same, holding on to the ends of the measuring tapes, or sending their children to help. For some plants, like bananas, I simply counted the number of clumps of stalks in the garden, and the number of banana bunches I could see growing in various clumps. By watching how long it took the bananas to grow, from the time I could see them until they were harvested, I could calculate a garden's total banana yield per year.

After returning from the field, I was able to combine the time allocation data with the garden productivities to get an idea of how hard the Mekranoti need to work to survive. The data showed that for every hour of gardening one Mekranoti adult produces almost 18,000 kilocalories of food. (As a basis for comparison, Americans consume approximately 3,000 kilocalories of food per day.) As insurance against bad years, and in case they receive visitors from other villages, they grow far more produce than they need. But even so, they don't need to work very hard to survive. A look at the average amount of time adults spend on different tasks every week shows just how easygoing life in horticultural societies can be:

| | |
|---|---|
| 8.5 hours | Gardening |
| 6.0 hours | Hunting |
| 1.5 hours | Fishing |
| 1.0 hour | Gathering wild foods |
| 33.5 hours | All other jobs |

Altogether, the Mekranoti need to work less than 51 hours a week, and this includes getting to and from work, cooking, repairing broken tools, and all of the other things we normally don't count as part of our work week.

During the evening leisure hours, I received visits from some of the women who accompanied me to the gardens. The men's indifference to my time with their wives owed nothing to their wives' purity. Several of the younger women offered themselves for sex. Every time I talked to Ngrwany, one of the village's more popular *kupry*, she assumed I was interested in a tryst, and walked out of the village on one of the paths behind her house, looking back with a sly smile now and then to see if I was following. Ngrwany was from another Kayapo group that eventually became extinct. Like most women who became *kupry*, she had lost her mother while still a child, and she had no relatives at all in the Mekranoti village. Perhaps because of her successful activities as a *kupry*, Ngrwany was rarely seen gardening, and earned a reputation as the laziest woman in the village.

One of the chief's daughters, Tykre, was also blatant about her sexual interests. She had been "married" twice and had a child by both "husbands," but neither of her spouses stayed very long. She had trouble with everyone in the village. After fighting with her mother, she moved to live with a sister who had married the chief of the smaller men's society. Here, too, she fought with the household members. To escape the tension, she made a couple of long trips with the young men to gather Brazil nuts for FUNAI. She said she wanted to gather nuts to buy a hammock, but everyone in the village thought her motives were otherwise.

Tykre was not only sexually indiscreet by Mekranoti standards, she was also shameless in general. She neglected her two sons, so her mother was forced to take care of one of them. During the middle of several ceremonies, she had temper tantrums and rolled on the ground. Tykre had spent several months in Belém, receiving medical treatment, and several Indians commented that she must have consumed alcohol at the time. How else could her deviant behavior be explained? they argued. Probably she also prostituted herself, but nobody knows for sure.

One evening I invited the missionaries over for dinner. As usual, we talked mostly about the Indians. Tykre's behavior soon became the center of conversation. I mentioned Kentỳxti's theory that she had drunk alcohol, and asked if the missionaries knew anything about her trip to Belém. They knew nothing about the Belém trip, but Mary, with a gesture of indignant resignation, said that she knew what had happened with the wayward woman. After a poignant pause, she explained that Tykre was possessed by the devil. Esther, who did not always see eye to eye with Mary, was a bit stunned, but quickly agreed that that must be what happened.

Another woman who made sexual advances was Ngrenhre, Kamerti's sister's daughter, who lived in Tàkàkrorok's hut. Ngrenhre was recognized as one of the more intelligent women of the community. While the men can demonstrate their mental abilities with their weaving expertise, women do it with body painting. Ngrenhre was an expert at creating designs that flattered both the wearer and the artist.

Ngrenhre was subtle about her advances. Arriving late at night in my house just behind the chief's hut, she spoke quietly of many things—her children, the season's foods, and future ceremonies. Sometimes she sang a quiet tune, one of the songs of the manioc juice ceremony. The tunes, with words borrowed from other Indian languages, were nonsense to the Kayapo. When sung by a group of women, they sounded terrible—much too nasal, but when only Ngrenhre sang, they were happy and gentle.

Ngrenhre's present husband, Ne'i, was a good-natured and generous spirit who liked to make friendly jokes with everyone. He had already abandoned three wives before settling down with Ngrenhre, and shared his wife's reputation for sexual escapades, although he was not considered quite as intelligent.

Several times during my fieldwork, the names of Ne'i and Ngrenhre came up in accounts of sexual scandals. As the entire village knew, Ne'i was spending a lot of time with Ngrwany, one of the *kupry*, while Kentỳxti and several other men enjoyed Ngrenhre's favors. Kentỳxti asked me for a hammock about this time so that he could pay Ngrenhre for her sexual services. He was quite fond of Ngrenhre, praising her sexual expertise and her personality. I was worried about how Ngrenhre was going to explain a hammock to her husband, and had no intention of getting involved in another of Kentỳxti's sexual escapades. I had been accompanying Ngrenhre to the gardens but did not want to explain that the hammock was in "payment" for the time she spent showing me things there.

The affairs were more open than I imagined. Ngrenhre and Ngrwany began going off together to garden. At times in the past, Mekranoti women agreed to share a husband, especially when the husband was away on warring expeditions. The custom was more a question of sharing gardens than of sharing a man's sexual activities, though sex was involved. Sometimes, also, husbands exchanged wives for periods of time. But Ngrenhre's gardening with Ngrwany was not a question of either of these more formal arrangements. I never unraveled the entire affair. Possibly the cooperation of the two women was simply a way of biding time until people could figure out what was really going on. Later in the year Ngrenhre and Ne'i's problems would come to a head, but now everyone was content to leave the matter as it was.

At this time I also began attempting some dietary studies with the families of the women who went with me to the gardens. Since the Mekranoti don't eat regular meals, I could not simply observe what they ate at mealtime.

At first I tried to weigh everything that came into or left the household, in the hopes of calculating food consumption by looking at the depletion of household food stocks. It did not take long to realize that this would never work. Most of the food the Mekranoti ate never even reached the house. Mothers and children ate sweet potatoes and manioc pulp on the way back from gardens. The men usually ate in the men's house, and everyone ate in neighbors' houses now and then. The few foods that did reach the house never lasted long enough to be weighed. As soon as a hunter brought home some meat it was cooked and eaten. Only if I spent entire days walking around with people could I hope to observe directly what they were eating. Few people would feel comfortable having me trail them like this.

I finally decided simply to ask people what they had eaten the previous day. It was a crude technique, but would have to do. I was interested mostly in protein intake, and so tried especially hard to find out how much meat people ate. After analyzing this data, I compared it with other data on hunting yields. The food intake studies showed that people averaged 63 grams of animal protein a day, while the hunting yield data showed 72 grams captured per person per day. The two kinds of data were not all that different. They both showed that the Mekranoti, despite their leisurely hours, enjoyed a fairly high-quality diet—certainly much better than the majority of Brazilians.

As the September rains grew more intense, people began to wonder about the trekkers who had left the village in early June. They had been expected back a long time ago. People began to talk about when and if they would return. A few of the trekkers had already come back to cut gardens, but most still remained at the distant campsite. Presumably they had gone off to collect palm nut oil for their hair, but the hunting in the area was good, so the trekkers decided to stay longer. The village had seemed empty all summer, and many people longed for more excitement. So, the arrival of a few young men announcing the return of the rest of the village was a welcome treat. It would be nice to continue those amorous affairs held in abeyance during the summer absence. It would also be good to resume again the women's *bijok* ceremony, suspended when the village split up.

# 11

# THE WOMEN SING

People had been gathering in the men's house all morning. Even the women ran in and out of the structure, bringing their menfolk bits of food and any messages they had heard. The trekkers would soon be entering the village. It was the end of September, and they had been gone only a few months—a short time by the standards of a few decades ago—but enough to make the event an exciting one. The men sat quietly, thinking of what they would say to their long-absent relatives and friends. Some of the *norny* had returned a week earlier and warned them of the imminent arrival.

Suddenly a few gunshots resounded in the distant forest, foretelling the entrance of the first returning trekkers. The villagers responded with a gun salute of their own, and within a few minutes a procession of men marched into the central plaza. Most of them went straight into the men's house, but a few walked into the domestic houses along the village circle. The wails of welcome began immediately. In the men's house most of the trekkers went first to Tàkàkrorok. Bowing their heads and holding the backs of their forearms across their brows, the men keened in high falsetto yelps, as they told one another how much they were missed, and brought each other up to date on all the news. They passed from one man to the other, repeating the same cries. Even a few of the women entered the men's house to wail for their relatives, adding to the noisy commotion.

Twenty minutes later, the long-absent women and children also marched into the central plaza. People stopped their wailing briefly as the marchers, heavy laden with baskets and children, came to a stop. Forming themselves into a circle, the women remained silent for a brief moment and then split up as each walked briskly to her village house, bottles of palm nut oil clanking gently against the cooking pots that hung from her baskets.

The loud keening resumed immediately, the women's wails augmenting those of the men. Tàkàkngo, who had earned a tape recorder for his linguistic help with the missionaries, tried to record the cries. People were not very interested in the recordings, and nobody wailed with Tàkàkngo. Several other men also remained quietly in the background as they watched the welcomes and the tears among the other men. They had no close relatives on trek who needed to be greeted this way, and so contented themselves with the news brought back by their friends. When the wailing finally stopped after an hour or so, the rest of the day was spent by both trekkers and villagers catching up on details of the past few months.

This ceremonial reunion was not as important as others in times past. In earlier days the Mekranoti could never be sure about how they should treat the return of a split-off group. Sometimes people held grudges about past murders and came back only to begin another round of feuding. Especially when absences were long, there was no way to know the aims of the returning group. Usually the trekkers shouted out the names of relatives or ceremonial friends before entering a village, in the hopes of receiving a friendly welcome. But sometimes even these reunions turned sour. The elaborate wailing helped people judge one another's true intentions.

Now that the village was whole, the Mekranoti could begin again the women's *bijok* festival, suspended during the dry season separation. Kaxre and Tàkàkngo, along with their wives, Nhàkkruw and Kokory, were sponsoring this festival to give special names to their daughters. For boys, the names seemed to have no effect on later prestige or influence, but women with ceremonial names were generally more influential than other Mekranoti women and less likely to end up as *kupry*. So it was especially important to give good names to girls.

Not every Mekranoti parent was willing to sponsor a ceremony. The job required months of hard work to feed the people who sang and danced "for the children." The sponsoring couple had to make their plans early enough to have time to cut gardens in order to feed everyone over the long course of the festival with manioc dough and bananas. The husband had to hunt arduously for months to supply daily meat to the singers and dancers. During all of this time, it was taboo for the sponsors and their children to eat meat. One boy receiving a name at a ceremony told me he would die if ever he dared consume animal flesh. A ceremonial hunter confessed to me that he broke the taboo almost every night by downing a few morsels of game behind his house where no one could see him. He insisted ceremonial sponsors always did this, even though they didn't like to admit it.

The first months of the women's *bijok* ceremony were simple enough. One of the women's societies periodically cleared the central plaza of weeds and dog manure. Every evening and every morning they lay banana and palm leaves on the ground near the men's house to serve as a sitting place for the singers. The women then sat around for one or two hours singing the songs different people suggested. The gathering seemed remarkably informal—people sat down or got up at will, sometimes leaving in the middle of a song. As they sang, always in unison, the women swayed forward and backwards to the steady rhythms, swinging their arms in a cradling position to and fro.

Anthropologists have discovered that steady rhythms are common in societies like the Mekranoti where infants are carried close to their mothers' bodies. The babies learn to associate the steady walking rhythm with the mother's warmth, and the music gives feelings of security and pleasure.

The women liked to begin the morning sings just before dawn and end at daybreak. But sometimes they miscalculated the night hours and began at one or two o'clock in the morning. In the spring, before the summer suspension of the ceremony, I had often found it hard to listen to the nasal singing. I was still suffering from diarrhea, and the oppressive droning somehow made matters worse, especially when I had to listen to it in the middle of the night. But now, better adapted to Mekranoti life, I found the singing more tolerable, if not actually pleasant.

The women were becoming more prominent in the village. In the late afternoons they dressed up in feather headdresses and paraded in couples around the plaza, singing the same tunes they intoned with the others just before nightfall or daybreak. At one point, one of the older women even gave a short speech to the villagers. The discourse was short but effective. It was the only time I ever saw a woman perform this traditionally male activity.

The women also began to meet more often with the other members of their women's society behind the houses of their women's chiefs (the wives of the corresponding men's society chiefs). In these meetings they hurriedly painted each other in traditional striped designs. Mothers still had to care for their children, who were none too patient with the makeup sessions. These body-painting assemblies were one of the few chances women had to meet as a group. The only other times they got together were when bathing their children at the river bank or when grating and roasting manioc in the manioc hut. At the end of the naming ceremony they would also go off with their women's society to harvest produce from the ceremonial sponsor's garden. They had nothing like the men's house for regular meetings.

As the rains grew more intense, the women sometimes held their morning sings in the men's house. When this happened, the men reluctantly gave them the center of the structure in which to arrange their sitting place of banana and palm leaves. In most South American Indian societies the men's house is strictly off-limits to the women, who are sometimes threatened with death if they happen to pass one of the building's thresholds, or even try to look inside. The easygoing attitude of the Mekranoti is a surprising testimony to the influence of the women in this culture.

It did not take long for the rains to become torrential. In October, thunder often shook the houses, and lightning lit up the dark skies. In times past, lightning bolts burned down several particularly susceptible villages in clearings on high ground. Now, when thunder crashes made the earth tremble, the men rushed outside with their shotguns to shoot back at the menacing celestial enemy. Ramming their war clubs into the ground, they shouted out their defiance to the blustering skies. But the threats were brief, for the men dashed quickly back inside the shelter of their homes.

In October it rained a total of 310 millimeters (12.2 inches). This was little in comparison with the 460 millimeters (18.1 inches) of December, but it was enough to change the Mekranoti landscape. Blue skies quickly became a rare treat as the low-hanging clouds gave an even more claustrophobic feeling to the dense forest habitat. In the dry season the paths had hard floors of sun-baked clay and the forest maintained a healthy distance from the center of the thoroughfares. But now the paths were often muddy, and the vegetation overtook its lost territory, closing in on the once ample walkways. I began to travel with a machete to cut away leaves and tree limbs that blocked my way. Even more dramatically, the rains flooded large areas of the forest. To go anywhere required wading painfully through vast stretches of knee- or waist-deep water, surrounded on either side by thorny palm trees that became torturous hand railings when I slipped in the muddy water. The rains made going to the gardens unpleasant. Fortunately, the Mekranoti finished planting most foods before the heavy rains began. Only rice remained for November, so I turned to other matters.

One of the things I wanted to check was the kind of personality that made Mekranoti leaders successful. Anthropological accounts often stressed that "primitive" leaders possessed personal qualities unlike those of leaders in stratified societies. But no one had collected systematic data needed for reliable cross-cultural comparisons.

Besides the leaders of the men's and women's societies, I also wanted to know about influential people in general, even if they had no formal positions. I could already guess who some of these people might be—Ajoba, Tàkàkrorok's oldest son; Teryti, one of the elders; and Kentỳxti, because he knew Portuguese. But I wanted to be sure the Indians thought these people were influential as well. I could have asked all the Mekranoti to tell me who "they listened to" to do things, but that would have taken a lot of time and bothered a lot of people. Instead, I decided to make up a miniature Gallup Poll. I called on Kentỳxti to help perfect the questionnaire, although my Kayapo was good enough by now to allow me to ask almost everything I needed. After spending a couple of afternoons with a table of random numbers, I drew a sample of Mekranoti adults to interview.

I asked each interviewee for the names of twenty people "who were listened to to do things." While I had informants in my hut for interviews, I also decided to ask people about other characteristics of their neighbors— Who is smart? Who knows a lot about the ancestors? Who is good-looking? Who is lazy? Who is fierce? Who is promiscuous? and so on.

I closed tight the door to my hut whenever I asked an Indian to come in to "tell me names of people." If someone walked by outside, both the Indian and I waited for the passerby to get out of listening range. I was determined to keep these interviews private. At first, some people hesitated to give names, especially when I asked about bad traits. "No one here is stingy," they told me over and over again. But with just a little prodding all the complaints came out—about neighbors who never gave anybody anything, or who were too stupid to learn how to weave, or who hated children.

Several times when walking around the plaza, I heard people chatting about what I had asked them. "Beproti asked me who was stingy," one woman said. "But I told him there weren't any stingy people here." Although everyone gave me names, it seemed no one wanted to admit it. I was delighted at the lies. I wanted to guarantee secrecy in the interviews, and so always refused to tell anyone what the others had said, even though I was asked many times. I was glad the Indians thought the same way. The interviews went so well that I eventually drew other samples of adults to ask other questions.

I had to make only one small change in my plans. Almost everyone hesitated to give the names of women. So instead of asking for twenty adults, I asked for names of ten women and ten men. Later I looked at the number of "votes" people received on different questions. I could then tell whether "influential" people were also generally "knowledgeable" "promiscuous" or whatever. I could also check out the reputations of the village's *kupry*, of its shamans, and of any other category of person I could think of. The ratings gave me an excellent idea of how the Mekranoti saw each other.

During one of these interviews, I asked Karàrti for the names of men who were good warriors. She answered immediately, tears swelling up in her eyes. "Bokrã," she said softly, "he killed my mother and my father." She then mentioned a few other Mekranoti men who had killed brothers and other relatives. I didn't have the heart to ask for more.

Karàrti was a Tapirapé, one of the most peaceful Indian peoples in Brazil. When a raiding party of Mekranoti invaded her village in 1947 there were only a few timid warriors around to fight. The Mekranoti plundered the village, carrying off machetes, guns, and several women and children, including Karàrti, a pretty maiden. The invaders burned what remained, sending the terrorized survivors into many years of forest hiding.

Karàrti began to tell me about how much she missed the Tapirapé and how much she hated the Mekranoti. She dreamed of going back some day to her native home. Although she remembered many Tapirapé words, she could no longer speak her native language. The other captives had all died, leaving no one to talk to. According to Karàrti, she managed to survive because the Mekranoti appreciated the many songs she could teach them. But she never quite felt at home. She spoke Kayapo with an accent, and at 1.4 meters (4 feet 7 inches), was much shorter than the Mekranoti women. Emphasizing the differences, the Mekranoti often referred to her as "the Tapirapé." Like the other stolen women in the Mekranoti village, Karàrti did not have a husband. As a *kupry* she had borne two children, but both of them had died. She managed to find a home of sorts in the house of an older couple and their married daughter and children. But she was not a happy person. The missionaries described her as "a bit downtrodden."

My "naming" interviews were not the only interruption to the women's ceremony. Without warning, one day a procession of masked figures marched into the village. The men had decided to begin a naming ceremony of their own called *koko* before the women finished their *bijok* naming ceremony. The two festivals would just have to overlap. Leading the procession was Ajoba, painted red with achiote and wearing a delicate red feather headband. He shook a gourd rattle and sang the songs he inherited from his mother's brother. The masked figures followed behind. Two full-length conical body masks with bent points, from which dangled bright red tassels, represented anteaters, I was told. They moved in a slow waltz, occasionally bowing to each other or to the audience. Behind them, men wearing pillow-shaped face masks and straw coats played the part of monkeys, and jumped playfully up and down, talking in falsetto voices to each other and to the audience. The procession stopped in the house Rik'o was building, while the anteaters went into a short dance and the monkeys jumped up and down around them.

The men had been preparing for this procession for weeks. After collecting the masking materials, they wove the costumes in the forest—out of view of the villagers. With the suggestions and help of others, each *norny* made his own monkey mask, adding any decorative details he could imagine—a string of beads around the eye holes, clamshells for a nose, or tiny bells hung on tassels to represent ears. The anteater role belonged to Kwỳrdjo and his brother Netire, who inherited it from their uncle. But the masks were harder to make, so more people helped out. The men even wove a few tiny anteater masks for some of Kwỳrdjo's nephews. The boys were beginning to learn the anteater's part for themselves.

For the next three months the anteaters danced around the village plaza. Their ballet was as quiet, serious, and dramatic as a tango. At first the anteaters were friendly, chasing the children without harming them. But week by week, as the masks began to wear out, the anteaters turned nastier. Carrying fish teeth, they attempted to scratch and frighten the toddlers, sometimes making them cry. The monkeys were more playful. The Kayapo were so fond of them that other Indian groups referred to them as the people who "resembled monkeys" (*Kaya-po* in the Tupian language), giving origin to the group's name. Visiting people in their houses, the monkeys played small pranks and asked for small gifts of food. Covered from head to foot and speaking in falsetto voices inside the heavy masks, the *norny* could easily disguise themselves. No one dared asked who was inside. In the past, the Mekranoti would have killed anyone who tried to find out the mask's secret.

The *norny* used the monkey masks more than the others, but the fathers also wore them at times, and sometimes even the *'okre* donned the heavy costumes to play pranks around the village. Still prepubescent, and still without the penis sheath that would graduate them into the *norny* age-grade, the *'okre* boys normally had to submit to orders from the older men. As a sign of their lower status, they kept their hair clipped short, while the *norny* grew their locks a bit longer, and the fathers let their manes fall below the shoulder. The masks were a wonderful opportunity for the *'okre* boys to escape this submissive role, and even become confused with the *norny* or the fathers.

Graduation from one age-grade to another is a big event for Mekranoti males. A boy lives with his mother until about nine years old. By that time a man who's not related to the boy decides to "paint" the youngster and accompany him to the men's house. From that time on, the boy, now known as '*okre*, sleeps with the *norny* and the young fathers who are tabooed from having sex with their postpartum wives. The youngster continues to eat with his mother but he must now serve the older men, bringing food to the men's house, or fetching tools for making arrows or other handicrafts. He must also build the temporary men's houses when the village goes on trek. Later, when his voice begins to change, one of the elders will take him outside the village, throw him against a tree to make him as tough as the hardwood, and fasten a small woody penis sheath around his foreskin, preventing the glans from showing. The boy then becomes a *norny*. In times past he would have had to go off on a warring expedition before graduating to *norny* status.

One night shortly after Bokrã had just performed this latter ceremony with a small group of the village's boys, the elder came into my hut. He decided I needed a penis sheath, too. After quickly fashioning a small sheath, he tried to put it on me. But as I've been circumcised, he could find no way to do it. Embarrassed at my "deformity," he was too polite to say anything, and simply suggested that, perhaps, whites didn't need the sheath after all. I explained the custom of circumcision to him, which he accepted somewhat disbelievingly. Undaunted, he then suggested that maybe I ought to have my lip perforated so that I could use the large lip plugs of the men. I replied that this would be fine with me and offered to circumcise him in return. The trade-off horrified him.

The women's *bijok* ceremony continued as before, but every now and then the men's *koko* ceremony interrupted the affair. One of the men's masked figures, a howler monkey, was required to make jokes of everything around him, including the women's singing and dancing. Like most ceremonial privileges, the right to wear the howler monkey mask and to play the clown's role was inherited by the men from a mother's brother. Several times one of the women grew irritated with the joker's shenanigans and ran after him, beating against the straw mask. I could not help thinking the men were simply jealous of the women's festivities and determined to sabotage them.

Toward the end of October, people decided it was finally time to end the women's *bijok* ceremony that had begun six months earlier. All Kayapo ceremonies require tortoises to feed the crowds during the final days of festivities, and getting the special treats requires a trip into the forest just before the ceremony ends. Sometimes the entire village goes on trek for several weeks, but this time people wanted to end the ceremony sooner, so only the men would go out. They could gather the tortoises much faster without the women and children along.

I was running out of supplies about this time, so I took advantage of a plane that arrived in the village—the first in four months—to hitchhike a ride out. The pilot would not charge for the trip. As he left the airstrip, he made a daring swoop over the village, thrilling the children, and frightening some of the adults who had lost relatives in a plane accident some years before. The pilot had already crashed once in the jungle, but since he survived that accident he felt confident he could survive others as well. We encountered rain on the way back, and so were drawn off course. Although I noticed the fuel gauge had been reading empty for half an hour, I said nothing. I figured the pilot must know what he was doing, and if he didn't there was nothing I could do anyway.

Suddenly, the pilot cried a loud sigh of relief. He had been searching the ground intently for some time, and just caught sight of another Kayapo village. "If we missed this place," he explained, "we would have crashed. The fuel is almost gone and there is nowhere else to land."

The Gorotire village looked very different from the Mekranoti. Houses were arranged along streets. A church stood at one end of the village, and cattle queued up at the FUNAI headquarters for salt. The men's house had no walls, so no one slept there anymore, and people went to their gardens in a canoe. Most of the men and some women spoke Portuguese.

We stayed only one night among the Gorotire—enough for me to get an idea of the difference a few years of contact can make. My biggest thrill at coming back to civilization was the taste of bread and butter at breakfast. I had forgotten how good this simple food can be. I spent only a week gathering supplies in Brasília before heading back to the Mekranoti.

The men were still out on trek when I returned. They would come back in a few days, I was told. The women began to make special preparations for the *bijok* ceremony's end. Body ornaments had to be painted with achiote and genipap, or glued together with beeswax. The women began to pester me for razor blades and scissors to shave their children's heads, and for string to make bead necklaces and to color red with thick achiote dye. They would wrap the colored string under their children's knees, to make their calf muscles grow. Through all of this preparation, the children also had to be told how to act during the ceremony's different phases. No one talked of anything else.

Even the death of Iredjo's other twin went almost unnoticed. There were a few wails when the infant died, and Tep'i, Iredjo's brother-in-law, fired two shots in the air. But most people didn't even hear the wails, and, if Iredjo had not clipped her hair in mourning, it would have been very hard to tell that her daughter had died at all.

On the day the trekking men were to return, the women went off by themselves to the forest outside the village. It was the largest gathering of Mekranoti women I ever saw. The women of one of the women's societies made a large clearing and placed leaves on the ground for sitting. They spent a couple of hours painting each other with genipap, achiote, and palm oil. Standing in the middle of the gathering, Tàkàkrorok's wife, Kamerti, bossed the others around. No one complained, but many women looked away, and most ignored the things Kamerti was saying.

Finally, the dancing began. Women slowly joined in a procession, walking two by two around the clearing they had prepared, intoning the melodies they had been singing for months, swinging their arms to and fro to the rhythm. The dance was much shorter than the preparation, and probably much less important. Soon the women returned to the village. The men claimed ignorance of the women's activities.

Later in the day, as the women were bathing by the river, they heard a shot in the forest. Quickly grabbing up their belongings, they rushed back to the village. Not long afterwards, the first returning trekkers arrived at the river. Supported by bands hanging from their foreheads, with the weight on their backs, most of the men carried 10-foot racks that towered above them and held as many as thirteen or fourteen tortoises lashed to the two side poles. Leaning the heavy cargos against trees, they quickly bathed and then returned to the forest to paint themselves for their grand entrance into the village.

Heavy laden with tortoises and baskets, the men silently walked single file into the plaza. After meeting for a few moments outside the men's house, they carried their cargo to the house of Tàkàkngo and Kaxre, the ceremonial sponsors. Then they began a short dance, imitating a battle between the two men's societies.

The women had been grating manioc for days in preparation for the event. Tàkàkngo and Kaxre knocked down almost the entire front wall of their house to allow people to arrive and depart. Now, Kokory and Nhakkruw, their wives, would have to work hard with their mothers to make tortoise pies for the crowds that gathered around the building. For the next four days, the oven at the entrance gave off the wonderful scent of roasting banana leaves as the ceremonial sponsors worked around the clock.

On the second day after the arrival of the tortoises, most people spent their time on body decorations. The feather headdresses, necklaces, armlets, and legbands had been made much earlier and stored in bags hanging from the household ceiling. Many of the women and children were already painted. Most of them had also already shaved the tops of their heads and decorated the tonsures with red and black tree gums. But now the men too needed painting. Completely naked, they lay for hours on household mats while their wives and sisters studied the contours of their bodies and painted elaborate designs to match their wearers. It was one of the most intimate experiences between Mekranoti men and women.

The genipap dye would last for weeks, but other decorations were more temporary. The red achiote and palm oil had to be replaced almost every day. Many Mekranoti had been raiding birds' nests all year so that they could paste the broken blue eggshells onto the faces of their nieces and daughters, and stick downy feathers into their hair. These decorations would last only a few days at most. It is no wonder that showing off finery is one of the most important parts of a Kayapo ceremony.

The women made a second procession in the forest the day after the men returned with the tortoises, but afterwards the festivities took place in the village, and both men and women took part. Kuture, Kamerti's son, had inherited the role of song leader for both the men's and women's *bijok* ceremonies. He led the villagers in processions around the plaza. Other people had other roles to carry out during the festivities. And everyone had inherited at least the right to wear a few ornaments from an aunt or uncle. Some of the young men donned their monkey masks from the men's *koko* ceremony and joined the *bijok* procession, much to the chagrin of the women who would have liked to carry out their procession in peace.

Many times the sight of a traditional decoration would cause fits of wailing among the older women who were reminded of past ceremonies and of dead people who once used these ornaments. The women then would grab a nearby machete and begin to hack away at the tops of their heads, in the same gesture they used at funerals. Fortunately, the others wrenched the machetes from their hands to prevent too much damage. The custom was so popular that one of the "howler monkey" clowns from the *koko* ceremony caused fits of laughter by imitating the keening women in the middle of their wails. Then the other monkeys increased the laughter by dutifully grabbing the machete from the keening howler monkey with the same gestures used by the women.

At night the ceremonial sponsors, Tàkàkngo and Kaxre, went to the houses of their ceremonial friends, known as *krabdjwỳ*, to give tortoise pies to their families. In return, the ceremonial friends carried around the sponsors' name-receiving children during the final festivities. The exchange was extremely formal. People offered their gifts, reciting set phrases, and otherwise talked little. I often got the impression that people became ceremonial friends because they didn't like each other. It is forbidden to talk directly to one's *krabdjgÿ*, and interactions with the *krabdjwÿ's* relatives are limited mostly to joking—Men feign anger with their *krabdjwÿ's* male relatives, and make sexual jokes with their *krabdjwÿ's* female kin.

Supposedly people inherit their *krabdjwÿ* from their fathers, but ceremonial friends come and go so fast that the formal inheritance seems to mean little. Most of the Mekranoti considered virtually everyone else in the village to be either a true relative or a fictive one. The fictive kin were simply people who "acted like relatives" and so were given kin terms, much as people in our society tell their children to call unrelated adults "aunt" or "uncle." The few people who weren't kin of one kind or another were usually labeled *krabdjwÿ*. Some Indians had no *krabdjwÿ* at all, and most had only a few.

Sex is prohibited between *krabdjwÿ*, but the taboo is easily circumvented. After Kentyxti grew fond of one of his ceremonial friends, Ngrwa'o, he simply declared that she was no longer his *krabdjwÿ*. "She's now my fictive niece," he reported, "so sex is okay." If he later needed a ceremonial friend to help him give special names to his daughters, he could always ask a fictive brother to find him one.

When the tortoise pies had all been distributed, the ceremony could come to its dramatic close. In the morning people gathered in front of Tàkàkngo and Kaxre's house. Inside, the young girls receiving names, and a few others as well, sat on fresh leaves surrounded by admiring onlookers who commented on the fine costumes of eggshells and downy feathers. Throughout the morning people came and went. Men fired gunshots in the air to add to the drama, and small children occasionally beat on the roof of the ceremonial sponsor's house.

Many of the older men sang and danced in front of the newly named children, sometimes two at a time, often each man by himself. As they shook their rattles and stomped on the ground, the audience suggested songs. The women, too, began to dance after most of the men had finished. Ireti arrived while the women were singing, looking a bit peeved at the others for not waiting. He fired a gun into the air and entered the house to do his dance. While the men performed in the sponsor's house, the women occasionally went off in pairs to the plaza to march around the circle, singing and swinging their arms. The gestures were the same as always, but now the body decorations were finer, the people more numerous, and the atmosphere more exciting.

As the day wore on the confusion grew greater. People joined in processions around the men's house. They walked two by two, the nephews, nieces, aunts, and uncles of the ceremonial sponsors on the inside, and the non-relatives on the outside circle. People wore all of the ceremonial paraphernalia they had inherited. One *norny* had an elegant hat of white down, another wore a finely woven headband of red feathers, and others sported large headdresses of the bright yellow tail plumes from the pe'jati bird, sewn into arched frames hung in tumplines from their foreheads. The women, painted blacker than usual, and with heads closely shaven, often carried brightly decorated children, along with the feather headdresses that trailed down their backs. The color and pageantry rivaled the best that "civilization" can offer.

To bring the ceremony to a formal close, the Indians joined in a procession that would last all night. I stayed up for a while watching as people went around and around the village, sometimes dropping out for a short rest, but then joining the crowd again for another circuit. In the predawn hours the procession, now only women, dropped to as few as twenty people, but quickly grew just before daybreak. To end the affair, Mydjêti, who had inherited this ceremonial privilege, took the women one by one out of the circle and removed their feather ornaments. The women quickly reformed their procession, but the men, armed with war clubs, recaptured them, swinging their bludgeons without hitting. Sometimes the women put up a mock battle, but usually they gave in meekly. When all the women were out of the circle, the ceremony came to a close, and people went home to sleep off the week's intense sensuousness.

# 12

# HONEY BEES
# AND MONKEY BUSINESS

In the late November morning Kukrytbam came by my hut with one of the other *norny*. "Let's get honey," he offered excitedly. He had found a bees' nest earlier in the morning while out hunting, but needed to return to the village to get an ax. Apikrã, his friend, and I were the only ones to know of the find. I felt honored. Ever since he helped me set up house during my first month with the Indians, Kukrytbam felt obligated to instruct me in Mekranoti customs.

We had walked only a short distance out of the village when Kukrytbam pointed to a treetop. "See the nest?" he asked. I could see nothing, but by this time Kukrytbam was accustomed to my ignorance, and simply told me to wait a bit. While Apikrã and I watched, he then began to chop down trees to make a clearing in order for the larger tree with honey to fall. When his target finally crashed to the ground, Kukrytbam ran to the nest site—a small hole in a large branch of the tree. From the ground, he must have seen only the bees, and inferred the nest. I was impressed by his vision.

Seemingly oblivious to the stingless bees swarming around his head and hands, entering ears and nostrils, Kukrytbam chopped a larger hole in the tree trunk, and stuck in his hands. With watery honey dripping from his fingers, he pulled out a dark brown, paperish sack, divided into egg-sized chambers, full of thin, mild honey. Puncturing the chambers, making all of the honey flow out, was difficult to avoid, so Apikrã rushed to bring some nearby wild banana leaves on which to set the honeycomb.

After gorging ourselves on the sweetest food in the forest, Kukrytbam stepped down from his perch on the fallen tree trunk to look for leaves to wrap up what remained of the prized honey and take it back to the village. He found wild banana leaves only a few yards from the site, but then could not figure out how to make a honey basket. He tried several times, asking Apikrã every now and then if he knew how to do it. Baskets for other things are easy, Kukrytbam insisted. But making a container to hold liquid is another matter. Finally, with a cry of glee at his discovery of the proper technique, Kukrytbam proudly tied the leaves together and slung the package over his shoulder.

Watching Kukrytbam's difficulties, I realized just how hard it is to learn everything needed to live in the forest. Wrapping material alone is a complicated business. Different kinds of baskets and rope are good for different cargos. A paca can be tied by its legs and carried on a tumpline, but transporting half of a large peccary requires special knots and leaves. Tortoises go on racks, and honey goes in a special watertight basket. Besides, containers are only part of the forest's tool case. I once saw an Indian grab a twig and split it in half. The result was a razor-sharp blade that could serve as a butchering knife. But in this case, the hunter used it to remove calloused skin to get at a thorn in his foot.

We walked rapidly back to the village. As we approached the houses, Kukrytbam began to strut a bit more and to sing the honey song, telling the villagers of his find. There were also songs for different animals hunters brought back, but men were not always so willing to advertise their catches. A hunter usually preferred to keep the meat for his wife and children, giving what little remained to his wife's family, or to his sisters. But Kukrytbam had a reputation to build, and honey is usually given more freely than game anyway. He gave part of his honey to Tàkàkrorok, and part to his girlfriend's grandmother and little sister. He left me with a 100-gram jar of the sweet liquid, warning me not to eat it all at once.

There was more to the warning than simply eating too many sweets. When collecting genealogies I was told of several ancestors who died "from honey." At first I thought the Indians were referring to some superstitious cause for disease. But later I talked to a photographer who mentioned that once, after she ate too much honey in an Indian village, a violent rash encircled her abdomen and she had fits of vomiting. Perhaps the reaction was due to an allergy in this case, but many honeys may be slightly poisonous as well.

After running out of the sugar I brought into the village, I asked people to bring me honey whenever they could. I was surprised at how many different types there were. Most came from bees, but some were from ants. There was even a syrup the Kayapo ate by biting off an ant's abdomen. The honey Kukrytbam collected was one of the better ones. Clean and sweet, it lasted for several weeks before spoiling. Other honeys were less interesting. Sometimes the Indians brought me honeycombs with more larvae than liquid. They enjoyed the larvae as well, but I ethnocentrically turned it down. Sometimes the Indians dug honey out of ground nests. Usually eaten mixed with dirt, it had a strong acidy taste, and I decided not to eat much of it, even though I craved sweets.

Every once in a while the Mekranoti brought me the thick sweet honey I knew from childhood. Stinging bees, like the ones that made this honey, were new to the Indians. They arrived in the area only a few years before my study. The Mekranoti were worried about this new addition to their forest. The stinging bees had invaded the nesting areas of the more harmless varieties, and seemed to reduce the honey supply. Besides, getting honey from the new bees required setting fire to the nests and running, usually suffering a few stings in the process. The only alternative to fire was putting a certain kind of bark in tree nests that killed some species. Apparently the famous "Brazilian killer bees" had left some modified descendants in the Mekranoti area.

The Kayapo recognize some fifty-five varieties of bees, and are keen observers of their behavior. One entomologist-turned-anthropologist discovered that the Kayapo divide bees according to much the same criteria used by Western scientists, such as ecological zone, or nest structure. Some bees build their nests in the ground, others inside tree trunks or tree limbs, and still others make external nests on tree limbs or leaves. There are even forest bees that make their colonies in termite or ant nests.

Honey is not the only reason the Mekranoti pay close attention to bees. They also like the wax for making artifacts such as the cap that holds a feather headdress, or for sticking feathers and points on arrows, and strengthening bowstrings. Although I never saw the Mekranoti do this, other Kayapo groups "domesticate" bees, bringing the nests back to the village to hang from houseposts. Also, after robbing a forest bee colony of its honey, the Kayapo sometimes leave the queen bee behind in the hopes that the other bees will return to reestablish their nest. In at least one group the Kayapo even dig holes near garden sites to encourage bees to nest near their plants, which they say is "good for the fields." They may not understand the details of pollination, but certainly understand the importance of bees in agriculture.

Other insects also have their uses. The Kayapo sometimes eat the dirt of ant and termite nests, and wasps are especially esteemed for their social behavior and for their fierceness. A long time ago, begins one myth, a man hunting in the forest once cut what he thought was a liana, but which turned out to be the earth's artery. Water began to pour from the severed duct until the earth was flooded. The Indians climbed to the treetops to avoid the rising tide. Remaining many days without food, they lost so much weight that they turned into wasps. Another time, when the Kayapo still lived in the heavens without villages, they were attacked by beetles under the leadership of the giant rhinoceros beetle. By observing the wasps, the Indians learned to live and fight together under the leadership of a chief, and to attack fearlessly like the wasp warriors. Thanks to the wasps' example, from that time on, humans became more powerful than other animals.

To celebrate their victory and to encourage fierce behavior, the Kayapo sometimes construct scaffolds under the nests of the fiercest wasps they can find. The scaffolds are made at night when the insects are inactive, but the following morning, the entire village goes to the site and waits while the young men climb, two by two, to the wasps' nest and beat on it with their hands. The young warriors sometimes fall unconscious from the stings they receive. Even those waiting below suffer. The test is worth the pain, because it "toughens up" the Indians and readies them for war.

The Mekranoti had not carried out the wasp ordeal for many years, but now they began to talk about it with more enthusiasm, anticipating a test in the near future. As he wrapped his arms over his chest and trembled with imagined pain, Kukrytbam talked about how bad the stings would be. "*Tokry*" (it hurts), he cried, exaggerating the word's last syllable with a mixture of glee and pride. "But after the stings," he went on "our wives and lovers come to take care of us, rubbing leaves over the blisters. Then they tell us how brave we are." That was the fun part.

While wasps are good warriors, and are used to make men fierce, ants are better hunters. To make them good at catching their prey, the Kayapo sometimes grind up stinging ants and mix them with achiote to paint dogs and men. Amakkry sometimes gave his animals this treatment after they failed in a day's hunt. Shamans, too, sometimes drew upon the "spirits" of fierce ants that "bite hard," to harness their power.

Even the more recent stinging bees have become a part of Kayapo ritual. Young boys, in preparation for the wasp test, sometimes go off to ground-dwelling bees' nests to practice getting stung. While bees, wasps, and ants are admired by the Kayapo, termites are held in contempt. They are not fierce like the other social insects, even though they also have their chiefs. The Kayapo pay little attention to them, simply noting that black termites are like black people, white ones like white people, and red-headed ones like other, less fierce Indian groups.

There are a few species of these normally social insects that are solitary. The Kayapo think of these in the same way they think of Indians who go off on their own in the forest, or like shamans who remain alone more than the others. They are still basically social insects that have gone astray.

The Kayapo usually pay less attention to solitary insects, except when they become pests, like the black flies that infest the area when the flood waters recede at the end of the wet season. But even a few of these insects enter into Kayapo folklore. One day, while sitting in the men's house on trek, I felt a slight sting on the back of my hand. Near me, on our sitting leaves, was a caterpillar with long, bristly hairs. I had accidentally touched the insect's hairy back. As they cautiously used long sticks to kill and carry away the bug, the Mekranoti told me to tie off my fingers. The poison in the caterpillar would spread to the rest of my body. Remembering the scorpion sting, I dreaded going through several days of terrible pain again, and this time in the middle of the forest, away from the care of the FUNAI personnel. Fortunately, I must have touched only a few hairs, for I felt no pain after-wards. One of the missionaries told me that after she once grabbed one of these caterpillars her whole body felt as if it were on fire. The pain evidently didn't bother the Kayapo too much, because young warriors sometimes rubbed caterpillars against their chests as a test of endurance, and displayed with pride the scars left by the insects.

Kukrytbam's interest in the traditional wasp test may have been a way for him to prove his "Indianness" to the others. He was not quite as pale as his nervous younger brother, and his hair was not quite as wavy. But still, the white genes of his father, Tedjware, made him stand out from the other *norny*. Fortunately, Kukrytbam also had a few traits the Mekranoti appreciated. He was taller and stronger than most of the young men, and many thought he was smarter as well. A hard worker, Kukrytbam was beginning to earn a reputation as a good hunter. As one of the oldest *norny*, he had to begin thinking about taking on the responsibilities of fatherhood, and he had to help his brother-in-law take care of his invalid father.

Since the first month when he had worked hard to set up my house, I always got along well with Kukrytbam. A happy young man, he enjoyed helping others and volunteered to do any odd jobs needed around the house. I would have relied more on the congenial young man if I hadn't needed to keep everyone happy with gifts of goods. So at times I asked others to help me with small chores. Nemyti, another *norny*, once volunteered to clear the area around my house of the weeds that had grown up rapidly since the beginning of the rains. He worked all day cutting the thick grasses and turning the soil with a hoe to prevent regrowth. When he left he showed me a broken blister on his hand as evidence of his labors. I gave him some merthiolate and thought little of the sore.

But a few days later I visited Nemyti in his mother's hut. He was lying on a sleeping platform, unable to go out hunting because his hand had swollen up to twice its normal size. I asked him if he had gone to the FUNAI medical attendant for antibiotics. He answered that he couldn't do this because his illness was an Indian one, and FUNAI's medicine would be useless. At that point Kentỳxti walked in and warned Nemyti that under no circumstance should he go to FUNAI. His hand had swollen up because tiny invisible fish had bitten him since he spent too much time in the water. FUNAI's medicine would kill him, Kentỳxti insisted. To back up his point he cited a couple of examples of how the FUNAI medicine had killed people before.

I was surprised at Kentỳxti's hysteria. But he seemed so sure of himself that I almost believed his account. Fortunately, Nemyti was less convinced by the arguments and eventually risked the foreigners' antibiotics. Later in the year I saw Kentỳxti again grow hysterical and condemn Western medicine, while the other Indians remained calm. I now knew one of the reasons this highly intelligent man did not enjoy greater prestige in the community.

Even if he lost his nerve with illnesses, Kentỳxti was still a big help when it came to language problems. Now I needed to interview all the women about the times they became pregnant, and would need him to help me with the questionnaire. From pregnancy histories I hoped to discover how Mekranoti fertility and mortality had changed over time, and how the Mekranoti compared with other groups in the world.

The Kayapo translations of my questionnaire went fine until I came to the question about first menstruation. Kentỳxti could not understand what I wanted. "There is the moment when a man breaks a girl's hymen and blood comes out," he explained. "But other than that the only vaginal blood is in giving birth." I tried to explain what menstruation was, and Kentỳxti seemed to understand. Already accustomed to the bizarre habits of civilized people, he agreed that white women might indeed pass blood every month, but Indian women, he insisted, certainly did not. Still, at my insistence, he agreed to make up a translation of sorts for the concept.

True to Kentýxti's prediction, the women could not understand what I meant about monthly blood. I realized how convinced they were about not menstruating when a new FUNAI medical attendant asked me one day to help him understand one of the Indian women. He thought his problem was with the Indian language. "She says she's sick, but I can't see any problem," the attendant complained. Suspecting a miscarriage, I tried to find out what was wrong. "You say you were hurt in the vagina?" I asked. "No, it doesn't hurt, it's just bleeding," the woman answered, somewhat peeved at my failure to understand. Finally, I realized that she had simply menstruated and thought she was ill. Later one of the missionaries told me that Indian women came to them every now and then with the same "problem." Probably the women began sex so early in life, and remained pregnant or lactating so long, that they hardly menstruated at all. The few times they noticed blood, it was natural they would think something was wrong.

Apart from the menstruation question, the pregnancy histories went well. The women liked to talk about all the children they had. A few got the births out of order, and often the mothers were distracted by the youngsters they brought with them to the interview. Whenever a child cried, the mother would pull out her breast, if she was wearing a dress, and stick it in the child's mouth. Some mothers nursed children as old as four years if the child was their last. If that didn't work, the mother got up and carried the child around a bit until it quieted down. The interruptions sometimes lasted longer than the interviews. Eventually the mother would sit uncomfortably on the bench in front of my table and answer my questions, her breasts still dripping milk.

The women told stories of years wandering from one place to another without husbands. Wars and epidemics had killed off many of the men. Even today, men are in short supply, they complain, but in the past the sex ratio was worse. Girls were older when they married, and the *kurerêr* (post-pubescent girls without children) followed the men on war expeditions.

Many women also talked of long periods without sex just after the births of their children. Many societies have sex taboos at this time to allow the mother a rest and to prevent another birth before the first child is weaned. Among the Mekranoti, the husbands have to sleep in the men's house at this time—"until the child can walk strongly" they say. Because the Mekranoti did not make ceramic pots, there was no way to boil food until metal pans made their way into the village. Most food was roasted, and small children could not eat it. As a result, mothers had to nurse their babies longer than they do today. Before contact, the women used to nurse babies an average of 20 months, but now the average is only 16. The sex taboo has also dropped from an average of 37 to 26 months.

Women were usually happy to have babies. No one was sterile, but one old woman lamented that she had given birth only once, and that baby had died. No one complained about having too many children, but sometimes women tried to avoid babies. Two women mentioned abortions they committed. One was sick, and took some medicine she knew would cause a miscarriage. I would guess the "medicine" was probably slightly poisonous. Another woman was angry with her unfaithful husband and aborted when he frightened her by firing a shot in the air. Several women also had killed their newborn babies. Two had eliminated one of the twins they had borne, and two others killed their newborns because their husbands had left them.

Most of the women said they took contraceptives, but the Mekranoti had little faith in this medicine. "In the savanna regions there is a contraceptive that really works," I was told. Later I discovered that scientists had confirmed the contraceptive powers of the savanna plant. Unfortunately, though, it was not commercially viable, so the scientists lost interest. In the forest regions, "the plants are no good," the Mekranoti complained. Most are boiled in water and drunk as a tea.

A botanist who once visited me in the field had already heard of the savanna plant and was determined to discover a new contraceptive from the Mekranoti forest. As we walked about collecting plant specimens, one of the Indians mentioned a certain plant's contraceptive powers. Excitedly, the botanist asked how it was used. "You boil the leaves and drink the tea," the Indian answered while the botanist frantically took down notes. "And then you abstain from sex," the Indian added as an afterthought. The botanist was crestfallen. Instead of discovering a substitute for the pill, he was urged to bring the Indians contraceptives from the city.

The pregnancy histories showed that life before contact with civilization was better than life afterwards—at least for Mekranoti children. Beforehand, eight out of ten newborns survived to age ten. During contact only 60 percent survived this long, and after whites moved into their village, only 54 percent survived to their tenth birthday. The figures showed just how bad "civilization" had been to the Mekranoti. Fortunately, since FUNAI gave them a resident medical attendant three years before my arrival, children have had a better chance of surviving.

Fertility also changed from one period to the next. Before contact with whites, Mekranoti women who lived to fifty-five could expect to become pregnant between six and seven times. During the difficult contact years this dropped to five or six times. More recently, women could expect eight or nine pregnancies if they lived to fifty-five. Tàkàkrorok and the other elders appreciated the increased fertility as a sign of the group's health and vigor, and they encouraged the women (and men) to have more babies.

The lower fertility of earlier years is best explained by the lack of husbands, due mostly to the many male war deaths. Of course single Mekranoti women—such as *kupry*—did not forgo sex, but they probably got less of it than other women who had husbands to sleep with them. Even the *kupry*, despite their promiscuity, had fewer babies than the married women. Probably they also had less sex, since they had to arrange trysts in the forest in order to meet their lovers. Since pregnancy is not certain from a single sex act, it generally takes more intercourse than most people think in order to ensure conception. That women who observed long postpartum sex taboos also had fewer babies confirmed this view.

Some scientists suggested that other factors, such as long nursing periods or use of native contraceptives, would reduce fertility, but they seemed to have little effect on the Mekranoti. Even the Indians didn't expect their contraceptives to work, so this finding was hardly surprising. It seemed lack of sex was the main reason some Mekranoti women had fewer babies than others.

While I was carrying out the pregnancy histories, village events showed that sex affected more than just fertility. The amorous adventures of Ngrenhre and Ne'i finally led to a confrontation. Late one night, some of the young men, wearing monkey masks and feeling less shame than usual, decided to walk into Tàkàkngo's house unexpectedly. There, they caught Ngrenhre *in flagrante* with Tàkàkta, one of her beaus.

Word got quickly back to Ne'i, whose pride was damaged by the openness of the affair so close to home. Marching into the village plaza, he began to shout his complaints to the entire village. He had known about the affair for some time, he began. "If Tàkàkta likes my wife so much, he can have her," he screamed out to his rival. Tàkàkta was none too happy with the pronouncement. He had no intention of marrying Ngrenhre, at least under these circumstances. He grabbed a club to confront Ne'i.

The confrontation between Ne'i and Tàkàkta could have started a traditional pounding duel, but some of the elders intervened. The speeches continued one after another until the two sexual rivals calmed down. The elders reminded the young men of all the times they had worked together, of how they were *norny* at the same time, and of how they were fictive relatives.

Just a few days before the fight, Ne'i had walked off with my flashlight. The men often borrowed it for hunting, but this time it disappeared without a word from anyone. I complained about the missing article and Ne'i showed up a few days later in my hut with the stolen item. He had taken it, he confessed, and was sorry, but he asked that I not tell anyone. At the time I had no idea that the affairs were coming to a head, but now I imagine Ne'i wanted the flashlight either to keep track of his wife or for his own sexual trysts. If I had lent it to him as I usually did, the others would have known, so he took it without asking.

Tàkàkta was also known for his sexual activities. He normally associated with the *norny*, but technically he was already in the fathers' age-grade. He had "married" Tykre and deserted her. Tykre claimed that one of her sons was Tàkàkta's, although no one was too sure about the claim. Tàkàkta had also supposedly married one of the village's *kurerêr*, but this affair was a short one. For a while he lived in these women's houses, but now he was back in the men's house with the young men, keeping his things in his sister's house. One of the better-looking young men, he enjoyed the sexual favors of several women and appreciated the carefree life of the *norny*.

Kentỳxti was also involved in the affair. Everyone knew he had been having sex with Ngrenhre, even though no one mentioned his name. After the fight, he nervously came into my hut and closed the door. He explained the whole incident and complained that Ngrenhre didn't know what she wanted. "Maybe she wants to stay with me," he pondered. "Or maybe she wants Tàkàkta or Ne'i. Maybe she just wants to be a *kupry*." Kentỳxti was looking for advice I couldn't give. So to stay out of trouble he decided to spend the day hunting.

The masked monkeys had already caused enough mischief in the village, so people began to think more seriously about finishing the *koko* ceremony. As with all the naming ceremonies, someone would have to go on trek to get tortoises. Many of the women complained that they didn't want to go to the forest because of·the risks their children would suffer from scorpions, snakes, and malaria. The December rains were heavy, and traveling would be difficult and unpleasant. Some began to suggest that the men ought to get the tortoises and leave the women behind in the village, but several of the men talked of other problems—sore feet, illness, or the need to make manioc flour.

The village fight finally settled matters. The trek would be a good way to relieve the tensions that had built up between the two adversaries and their supporters. So the day after the incident people began to pack their belongings and prepare for another long excursion into the forest. Only this time almost the whole village would trek together—except that Tàkàkta would stay behind while Ne'i accompanied the villagers.

As with all ceremonial treks, people had to be invited to trek by either the ceremonial sponsors or their "helpers." This time there were several different sponsors, so they dispensed with the helpers altogether. In a small ritual resembling the choosing up of softball teams, the sponsors and helpers went to the men's house and selected men to accompany them and bring along their wives. Not everyone was chosen though. Tàkàkdjamti told me later that he would not be going on trek because he felt ashamed that the ceremonial sponsors had not asked him. Although he may have been asked, Bepnĩ, one of the *norny*, also decided not to trek "out of shame" for having left his wife. Except for these two young men and a few elderly men and women, the entire village prepared to spend several weeks wandering in the jungle.

# 13

# GATHERING TORTOISES

The path behind Kaxti's house led west. Higher and less flooded than the other trails, it was a good walkway for the wet season. The trekkers who left a day earlier had already beaten away the dripping leaves that closed up the path. Kokokà, Amakkry, and the rest of my family had no trouble hauling the baskets of manioc flour, medicine, and bananas to the new campsite. As usual, I carried a knapsack with my hammock, an extra pair of pants, socks, plates, notebooks, and unfinished pregnancy histories. Remembering how much I missed sweets on the dry-season trek, I had also tucked away a few chocolate bars deep where no one would find them. In an hour, after passing the encampment where the others had spent their first night, we arrived at the new site.

The bustle of the December wet-season camp looked very different from July's dry season calm. Women ran about gathering saplings and wild banana and palm leaves, while their children stayed behind playing with their gear and anyone around them. Many of the men helped out by finding the smooth tree whose inner bark makes a good lashing rope. After a small cut, they pulled on the bark until, rising up the tree trunk, a two- or three-inch-wide sliver gradually separated from the tree. Then, standing on a stick or machete with the long strip of bark underneath, they pulled the inner fiber until the outer bark, moving straight along the ground, separated from the valuable inner bark. If they were lucky, they could get a cord as long as thirty or forty feet to use for lashing.

The ceremonial sponsors shouted to the others, trying to coordinate the construction of their lean-to. One long building had to shelter all of the people invited by one of the sponsors, while two other structures, facing it, housed all those invited by the other sponsors. Sometimes rocks, water, or ants got in the way, making it impossible to build where originally planned. Then women argued back and forth, shouting across the large clearing.

After deciding on a few trees to anchor the structure, the women lashed crossbeams from one trunk to the next until they had formed a long, arching line about five feet from the ground. Once this was done, the house's basic structure was settled and the ceremonial sponsors could calm down. The women would build the sleeping places for their families on their own. A few of the women waited till later in the afternoon to finish their house, but most tried to complete the job by midday. After placing a few leaves on the ground for their children, they vigorously pounded forked tree trunks into the earth, six feet behind the main girder of crossbeams and pointing diagonally back. These were used to place a second beam parallel to the first. Then thin, supple saplings with their branches and leaves still intact could be placed in the ground behind the girders. Bent over the back joist, their tops were lashed to the front beam, forming a curved roof and back, with an open front. Only banana and palm leaves needed to be placed on top to keep out the rain, and on the ground to make a sleeping place for the family.

In most sedentary societies men build the houses, while in nomadic groups women take over the job. Sedentary groups usually have larger, more solid buildings that require more intense labor. Burdened with children, women would have trouble finding the time to do the job. But in nomadic societies, the house goes up much faster so women complete the job quickly without interfering with their child-care duties. This leaves the men free to hunt or do other jobs. Among the Mekranoti, the men's societies put up the large, semi-permanent village dwellings. This leaves the women more time to garden. But on trek, the temporary shelters are women's work, leaving the men more time to hunt.

Most of the trekkers were housed in one of the three long lean-tos. But the 'okre boys, the norny, and the men observing post-partum sex taboos slept in an improvised men's house. Actually, there were different "men's houses" for each of the different groups. With a good deal of help from their mothers, the 'okre were charged with putting them up. A few other people also separated off from the long lean-tos—some because they had not been invited by the sponsors or the helpers, others because they didn't like their neighbors' dogs. Amakkry and Kokokà built a separate lean-to because they had me to take care of. My hammock had to be strung between two trees, which weren't always available at the place where Amakkry and Kokokà would sleep in the long lean-to. With a roof next to Amakkry and Kokokà's, it was easy for me to share the family's food and yet also remain independent enough to interview informants and to take care of the medicine.

Feeling a little more confident about my medical abilities, I decided to bring a syringe along on this trek. If people got bitten by snakes, or contracted pneumonia, only injections could save their lives, I reasoned. It was irresponsible not to be prepared, even though I hoped I would never need to use the needles.

A few days after the trek began, my blood curdled on hearing a woman begin that chilling Kayapo wail that indicates injury or death. Soon the keening multiplied to include most of the women in the area. I rushed to the crowd, fearing the worst. The Indians surrounded a mother and her baby. The infant had just been stung by a scorpion, I was told, and looked as if it was going through the spasms I had experienced.

Remembering the trouble Ronaldo had when a young girl died after a scorpion sting, I realized that the insects could, and did, kill children, and felt obligated to give medicine, even though the thought terrified me. I also knew that the Indians would expect me to do something about the ailment since I had gone through it myself. Fortunately, I had brought along scorpion antivenin. As I boiled the syringe and needle, I read over and over again the instructions on giving the medicine. For a large person, one vial of the antivenin was enough, and it could be injected subcutaneously, but smaller people had to be given more to neutralize the insect's poison. For a baby, I would have to give up to ten vials of the medicine, and would have to inject it intravenously. Finding a vein in a baby is difficult. Usually doctors give them intravenous injections in the head veins.

I could not imagine myself injecting shot after shot of medicine into a baby's head. I tried desperately to find a way out of the problem. I searched for other remedies in the medical handbook I had with me, and talked with the Indians over how to treat the case. Finally, one of the women told me that the infant had really been stung by one of the large two-inch ants that make holes in the ground. It would cry all night, she told me, and would feel pain like that from a scorpion bite, but would not die.

The relief was overwhelming. I packed up the syringe again and simply ground up some aspirin with sugar and a little of the baby's mother's milk and tried to get the infant to swallow. The child did indeed cry a lot, but did not die.

Trekking during the wet season was not nearly so pleasant as during the dry season. Several days we had to move camp in the middle of the rain, and almost every day we waded through stretches of knee-high water. I soon grew accustomed to putting on wet socks in the morning, and pants that were soaked up to the knee or thigh. Camps had to be set up on the high grounds, so despite all the water we encountered on our way we usually had to walk a good distance to find drinking water or to bathe. Often the water source was simply a spring at the bottom of a wide pit lined with slimy reddish clay. After struggling to get drinking water to flow into the vessels I brought with me, I would attempt a bath, but to no avail. Climbing out of the pit I ended up dirtier than before.

Stinging ants almost always infested the high-ground campsites. I tried to set up my hammock off the paths of the insect armies. But sometimes, when a longhouse was built through the paths, the women blew smoke on the ants until they changed direction—often toward my hammock. The insects climbed up the trees and onto the hammock ropes. Then I had to untie my bed while ants crawled up my feet and down my arms, biting anywhere they could. My feet were sore for days after these adventures.

The Indians were more accustomed to the ants. Once, while interviewing Pãxmry about her pregnancies, I suggested that we go off to the village periphery, a bit distant from my hammock, to avoid the ants that swarmed underneath. But Pãxmry replied that she could sit on the ground and the ants would go around her. During the interview, she nonchalantly crushed one ant after another, telling me that this would make them go away. After we were finished I asked if the ants had stung her. "Yes," she answered, "I've been getting bitten all along, but the insects are going away now."

Pãxmry's life had been difficult. She became pregnant eleven times, but one pregnancy resulted in a miscarriage, and six of her ten children had died—one of malaria, one of measles, another of an epidemic, a fourth of drowning, and a fifth of an infection after its ears were pierced. The sixth death was from "rice," I was told, although I never understood quite how the grain could kill. Although her face showed signs of stress, Pãxmry was a generous woman, both to me and to the other Indians. Like most talented body painters, she was also thought to be exceptionally intelligent.

The wet-season trek was full of problems, but it also had a few advantages. Most of the forest's fruits came into season at this time, so every day I had exotic foods to eat. When building houses, the women often gave their children heart of palm from the trees they chopped down in their search for leaves and saplings. An expensive delicacy in America, the soft inner shoot of the palm tree was considered "junk food" among the Mekranoti. "Why would anyone like to eat trees?" one Indian asked after hearing about the strange American food taste. "Wild bananas" were large nutlike fruits with hard outer shells and edible seeds inside. They came from the same plant that gave leaves for trekking roof shingles. It took a long time to eat the seeds, but the flavor was good. There were also "beans" that grew from tree branches and lots of tiny yellow fruits with a sweet taste, but, as usual, little flesh.

One of my favorite fruits was the enterpepalm berry, known as *açai* in northern Brazil. Collected from the tops of a small palm tree, the berries are dark purple with a large seed in the middle and little flesh. It's not worth trying to eat the berries raw, but pounded in a mortar, added to boiling water, then run through a sieve, the berries give a wonderfully rich juice that Brazilians use to make sweets and ice cream. The Mekranoti mostly mixed the liquid with their coarse manioc flour.

It was while eating manioc flour with *açai* that I accidently bit down too fast on the hard manioc pellets and broke two of my molars. There was nothing I could do about the resultant toothache except put aspirin on the teeth and hope the pain would go away. I would have to wait a few more months before I could go to a dentist.

Apparently, I was not the only one in camp with a toothache. One day Tàkàkrorok, who had brought a load of freshly ripened corn from the village gardens, made a speech in the center of the trekking village. He mentioned that many people were suffering from toothaches, and blamed sugar cane for the problem, warning the Indians to avoid sucking on the sweet stems too often.

During the dry-season trek I missed sweets, but now honey came into camp almost every day, so I could have as much as I wanted. I need not have bothered with the chocolate bars I'd brought along. Since the sugar made my teeth hurt, the sweets came at a very bad time. Even the roasted game was too tough to eat, and I began to long for meat. I realized how bad things had gotten when I caught myself dreaming of McDonald's hamburgers.

Everyone began complaining about the lack of meat. Hunting was unusually bad for a forest trek, even for a wet-season trek. I nibbled on recooked tapir liver and spleen for several days. When meat did come into the campsite it went immediately to the community oven, managed by the female ceremonial sponsors who spent most of their day gathering firewood and heating stones. There, the overworked women made meat pies. When the pies were ready, the sponsors called out to the other women in the camp.

One by one, each came by to pick up her family's share of the food. Sometimes people grew too impatient with the roasting and tore apart the earth oven before the meat was done. Then the sponsors had to make a new fire to heat the rocks, and once again cover the pies and hot stones with banana leaves and earth.

Tortoises, too, went to the ceremonial sponsors. Every campsite had a tree on which to hang the prize. Every now and then people would comment on how many tortoises were brought in that day or who contributed. At night the men arranged them by size and attached them to carrying racks. Two long sticks on either side, slipped between the tortoises' upper and lower shells, were simply lashed together between each tortoise until thirteen or more of the reptiles fit on each rack. Sitting in the men's house, the returning hunters liked to admire the different racks. Some of the young men tried to count them. Every night the young men covered the tortoises with leaves to prevent the rain from wetting the lashings which would make the cargo heavier. Incredibly, the tortoises stayed alive without food or water for the trek's several weeks.

Tortoises are festival food, and people are especially fond of them. The first to come into camp are irresistible, and trekkers usually succumb to the temptation to eat them. Tortoise meat is mostly organs like heart, liver, and lungs. Only the tiny legs and neck have any muscles. The only part I liked was the eggs, sometimes still inside the mother, but the Mekranoti adored everything. One night Teryti, one of the elders, made a speech complaining that too many tortoises were being eaten. If meat was in short supply, he argued, the men would just have to hunt more. A few members of his audience responded by adding a few cutting remarks about Teryti's own bad luck in bagging game.

One of the reasons the Mekranoti link their trekking to the ceremonial gathering of tortoises may be ecological. Tortoises are probably a good indicator of the amount of game in an area. If there is little game and consequently few tortoises, it takes the Mekranoti longer to gather the tortoises needed to complete a ceremony. This keeps them out on trek longer and allows the game back in the village area time to recover. But if there is plenty of game, then the Indians can quickly gather the necessary tortoises and return sooner to the village. As a result, the Mekranoti enjoy local game without fear of overhunting it.

The wild foods and the fresh corn brought from the gardens made the forest excursion a refreshing change from village life. But the hardships of trekking began to grow more intense as the days wore on. The path we had been following eventually came to an end, so the *norny* had to begin cutting a new trail. With the elders' advice, they chose whichever direction they thought best. It was difficult to walk through stretches of flooded land. It was even more difficult to hack paths through it. The young men exhausted themselves cutting away obstructions under the water. The only way to maintain balance while doing this was to grab onto one of the thorny palm trunks that grew in the flooded land, getting a fistful of splinters in the process.

Illness also became a problem. Several of the children, including 'Okàre. Kokokà's daughter, had what Kokokà called "the crying sickness." The infant's constant sobs worried and irritated Kokokà as well as everyone else around. Amakkry went several days into the forest to look for leaves and roots to cure the illness. After soaking the plants in water, he poured the mixture over the child, but to no avail. The sickness continued, periods of shivering and fever indicating that the baby probably had malaria. I tried to give some of the chloroquine I brought along, but the baby would not keep down the bitter pills, even when mixed with sugar and milk. The FUNAI medical attendant usually gave injections in these cases, but I had none of this medicine.

Earlier in the trek I asked a few people when we would be going back to the village. Some mentioned that the women would return first and let the men finish the trek. "When will the women return, then?" I asked. "When they've had enough meat to eat," I was told. But the meat had been poor, and several of the women, along with a few men, began to complain about the trek. The rains were miserable, there were too many ants, hunting was bad, and now sickness had attacked many of the children.

Finally, Amakkry and Kokokà gave up because of 'Okàre. "We're going back to the village tomorrow," they informed me. Several families had already left, and a few others were planning a return. I was sorry not to stay until the end of the excursion, but also glad to get back to my hut where I could avoid the rain, and cook my own food soft enough to eat it despite my broken teeth.

The trip back was the worst part of the trek. The heavy December rains had flooded the originally dry paths that we would reuse for our return. We had to wade for hours through water up to our knees or thighs. The ground underneath was loose, slimy mud, with an occasional rock to trip us up. I never quite learned to avoid catching my balance on the nearest support whenever I slipped. The Indians thought it hilarious that I grabbed the thorny tree trunks time and time again. Often I fell in the water, soaking my hammock and backpack, which only made the burdens heavier. We had been traveling away from the village for two weeks, but now we made the trip back in one day. My legs had never felt so sore and tired. It was already dark when I finally made it to my hut. I put up my hammock, made a glass of chocolate milk from the powder I'd brought, and slept until late the next morning.

In the next few days most of the trekkers returned, but some continued for another week. The children talked of nothing but the coming *koko* ceremony. Whenever they came into my hut they asked for paper and colored pencils to draw the different masks used in the festivities. Anxious to eat good food and forget about the humdrum activity of the partially abandoned village, the adults, too, looked forward to the ceremony.

The men's entry into the village was much the same as for the women's *bijok* ceremony. After bathing at the river and painting themselves with achiote, they formed a solemn procession, carrying the towers of tortoises on tumplines supported by their foreheads. As always, the thick-shelled reptiles were laid up against the houses of the ceremonial sponsors in a grand display of their numbers. The first night after the arrival of the tortoises, the anteater masks danced till dawn. They moved in an elegant side shuffle, with a slowness and deliberateness that gave the ballet a deadly serious feel. The ceremonial sponsors spent the whole night pounding manioc to make dough for tortoise pies, listening to the bells that hung from the tassels on the anteaters' pointed noses tinkling with a strangely threatening gentleness in the still night air. In the following days, the monkey masks began to visit houses again, and the anteaters frightened the children even more than before.

There were also *koko* masks made of green leaves with a woven mat facade in front. These represented neither animals nor people. They appeared in pairs at the four cardinal points of the compass during morning and evening dances. The first time I saw the masks I assumed there was no one inside. Seemingly inanimate, they were much more like theater props than like actors. But, in tiny imperceptible steps, they gradually made their way into the village center. Inside the masks were the ceremonial friends of the children receiving names. Women stood in front of the masks somberly waving away the evil spirits that could hurt them. In their simplicity, I found the *koko* masks the most dramatic of all. They were certainly the masks the Mekranoti took most seriously.

As with most ceremonial paraphernalia, the right to wear masks is inherited from a mother's brother or a grandfather. The Mekranoti call these inherited privileges *"nekrêx"* (belongings), and place great value on them. In a neighboring Kayapo village, a violent fight once broke out between two men over the rights to ceremonial privileges. One man argued that his son had received the rights from a former chief. The other accused him of "stealing" the ceremonial privileges because, like most orphans, he was envious of the others. As the two were arguing, a son of one of the men goaded them on, encouraging them to fight rather than just argue. He aggressively shoved them toward each other until they finally came to blows. One of the disputants grabbed a hoe and slashed the other's head, beginning a battle that soon involved the friends of both. FUNAI intervened, but the ill feelings never died down.

The Mekranoti inherit more than just the rights to wear ceremonial ornaments. They also inherit the rights to store masks, to perform dance steps, to eat certain parts of game during ceremonies, and even to raise different pets. Because these privileges, as well as names, are inherited from uncles, grandfathers, aunts, or grandmothers, they are usually associated with certain households. People often like to point out where their ceremonial privileges are located in the village. If visiting another community, they can mention what their privileges are and find lodging in the household that possesses these *nekrêx*. Now that some of the young men are writing letters to other Kayapo villages, they also like to state their ceremonial assets as a way of identifying themselves. The transmission can get very complicated, but the women attempt to keep track of who "owns" which privilege. It is also usually women who actually "say" the name or transmit the ceremonial privileges from the owner to the child.

When the owner of a name or a privilege fails to pass on his rights to a future generation, then the privileges die out in the community, so the Mekranoti have to arrange their ceremonies based on whatever privileges are still around. For example, the *koko* festival would be very different if there were no one to play the comic part of the howler monkey. Very likely the Indians would drop the ceremony altogether. Different Kayapo villages often end up specializing in different ceremonies simply because they have more people with the paraphernalia needed for those rituals. FUNAI once helped bring a festival back to life in a Kayapo village by transporting important ceremonial "owners" from a neighboring community to carry on the tradition. Another way to continue ceremonies is to compensate for losses of traditional rights and duties by inventing new ones. For example, the right to wear red cloth during festivities has now become an inherited privilege in some villages.

Besides transmitting "good names," some ceremonies also serve to arrange marriages between children, and to advance boys to new age-grades. The different events do not always coincide, but if they can arrange it, the Mekranoti like to add to the ceremony's excitement by doing more than just passing on names. The infant betrothals are supposed to precede the advancement of a boy to a new age-grade, but today, the betrothals are much rarer than in times past. Even though the "marriages" may never have been consummated, it was once a point of honor for a boy to be selected by a girl's mother for a future marriage and a source of shame not to be chosen. The practice seems to be dying out and most ceremonies do not include such marriages. The use of naming festivals to advance boys to new age-grades also appears less common nowadays, although it may never have been very common. When villages were small, ceremonies were rarer and the progress of boys through the different age-graders had to skip this step.

The final days of the *koko* ceremony were as exciting as the women's *bijok* festival. The masks appeared constantly in the village, and the joking grew bawdier, not only from the "monkeys," but also between the relatives of *krabdjwỳ*, ceremonial friends. I saw men hurl corn cakes at old Bekwỳnhnor whenever she walked by. She accepted the challenges and threw back bananas or whatever was available, screaming out aggressive insults all along. Good food was also plentiful, and seemed even more abundant after the trek's bad hunting luck. The tortoises were slaughtered by the ceremonial sponsors in the central plaza. Using axes, men and women broke open the animals' undershells and tore out their hearts, throwing the reptiles upside down on top of the burning rocks that would later heat the oven. Some of the tortoises were so hardy that even after weeks without food and water, and with their hearts torn out, they still managed to turn themselves over and walk away from the flames.

On the final day of the ceremony, Amakkry and Tàkàkngo lay on the ground in the plaza, covered with mats of leaves. They were soon forgotten in their hiding place. The others stood around in their ceremonial finery watching the anteaters dance. The ballet began with offerings of corn and tortoise pies carried by the masked anteaters from the houses of the ceremonial sponsors to the village center. Some of the women helped the masked creatures by tying the food around the anteaters' pointed noses. Then the serious dances began. The two brothers, Kwỳrdjo and Netire, passed the anteater masks to a man and a woman, who, after donning the heavy costumes, danced around the plaza, and then passed them on to other men and women. After several couples had danced, the masks were finally returned to their owners, Kwỳrdjo and Netire.

It was still early afternoon, but this was the beginning of the *koko* ceremony's finale. For Pãxajk, one of the old women, the dramatic moment brought back memories of past ceremonies and people, and she began wailing loudly and hacking away at her head with a machete. Then, without warning, Amakkry and Tàkàkngo, who had been forgotten under the covering of leaves, suddenly threw off their camouflage and ran to the anteaters, grabbing the masks and hoisting them violently onto the two long poles that had been set up at the plaza's periphery. A crescendo of loud cries accompanied the aggressive rush of the villagers to the site. Men began thumping the poles and their feet rhythmically into the ground, as they gradually made their way around the village. I could not help imagining that they had just hoisted their enemies' heads onto their spears and were celebrating their victories.

The ceremony ended as the thumping side steps with the poles finally died down. There was a small disagreement in the middle of the drama about where to carry the masks, but Tàkàkrorok finally intervened to settle the matter. Like the women's *bijok* ceremony, the *koko* festivities ended on a dramatically violent note. It was at these times that I most easily imagined the terror the Mekranoti could instill in their enemies, and conjured up visions of their warlike past.

With the women's ceremony and the *koko* festival out of the way, the Mekranoti settled down to a calmer life style, but they did not completely stop their ceremonial life. Just a few weeks after the *koko* finale, 'Orwỳkti decided to sponsor a "samba" festival. The ceremony was brief, strictly for entertainment. During the day the men went fishing to provide enough food for the participants. At night, they decorated the area in front of 'Orwỳkti's house with pieces of cloth hung from cord strung between four posts.

I received visits at this time from a botanist and another anthropologist with whom I would be gathering soil and plant samples. The samba festival was the only "native" ceremony the two would see during their four-day visit. Watching the young men and women leave their houses dressed in their finest imported attire—pants, shirts, shoes, and dresses—the anthropologist turned to me and lamented the boy-girl waltzes, clothes, and dance floor decorations. "I suppose it's ethnocentric of me to expect only native ceremonies when they obviously like the samba," he rationalized. "But I just can't help feeling disappointed." Since I had already seen the native ceremonies I was less upset about the samba. I knew the Indians could put on better shows of their own when they wanted to. I learned to see the samba as the Indians did—as a simple diversion from the daily routine, not a substitute for the rich native ritual.

I spent the next few days helping the visitors. Our job was simply to take soil samples from gardens of different ages and from the nearby forest. Walking in a straight line, I dug up a cube of dirt every ten paces wherever my foot landed. After noting the color and wetness of the hole, I put the dirt in a large sack, until I had completed twenty samples. Then the sack's contents were mixed on a large tarpaulin and a portion of the dirt—about the size of one sample cube—was put in a small cloth bag with the number of the garden site written on the front. The rest of the dirt was thrown out. It was a crude but effective sampling procedure.

I imagined Kentyxti, who accompanied us, would think the whole procedure rather bizarre. After all, we spent hours digging up holes and putting dirt in a sack, only to throw most of it away in the end. So I asked him what he thought we were doing. "You're probably digging up this soil to take it to the city to see what grows best here," he explained in a matter-of-fact voice. As usual, Kentyxti's reasoning was impeccable; I should never have doubted him. Earlier in the year I saw Kentyxti run an experiment with some beans I had brought into the village. Neither of us knew how to plant the seeds, so Kentyxti decided to put some of the beans in the middle of the garden where they would get sun, and some along the shaded edge. Not knowing whether planting would work better in the rainy or dry season, he repeated the comparison during the two seasons. If he could understand controlled experiments, he could certainly understand soil samples. Fascinated with the magic and religion of primitive peoples, we sometimes forget their science.

The Indians had planned no ceremonies for the near future, nor any special wet-season activities. On my last trip out of the village I agreed on a meeting in Brasília with other anthropologists in late January, so I took advantage of the post-*koko* lull to make another trip to civilization. I had been away from my own culture for a long time, and felt I might be losing perspective on my work with the Indians. A little exposure to a modern culture would do me good, I thought. Besides, I desperately wanted to get to a dentist. After closing up my house and saying a short farewell to the Indians, I left on the plane that took out the visitors. I would not be coming back for more than a month, but felt sure the things I left behind would be safe. The Indians had treated me well up to now, and I had no reason to expect any problems.

# 14

# BACK IN THE VILLAGE

It was March when I finally returned to the Mekranoti. The village had been calm during my absence. A few days before my arrival the young men left for the forest to collect the Brazil nuts they would sell to FUNAI in exchange for guns, ammunition, pans, beads, and cloth. They would not return until several months later.

In the early evening I walked past the lemon tree behind my house. It had been planted many years before when a missionary brought the seeds into the village with promises of abundant fruit. The Indians thought it odd to have trees so close to the village, and planted the remaining orange and lemon seeds in the distant forest where fruit trees belong. Sometimes the Indians even planted Brazil nuts or the seeds of other native fruits in the forest just in case they or their descendants ever passed through the area again. A few of the forest lemon trees bore fruit, but the village tree never fulfilled its promise. Still hoping that it might someday yield a few lemons, the Indians refused to chop it down. It was the only tree still left close to the village houses.

When I was within a few feet of the lemon branches I heard a loud rustle, and a huge flock of birds darted out from the boughs, just over my head—at least I thought they were birds. It did not take long to realize that the tree and the village had been invaded by bats. The Indians were upset about the invasion, but there was little they could do about it. A few people thought the hideous-looking mammals came from a neighboring Indian village where Indians had lost considerable blood after being cut by the creatures' razor-sharp teeth and injected with their anticoagulant.

Since I arrived late in the afternoon, I decided not to hang up my mosquito net this first night. It would be easier to hang my hammock as it was and leave the net for the next day. During the night the bats whooshed past my head and feet, both above and beneath my hammock. Remembering all the rabies reports that cited bats as the main carriers, I pulled my blankets over my head, hoping the newcomers were not really the vampire type. The Indians had fires in their houses to keep the pests away, but I had nothing. I could hear the lip-smacking sound of their nibbling away at the bananas that hung next to the oven. Turning on a flashlight, I saw them hanging upside down, completely covering the banana bunch as they ate their meal. It was a grossly ugly sight, but at least I felt a little better knowing they were mostly fruit bats and would not be looking for blood.

The bats never went away. A couple of times I went to bed only to find that one had made its way into my net. Then I had to get out of my hammock and chase the thing away. By refusing to keep large bunches of bananas in the house, I managed to reduce their numbers, and eventually got used to their noise-making at night.

I also discovered that the house rats had multiplied. Anticipating their mischief, I had put some of my goods in tins and hung all of my bags on long cords from the roof rafters, as the Indians do with their valuable ornaments. But even so, the rats crawled down the cords and made their ways into the tops of sacks that held the goods I had not yet given away. I could hear the high squeaks of the babies deep within the sacks. The nests had been made out of fibers nibbled from a new hammock I planned on giving away. I gave the pinkish babies to some of the Mekranoti boys, who liked to use them as fishing bait.

In the next few weeks I experimented with different techniques to keep the rats out of my goods. I made "rat guards" out of tin cans to place on my hammock cords and on the cords of the sacks hanging from the ceiling. At times some of the boys came into my hut at night to use their tiny bows and arrows to hunt the brownish rodents. Occasionally they got one and cut it up for bait, but their luck was usually not very good. Eventually they helped me set up the rat traps I brought back from the city. Afterwards, they came into my hut almost every morning in the hopes of receiving a dead rat as a present.

The only other pests were scorpions, which sometimes nested in my bags. The growth of weeds around the building during the wet season seemed to encourage their migration. I could hear their squeaks in the early morning hours, and then had to cautiously empty my belongings and shake out the dangerous insects.

Sometimes Ropnhỳ helped me figure out how to handle household problems. A short, thin man with a gentle, open smile that looked even more charming when his lip disk touched his nose and set off his sparkling eyes, he was always a welcome guest in my house. For a while he came by every night to chat with me quietly about anything or everything. Sometimes, if we had nothing particular to say, Ropnhỳ just sat contentedly patient, as if he had absolutely nothing else to do, and was enjoying the night air. When not chatting with me, he usually spent his evenings with the FUNAI personnel. I never quite understood why he found us foreigners so interesting, but he made all of us feel at home with the Indians.

Ropnhỳ had been married several times. He separated from his first two wives and was widowed from the third. All of the children from these marriages had died. In his late forties, Ropnhỳ was already called an elder by the Indians, but he had a surprisingly young wife. She had no relatives in the Mekranoti village, so the couple lived in Ropnhỳ's sister's large household. I suspect Ropnhỳ found the arrangement uncomfortable. Most Mekranoti men feel ashamed to be around their sisters too much. Perhaps this explains why he visited foreigners so often. Too quiet to feel comfortable in the lively men's house, he had nowhere else to go at night.

Ropnhỳ sometimes liked to tell me Mekranoti myths. The stories were rarely very long. Ropnhỳ was not a man of many words. And then the tales were for children anyway. "Well, this is what the adults told me when I was young," Ropnhỳ would add with a slightly embarrassed laugh after finishing his myth, as if he didn't really quite believe the stories. Perhaps the Mekranoti, like other people, have their share of agnostics. But even if he had doubts about the stories, Ropnhỳ was not beyond using a little magic when he thought it would help. He once showed me all of the charms—bits of cotton, a few dried leaves and some colored string—that he kept tucked away inside the butt of his shotgun to bring good luck in hunting.

After Ropnhỳ helped me set myself up in the village again, I began to think about some psychological interviews I wanted to do. From the "polls" I had carried out earlier I already knew the reputations people had for some personality traits, but I had no guarantee that these reputations would correspond to behavior. There were also a few traits I had never asked about, and couldn't, because I could find no easy way of expressing the ideas. I once tried to find out who was "exploratory," but my translation of the concept was so strange to the Mekranoti that the results were entirely unreliable. Finally, I wanted to know if Mekranoti ideas about smart behavior corresponded to any abilities we, in a more complex society, would associate with intelligence. The only way to answer these questions was to interview all of the 136 adults in the village.

Earlier, I had asked a friend to take slightly out-of-focus pictures of Indians in another area of Brazil. I would use the photographs as a stimulus to get the Mekranoti to make up stories. Hopefully, I thought, I could then use the stories' contents to make judgments about who was more aggressive, original, passive, thoughtful of others' needs, or any other trait I could think of.

I had no idea what "smart" behavior might mean among the Mekranoti. Psychologists suggest that there might be more than one kind of intelligence, and that different societies might stress different mental skills, according to their needs. Hoping to discover a native "test" for the Mekranoti, I finally decided to ask several of the Indians how they could tell if someone was smart or not. The Indians told me that smart men were those who picked up weaving techniques right away. Stupid men had to be shown several times, and even then didn't always learn. I reasoned I could modify this native "test" to invent a test of my own. I could ask the Mekranoti to point to things in the same order I pointed—a test that, like weaving, would require remembering the hand movements of another person. Beginning with three dominoes, I would add one each time someone got the series right, and use as a score the maximum number of dominoes a person could accumulate. Then I could check whether reputations for intelligence were related to scores on this test.

Everyone agreed I should start the interviews with the men. The women thought their husbands ought to have first pickings on any goods I brought into the village, and the interviews would add to the "accounts" I kept on my cards. I was happy to agree with their sex priorities. I knew the Mekranoti men would be harder to track down if the Indians decided on a trek. And the interviews with the men would add a seriousness to the task that would make it possible for me to ask the women not to bring their children along when their turn arrived.

The interviews started out fine. There was enough variety to prevent too much boredom. Even without my saying anything, people seemed to understand the purpose of some of the things I was asking them to do. When I invited a man to come into my hut for an interview, the others goaded him on, telling him I would find out how smart he was. They even played among themselves with the domino test.

I usually managed to interview only three people a day. Besides the time for the interview itself, I also had to add another hour per interview just to transcribe and translate the stories I tape-recorded. I could not possibly expect Kentỳxti to spend three hours a day, day after day, helping me with the transcriptions, so I also drew on two other Indian helpers, Tàkàkngo and Kute'o. Both of these men had worked with the village's missionaries and were good friends with Kentỳxti and each other. They could not speak Portuguese, but they were learning how to write and knew how to be patient with academic work.

After Tàkàkrorok and Pãxkê, the leaders of the two men's societies, Tàkàkngo and Kute'o were probably the most influential men in the Mekranoti village. Although they were too young to give speeches in the village plaza, most people already called them "chiefs" of the younger section of their men's society. The Indians also thought the two young men were the most intelligent people in the village—a belief confirmed by their talents at weaving handicrafts and by their scores on the domino test. Known for their generosity and for their hard work, they were the most sought-after work companions in the village, and were also good friends for conversation. Their closeness to the missionaries apparently did not affect their sexual habits, because both were also known for their extramarital affairs. The two friends had a lot in common, but their careers were very different.

Coming from a small and unimportant family, Kute'o was a self-made man. Neither of his two half-brothers enjoyed prestige—Nokinh was too lazy, and Ireti never recovered esteem after running amok and shooting Kute'o. Since Kute'o married the sister of Ireti's wife, the two brothers lived in the same house, apparently without problem. But the facial and chest scars from Ireti's rampage detracted from Kute'o's otherwise handsome features. He was not considered as good-looking as Tàkàkngo.

Perhaps Kute'o's social success was due to his intelligence, or perhaps to the sternness that earned him a reputation as even more fierce than Tàkàkngo. Undoubtedly his association with the missionaries also helped his career. The American Protestants generally preferred not to preach directly to the Indians. Instead, they liked to make a few strong converts who could give the sermons for them. This way they maintained a low profile in the community, and guaranteed continuity to their teachings even if they were gone from the village. Kute'o was obviously their strongest convert. He took the religious teachings seriously and sometimes preached to the rest of the Indians that they should give up their warlike ways.

Like the wives of most influential men, Kute'o's plump wife, 'Oken, was one of the more influential and intelligent Mekranoti women. She was normally quiet and gentle, but she could fly into fits of rage if offended. Following her husband's lead, she also accepted wholeheartedly the missionaries' teachings, a fact that perhaps explained her unusual seriousness, in contrast to the playfulness of other Mekranoti women.

Remembering his own struggle to get ahead, Kute'o tried hard to give his sons any help he could. He sponsored naming ceremonies, and spent an unusual amount of time carefully explaining hunting and gardening techniques, ceremonial rules, and history. He also tried to teach his children to read, although the missionaries preferred to let the adults learn first. The extra attention seemed to be paying off because Kokowakõ, his twelve-year-old son, became the undisputed leader of his age-mates. The boy would come into my house with his friends and decide to draw pictures, listen to music, or leave. The others simply accepted his opinions; he never ordered them around. Extremely polite, generous, and forever smiling, he was a good leader for the boys. Sometimes he tried to teach them the things his father had shown him.

In many respects Tàkàkngo's past was the opposite of Kute'o's. As Tàkàkrorok's son, he came from a large and prestigious family. Several years younger than Kute'o, he was a handsome man, with long wavy hair, a broad face and an open smile. He was also extraordinarily energetic. At the ceremonial morning sings when everyone else had to be prodded out of bed, and when Kute'o failed to show up, Tàkàkngo was as alert as always. With his usual toothy smile, he encouraged the others to join in the singing and tried his best to keep everyone awake.

Like Kute'o, Tàkàkngo was married to his brother's wife's sister. Since men normally move in with their spouse's family, this meant that the two brothers lived together. Tàkàkngo's wife, Kokory, was an oriental-looking beauty with long silky black hair and slanted eyes. Together with her sister, Nhakkruw, she was one of the most desirable Mekranoti women. According to the Indians, she was also one of the most intelligent and friendly, qualities her more selfish sister did not share.

Tàkàkngo's son was a few years younger than Kute'o's, and seemed to have less influence on his age-mates. Much more bossy and ill-mannered, he made his way around by bullying. Coming into my hut, he would demand that I give him small things—pieces of paper for kites, beads, and anything else he could think of. When I saw him on a path, he would make the high squeaking sound of a scorpion and tell me the insect was lurking nearby to sting me. One day, after he irritated me with his usual insults, including pulling his buttocks apart to show his anus and drawing his foreskin back to reveal the glans, I jokingly picked him up and ut him on top of the eaves of my house. I expected the little boy to continue his blustering, but instead he was overcome by fear. After the incident he was friendlier to me, but still treated his age-mates the same.

Tàkàkngo's four brothers enjoyed high prestige in the village. Like Tàkàkngo, they got along well with the village's resident foreigners. Kaxre and Pãxtu had worked with the missionaries, and Mydjêti and Ajoba, the oldest of the siblings, felt at home with the FUNAI personnel. Probably this association with important outsiders was one of the main reasons for the success of Tàkàkrorok's sons. I doubt that the missionaries or FUNAI were fully aware of how much they encouraged leadership inheritance. Because they had to deal so much with the village chief, they probably simply got to know his family better than any of the others, so it was natural for them to choose his sons as helpers and informants.

Kentỳxti, Tàkàkngo, and Kute'o worked diligently every day for more than a month. At first it was fun to hear what people had to say, but after a while, the Indians began to talk to each other about what they had told me. Eventually informants came to my interviews with pre-prepared stories to tell. Because the narratives became so much alike, I got very little out of them. I discovered that the men who talked most about violence in their stories were also those most often named as aggressive, which helped validate the peer ratings I obtained earlier, but the stories were generally disappointing. Perhaps I would have done better asking people to tell me about their dreams, or about their life histories.

Fortunately, other parts of the long interview—such as the dominoes test—gave better results. Only one old man, Bànhõr, seemed to have trouble understanding my instructions on the "intelligence" test. I tried over and over again to explain, but finally gave up and asked Tàkàkngo to help. The chief's son had no more success than I. Finally, with his usual smile and calm self-assurance, Tàkàkngo looked at me and reported matter-of-factly that Bànhõr was too stupid to understand anything. Bànhõr couldn't even weave the simplest things, he added as a point of information. I was shocked by the directness of the insult in front of the poor old man, but Bànhõr simply sat quietly, accepting everything Tàkàkngo said.

Bànhõr was not very well liked by the Mekranoti. Like other "stupid" men he was harmless enough, but he was much too lazy to make a very good work companion and too bitter about life to be fun to talk to. Although he married three times, he never had any children, and regretted his failure to become a father. His current wife, Kokonhỳ, henpecked him no end. Much smarter than he, she had a reputation for her knowledge, especially about the ancestors. Perhaps because she had no children to distract her attention from the others, she was also one of the most generous and best liked Mekranoti women. The two lived with an adopted daughter and son-in-law, whom Kokonhỳ treated well.

Luckily, the young men who had been out collecting Brazil nuts for FUNAI returned while I was still doing the interviews, so I could include them in the study. In the previous nut-collecting expeditions, FUNAI simply paid the Indians a lump sum that Tàkàkrorok and Pãxkê, the two village chiefs, spent in Belém. Some of the Indians complained that this was unfair to those who had worked most or had not received their share in the chiefs' redistributions. So this time FUNAI kept individual accounts and asked each man what he wanted from the city. The young men made arrangements to give some of their earnings to the older men who stayed behind to hunt for their wives and children. The villagers were excited about the young men's return, and about all the presents they expected.

Most of the returning young men had gained a lot of weight on the trip—probably from eating so many Brazil nuts, which are very high in calories. I teasingly mentioned to Ne'i that he had grown a paunch. Laughing, he put his hands on his belly and joked that he had crammed a lot of animals there. The hunting had been good.

Now that the village was complete again, the Indians decided to begin yet another ceremony. There was no reason not to enjoy oneself while in the village. This time the men would sponsor their counterpart to the women's festival that took place in the fall—the men's *bijok* naming ceremony. They began with the usual morning and evening sings, but added a few dances as well. Stooped over with their legs bent at the knees, the men stomped vigorously from one village house to the next, zigzagging to the men's house between each stop. I joined in the dance but gave up, exhausted, after just a few household visits. The first few nights some of the Mekranoti also gave up the grueling exercise before finishing the village circle, but gradually, as they repeated the dance every day, their endurance grew and they finished the visits. I could not help thinking that Mekranoti ceremonies serve primarily as basic training for warfare.

Another addition to the festival was a ceremonial rape. One day, the *kurerêr*, some as young as ten or twelve, lined up by size at one end of the village. Rubbing their breasts seductively, they waltzed slowly toward the men's house. After they cautiously stepped inside, the men quickly barricaded the entrance ways with mats and leaves. In the past this was the moment for gang rapes, but with outside observers in their village, the Indians decided to drop the custom. Still, a few older men made attempts. Paken, in his usual coarse and brusque manner, grabbed one of the older girls and embraced her from behind. In a society where men almost never touch women in public, this was an extremely immodest act. The girl struggled to get away, but Paken held on. Finally, some of the other men persuaded the old man to give up. The custom had changed, they insisted. Rape, at least in the men's house, was no longer acceptable.

To add interest to the ceremony, the men also decided to make some masks for dancing. Dividing into their two men's societies, they went off to the forest to look for leaves. They were gone only a day or two, but returned ceremoniously painted with achiote and decorated with feathers. On a long pole hoisted onto their shoulders, they proudly slung some of the game they had killed—six macaws, five armadillos, one hawk and one paca. Marching into the plaza with their shotguns, they performed a few warlike dances amidst violent shouts and the heavy stomping of their feet on the ground. The meat they brought back was for them alone. The women and children would get none.

After arranging the leaves on rooftops and allowing them to dry for several days, the men excitedly joined together one evening in the men's house. The structure was bustling with activity. Working until dawn, the men would turn the leaves into *bô* masks that would emerge at the first light of day. After borrowing lanterns from me and from FUNAI, the men closed off the hut's four entrances. Standing in the middle of the confusion, talking to some of the elders, Tàkàkrorok supervised the work. He mostly just watched, pleased at the excitement of the others, who rushed about plaiting grasses, gluing feathers, weaving rope, and tying straw together into thatchlike mats. I thought of last-minute Christmas Eve preparations—of gift-wrapping, of final choir rehearsals, of decisions about where to stand or what to sing during the church ceremony. Tàkàkrorok played every bit the part of a preacher, calmly verifying that everything was going according to plan and that everyone was enjoying the work.

The two masks that emerged at dawn looked less impressive than the many different costumes made for the *koko* ceremony, but the Mekranoti esteemed them even more. Each costume had a conical top, finely decorated with colorful feather down and connected to a mass of straw sewn loosely together to make a heavy cloak. There were none of the fancy arm or facial ornaments associated with the *koko* festival. It was not the mask itself that was important, but its use. The men wearing it had to perform a vigorous dance requiring that they jump up and down until thoroughly exhausted. A couple of the young men excitedly volunteered to go into the plaza with the masks, but Tàkàkrorok told them to wait a bit since their "feet were still too soft." The disappointment in their faces showed how important the dance was to them. There was no mistaking the machismo associated with the *bô* mask. A couple of men maliciously chanted the songs they would intone before killing any woman who dared to ask what the mask was all about.

Another macho aspect of the men's *bijok* ceremony was the wrestling match that pitted one men's society against the other. In the late afternoon, the young men of each group stood with their arms crossed at opposite ends of the wrestling area, surrounded by onlookers. Amidst cries of encouragement and challenge from the audience, men strutted over to their opponents to challenge a match. In the center of the cleared area they locked arms and tried to throw each other to the ground. No one announced winners or losers, and no one kept score, but everyone could tell who was the better wrestler or who was unexpectedly good or bad.

At one point Kaxre arrogantly challenged Apikrã, one of the younger *norny*, to a tussle. Apikrã hesitated. He was no match for the older and stronger man, but could not refuse. The two men walked slowly to the center of the wrestling area. Several men and women shouted that the contest was unfair. Apikrã's sister, Ngrenhka, screamed insults at Kaxre, but the two men began grappling just the same. Suddenly, Ngrenhka tore out of the crowd, violently waving a firebrand in her hand. She rushed to Kaxre and tried to burn him, pulling down the short pants he was wearing and thrusting the burning stick at him. The crowd roared with laughter while Kaxre tried to ward off both brother and sister. The Indians took Ngrenhka's attack as typical of the joking between the relatives of ceremonial friends, but no one could say just who the linking ceremonial friends might be. It didn't really matter, since everyone—except Kaxre—was having a good time.

The excitement for the men's *bijok* ceremony grew every day. People began to talk of the orgy scheduled for the ceremony's finish. Then the nephews and nieces of the ceremonial sponsors, Pãxtu and Ireki, would "give" their aunts to non-relatives in a grand sexual exchange. As it was already the end of April, people also became optimistic about the coming dry season. Only one note of sadness dampened the festive mood of the villagers. Mrotityk's newborn baby died unexpectedly one night.

Like other *kupry*, Mrotityk was thought lazy by most of the Mekranoti, but she was well liked just the same. This was her second child. Her daughter had been born three years earlier, and Mrotityk wanted very much to have more children to take care of her in her old age. Children "pay back" their parents when they grow older, the Mekranoti liked to point out. It would not be easy for Mrotityk, already thirty years old and a *kupry*, to bear many more children, so she felt the loss deeply.

It was seven o'clock when I first walked into Mrotityk's house. The grieving mother sat quietly, tears streaming down her face while the others around her wailed loudly. Kokonhỳ chanted a long litany while Teptykti stepped in to scold Mrotityk lightly about her bad mothering. Afterwards, several women commented to Mrotityk that her mothering had not been so bad, and said it had little to do with the child's death. Simultaneous long litanies were also performed by some of the dead child's male relatives, such as Wakõni, Mrotityk's sister's husband who, by Mekranoti kinship reckoning, was also the child's "father." All morning people roamed in and out of the hut, stopping to wail briefly for the dead child. No one wanted the baby's ghost to come back looking for relatives to kill and take to the home of the dead. One old woman asked me to fetch my camera to take the lifeless baby's picture. The Mekranoti call photographs and souls of the dead by the same term. They are both images of live people. "You can take the baby's picture [soul] and leave it in the city where it won't come back to harm us," she suggested amid sobs.

As Ropnhỳ, one of the household's men, fired three shots in the air, Ngrenhnî, Mrotityk's sister, prepared black genipap dye and then took the dead child to paint. Mrotityke searched through her belongings for any ornaments she could find, and the other women, along with Ngrenhnî's husband, Wakôni, began the long job of stringing the loose beads. Using achiote-colored string, together with beads, Wakôni wove tiny arm and leg bands to place on the infant. Mrotityk used every bead she had to ornament the baby's body. At noon, when the child was finally garbed better than it had ever been in life, Mrotityk took a gourd bowl and began milking herself. The others made their way to the gravesite just behind the village houses.

The men of Mrotityk's house, Wakõni and Ajoba, cleared the gravesite area of the tall grasses that made passage impossible. Kokony, one of the village's *norny*, dug the grave. I never found out why he should have been saddled with this job. Perhaps the child was the product of his sexual ties with Mrotityk. He was not related to the *kupry* in any way.

After ritually wailing and cutting her head with the machete brought along for the purpose, Ngrenhnî took the dead baby from Mrotityk and placed it on top of the old clothes at the bottom of the grave. Next to the child she carefully laid the gourd of milk Mrotityk had provided and the sling used to carry the infant next to Mrotityk's breast. A horizontal row of sticks, placed halfway up the grave and covered with mats, prevented the dirt from falling on the infant as the tomb was finally filled in. A stick topped with another baby sling placed on top of the resultant mound marked the gravesite for the next few weeks.

The funeral was a sad but quiet affair. It had none of the tension that marked the earlier death of Tep'i's child. Most of the Mekranoti simply paid their obligatory visit to the grieving mother and then left to go about their daily business. The baby was so young that nobody gave it too much importance, and the death happened so suddenly that there was no anguish over what kind of medical treatment to give it.

The next few weeks were spent calmly in hunting and gardening with singing and dancing in the late afternoon. As people began to talk about the trek they would need to finish the men's *bijok* ceremony, I hurriedly tried to finish the interviews I was conducting. On earlier treks I had managed, without problems, to interview the women about their pregnancies, but this time I was using a tape recorder and the interviews were much more complicated. I hoped I would finish before we departed once again for the forest.

Perhaps it was luck that the Indians decided to begin their trekking only a few days after I finished my psychological studies. No one ever expressed the least concern about my trekking preferences. Possibly the people who had not been interviewed had asked the others to wait until they had a chance to talk to me and add a few items to their economic accounts. I'll never know why things worked out the way they did. In any case, the timing was perfect. It was May already, and I was ready for a change of pace. I was actually looking forward to the more intimate life on trek.

# 15

# ON TREK AGAIN

The delicious aroma of roasting meat and banana leaves wafted through the sun-dappled forest as we approached the first night's encampment. Amakkry, Kokokà and I left the village late so most of the trekking houses were already up when we arrived in the cluttered but happy clearing. Men lounged lazily in hammocks and women rushed about cooking the game their husbands had brought in. The excited play of the children at the forest edge added to the picniclike feeling of the late afternoon.

Amakkry, Kokokà, and I quickly set up camp. Our evening meal came from the ceremonial sponsors who busily managed the communal oven, distributing meat pies until well after dark. The two long lean-tos that housed the ceremonial sponsors and their helpers were close enough to allow conversation between them at night. Lying sleepily on their bedding of mats and leaves, everyone listened quietly while the elders told stories of past hunting adventures and of exciting battles. Tàkàkngo added to the evening's entertainment by telling stories that seemed even more fantastic about his adventures in Brazilian cities.

"Everywhere you walk on rocks," he told the disbelieving crowd.

"Didn't your feet hurt?" people asked.

"No, not at all, the paths are all smooth," Tàkàkngo explained.

Modern toilet facilities seemed incredible. "Where does it all go when you flush?" asked several men, suddenly awakening from their dreaminess.

"I don't know," responded Tàkàkngo, delighted at the attention he was getting. "It just disappears—whoosh."

The conversation gradually died down again until only a few murmurs could be heard now and then in the quiet encampment. The trek promised to be good this time—much better than the others this year. The first day's hunting had been successful. There was not too much water to wade through, and the coming dry season meant that things could only get better. Now that my Kayapo was fairly good, I felt at ease joining in the conversations, and was enjoying being part of the group.

As the days wore on, the early prognosis was confirmed. Even the bathing spots were unusually good. At the beginning we followed close to the river that meandered out of the Mekranoti village. The children were usually the first to find accessible beaches or fallen trees that could serve as diving platforms.

Gradually we moved farther away from the river and depended on small streams for water and bathing. Remembering waterholes like the ones we passed during the December trek, I was not enthusiastic about the change in direction, but my fears were unfounded. Sparkling water flowed gently in the shallow, sandy-bottomed streams. There were no dangers of stingrays, snakes, or piranha fish to worry about. On clear days it was always possible to find a spot where the sun found its way through the leaves and lianas overhead to bounce off the cool water underfoot.

Fish were plentiful. Beptu once returned to camp with a basket of twenty-four piranha, each weighing about four pounds. Later the others went to the same spot and brought back equivalent baskets teeming with the black, toothed fish. The women quickly made babracots to smoke the excess meat. With a little stirring the coals glowed all night underneath the makeshift racks. The dried flesh would last for several weeks, but the women gave most of it to the people making return trips to the village to fetch sweet potatoes or bananas.

Meat was also good. At the prodding of their elders, all of the young men went out to hunt virtually every day. Only the carrying of garden produce from the village was considered an acceptable alternative. The men gave their game and any tortoises they came across directly to the ceremonial sponsors, who supervised the distribution of food. Eventually, the sponsors would receive as many as three hundred tortoises, according to Kentỳxti, who had counted them on past treks. Sometimes the hunters kept an animal's head for themselves or their family, but on a ceremonial trek it would have been improper to keep the good meat.

Sharing the ceremonial sponsorship with her sister, Nhàkrop, Ireki was heavily burdened with responsibilities. A plump and friendly woman, she seemed to enjoy the prestige the sponsorship was giving her, but her work never ended. As soon as people moved camp she had to supervise the construction of the long lean-to that would house her group. Sometimes she had to order people around a bit. Once she made Kokokà tear down the structure she had been building because it was in the way of her long house. Ireki gave the orders as quietly as she could.

Even before finishing her own sleeping place, Ireki had to bring in wood and rocks to make the communal oven. When it rained she had to make sure the kitchen had a roof as well. Manioc also had to be grated for meat pies, and banana leaves had to be gathered for the wrapping. When hunters brought her game, Ireki gave it to the elders to butcher, or if there were no men around, to one of the women who could do the job. She then spent the rest of the afternoon arranging banana leaves in which to wrap manioc dough and pieces of meat or fish to be roasted in the oven. If there was still meat left over, she divided it into small pies, and called out the names of the other women, asking them to pick up their share to boil for their families at home. Throughout the trek, while everyone else rested or chatted at home, Ireki worked well into the night, watching the oven and carrying load after load of meat and fish pies to the men in the men's house. It was no wonder she was the woman the Mekranoti most sought as a work companion.

Ireki's husband, Pãxtu, was one of the chief's sons. Trimmer than most Kayapo men, he looked more attractive to outsiders than his huskier companions, but the Indians thought he was too skinny. For a while, Pãxtu worked with the missionaries, but eventually he lost interest. Still, the missionary experience left him with one curious quirk. Instead of saying "Nà," or inhaling sharply with a quick raise of the eyebrows like most Kayapo when they want to say yes, Pãxtu somehow picked up the American "uh-hum," a habit that always made me think I was talking to a compatriot.

Pãxtu was respected for his intelligence and his knowledge, especially about foreigners. In times past he was also a renowned warrior, although his friendliness and his small frame would make you think differently. As ceremonial sponsor, Pãxtu had to spend most of his time out looking for game. This only enhanced the reputation he already had as the best hunter in the village. I always liked talking to Pãxtu but he was usually so busy that he gave me little time.

Ireki and her husband lived with her father, Bokrã, and her mother, Pirã, in an old house with rickety thatched walls full of roaches. The flimsy structure reflected Bokrã's growing frailty and his declining energy. Although many years younger than Tàkàkrorok, he looked much older and the medical attendant did not expect him to live long. Pãxtu planned to finish a new house after ending the ceremony, but the family had to settle for the torn leaves in the meantime. Ireki's younger sister, Nhàkrop, refused to live in the decrepit structure and moved off with her husband to a smaller but more solid dwelling.

Nhàkrop was supposed to be a cosponsor of this ceremony, but she was not very interested and was not smart enough to manage a festival in any case. Only Kentỳxti's wife was thought dumber. Still, people seemed to like the jolly fat woman. She always greeted them with a friendly, although stupid smile. Besides, Nhàkrop had five children to take care of, and was an excellent mother. I never saw her free of her babies and toddlers. She seemed to delight in sitting with the noisy children climbing all over her ample body, as she nibbled on a piece of fruit or a handful of manioc flour.

Nhàkrop's husband, Kamti, was a burly muscular man well suited for Nhàkrop. He had been married once before, but his previous wife and their child died. Kamti seemed pleased at all the healthy children Nhàkrop had given him. But the other men sometimes teased him for carrying water, which is usually women's work. With so many children, Kamti had to help his wife around the house. Kokoka, Kamti's sister, sometimes watched one or two of Nhakrop's children for short periods of time so that Nhàkrop could help her sister Ireki. But the Mekranoti think it's poor mothering to leave children very long in the care of others, so Kokokà's help was limited. As a result, Ireki ended up doing most of the work.

Ireki and the good weather kept the trekkers happy most of the time, but there were a few sad moments. Old Tyrre began wailing one day because her pet peccary went off on its own into the jungle and refused to come back. Amakkry complained she was being silly to cry for a wild animal that wasn't a very good pet in the first place.

Another day Pãxkê had to kill a dog that had bitten a child once too often. Grabbing the unsuspecting animal by the scruff, he carried it just outside the campsite and beat it to death with a war club. The owner complained, but there was nothing he could do against the community's guilty judgment.

Perhaps Pãxkê dispatched the dog as part of his chiefly duties—perhaps because he liked the job. A rugged, ill-kept man in his forties, considered "hard" by the missionaries, Pãxkê was one of the best Mekranoti hunters, and one of the best warriors. I suspect he liked the cruder side of life. Never very attentive to grace or manners, he always left a few stray chin hairs on his broad and homely face. His indifference to this basic matter of personal hygiene grated on the sensitivities of most Mekranoti men, who tried hard to keep their facial hair, including eyebrows and eyelashes, cleanly plucked away. Still, Pãxkê was a generous man and the Mekranoti liked him enough to make him chief of the smaller men's society.

Pãxkê's father, Angme'ê was a famous Kayapo chief. Because of fights in the village, Angme'ê and his followers separated from Tàkàkrorok's group to live in another part of the forest. Those were the stormy times mentioned earlier, when battles between different factions killed off many of the men. In one violent skirmish, almost half the warriors in each group died of arrow, club, and gun wounds. As a young bachelor, Pãxkê fought fiercely, defending himself and his people.

Tired of all the fighting, Angme'ê was open to gifts of pacification offered by Meirelles, the famous Brazilian Indianist. The group followed Meirelles to a village on a navigable waterway, that eventually flowed into the Xingu River. There, Pãxkê got to know Meirelles well. The young Indian and the older Indianist went together to Belém to buy shotguns and other things for the pacified Kayapo. On their return they discovered that Pãxkê's father had died.

Pãxkê was already gathering influence among the Indians when Meirelles sent him along with a group of older men to offer peace presents to the rest of the Mekranoti still in the forest. The young warrior's renown grew with the added contacts between Brazilians and the different Kayapo groups. It was not long before he eventually moved in with the Mekranoti.

After all of the separations, and the population losses due to battles and epidemics, the old Mekranoti men's societies had gradually fallen apart. There were simply not enough men to make divisions into men's societies worth the trouble. The men's organizations had come and gone many times before in Mekranoti history, so there was nothing new in the loss, and no one worried about it. Generally, when villages were large the Mekranoti had several men's societies, and sometimes even two men's houses, but there were many times when fighting split up the groups, and the men's societies disappeared.

After their population recuperated a bit, the Mekranoti began thinking more about forming men's societies. Now that contact had been established, and the new village seemed more stable, societies would make more sense. Finally, one day in the late sixties, some of the men simply noticed that friendship cliques had formed in their men's house. In one of the cliques the men were wearing lots of armbands, and so, they decided, these friends ought to be called *mẽ pa'ã kadjàt*, "the armband people." The other clique was eating a lot, and so would be called *mẽ 'õtoti*, "the long-tongued people." Men's society names always seemed to have these half-comic origins. Past societies included "the black people," "the small people," "the people with happy heads," and "the big-nosed people."

Already an influential leader, Pãxkê became the chief of the armband people's society, while Tàkàkrorok, already village chief, became leader of the long-tongued society. Today, Pãxkê sits with his society in one corner of the men's house, goes with them on hunting expeditions and men's treks, and gives speeches at night in the village plaza. But he also spends a good deal of time with FUNAI, managing Brazil-nut-collecting, advising handicraft sales, and shopping for guns and ammunition in Belém.

Although his unkempt appearance makes him an unlikely choice as intermediary between Indians and Brazilians, Pãxkê built his reputation on his contacts with influential outsiders. Even today people think Pãxkê especially knowledgable about how foreigners think. In this, Pãxkê's career matches Tàkàkngo's. Both got to know outsiders well because of their chiefly fathers, and both gained from the contact.

I saw little of Pãxkê during my fieldwork. He was gone much of the time on treks with other Indians, or on trips to Belém. When in the village he preferred spending his spare time with the FUNAI personnel. He was always pleasant but direct, and seemed to have little time for idle chatter. Even on trek, when the others felt free to joke around at night, Pãxkê thought about making artifacts to sell to FUNAI. Abounding in self-confidence, he never worried much about his actions, either in front of others, or on his own.

Others were less independent than Pãxkê. A couple of times on trek men failed to return home at night. Then relatives panicked. When Kokony lost his way in the forest, his grandmother and sisters wailed loudly. Perhaps something had happened to him, they feared. Since the women were all *kupry* and there were no other brothers, he was their only male relative. He was too young to manage his way in the night forest, they cried, and he had not even taken a machete or matches to build a fire. Since he was the family's only hunter, they would lose more than just a loved one.

Several men fired their guns into the air in the hopes that the *norny* would hear them and find his way back to camp. A couple of men took flashlights and walked out of the village along the makeshift paths, shouting his name and firing more shots into the air. Amidst the wails of Kokony's relatives, the men searched unsuccessfully all night.

The next day the camp was quiet as people went about their business, talking little of Kokony's absence. Then, about noon, I heard a loud scream.

It was Kaxtykre, welcoming back Kokony, who walked embarrassed into camp. Aside from his grandmother, no one greeted him as he went to the men's house to sleep. He had been walking around all night looking for signs of the trekkers.

Others also had trouble in the forest. Kamrekti, a middle-aged man with lots of hunting experience, also lost his way in the jungle, but luckily wandered into camp during the night. The lost hunters created a confidence crisis in the camp as many men began to worry about wandering astray in the forest. Tàkàkdjamti complained about not knowing the paths the elders wanted him to follow in his hunting. One day the *norny* cut a path in the wrong direction. The area where the elders wanted them to cut was too flooded, they argued. The old men disagreed. It was better to cut through water now and avoid the larger flooded areas later. The path the young men chose would lead right into a badly flooded marsh. Some of the young men complained that the elders didn't even go out hunting and so couldn't know the terrain that well. But the old men defended themselves. To show that they knew the terrain they pointed out landmarks that the *norny* would recognize—a grove of Brazil-nut trees, a white sandy open area, and an area with lots of termite nests. The *norny* finally gave in and recut the path through the water.

Wakõni was the brunt of an entire night's discussion. The middle-aged man was a good work companion, and as intelligent as anyone else, but he had a terrible sense of direction. Half in frustration, and half out of teasing. Tàkàkngo asked Wakõni to point to different places in the forest. "Where's the new campsite?" Tàkàkngo asked. "And where's the large flooded area in the forest?" As soon as Wakõni made a wrong guess everyone jumped on him until Wakõni, thoroughly confused, gave up and refused to answer any more questions.

The haranguing of the poor man continued until everyone at the men's meeting joined in. Tàkàkngo tried to explain to Wakõni why he was having trouble finding deer in the forest. One of the elders scolded him for not finding armadillos, and because he had avoided hunting a couple of days, Tàkàkngo hounded him even further. "If you don't want to bring back game like the young men, then carry garden produce like the elders," he said in his most recriminating tone.

Because of all the harassment, Wakõni tried harder at hunting, but was soon foiled in his efforts by another problem. In one of the campsites, in the exact spot where a woman was about to place her lean-to, Wakõni stepped on a poisonous snake and was bitten in the leg. The men rushed to kill the other snakes in the nest, while Wakõni's relatives wailed over him. I quickly prepared syringes and needles to give him the antivenin I had brought along. I would have been more nervous except that Wakõni himself seemed unconcerned about the bite. He sat quietly, giving the impression that he didn't even notice as I poked the needle under his skin time and time again.

The other men also said nothing of Wakõni's bite. They simply left him alone, knowing that he would feel pain all night. Kentỳxti explained how he treated snakebites in dogs, but no one seemed to pay much attention. Eventually, the swelling that had already begun in Wakõni's leg went down and he slept well that night, complaining later only of the injections.

I had been traveling about with the Mekranoti for a year but never saw any poisonous snakes. Now, suddenly we were coming across the dangerous reptiles in one campsite after another. Everyone had to be careful, but no one else got bitten.

There were other accidents besides snakebites. One day while chopping firewood, Ngrenhkorre sent a six-inch sliver of dirty bark and wood through her thigh. The wound was deep and needed to be cleaned. Several women ran to me telling me to rush with the medicine. When I arrived, Ngrenhkorre was surrounded by keening women, but refused medical treatment. Finally, at the insistence of the others, she let me dress the wound and give her a preventive shot of antibiotics. When I asked her not to walk around she simply grunted in disdain. Two hours later I saw her carrying another load of firewood back to the campsite.

Ngrenhkorre was probably the most macho female I've ever met. A large, barrel-chested woman, she almost never smiled, and seemed to pride herself on looking mean, which earned her a reputation as the fiercest woman in the village. At times she liked to go out hunting with a club looking for armadillos, porcupines, or any other small game she could find. After the wives of Tàkàkrorok and Pãxkê (the women's chiefs), she was the most influential woman in the village, and was respected for her intelligence and her ceremonial knowledge. But many thought she was a poor mother and that she disliked children. Her pregnancy history bore this out. She had given birth nine times, but only two of her offspring were still alive. The others all died young. Child care required a certain patience and gentleness that Ngrenhkorre probably just did not have.

Ngrenhkorre's husband Teryti, recognized his wife's masculine qualities. I once asked him to give me the names of women who were "like men." "Can't you tell?" he asked, looking at me in feigned surprise. "Ngrenhkorre! She acts just like a man." He then added with a sly smile that this made sense because he was more like a woman than most men. Teryti liked to joke about himself, and he could tell I was amused at his response.

In the past Teryti was one of the Mekranoti's fiercest warriors, and he loved to act out historical battles for audiences in the men's house. Before beginning his stories he stood absolutely still, holding his wooden sword club aloft in his hand, deep in concentration. Then suddenly he would begin with a wild sweep of the sword and a deep resonant shout. Teryti played all the parts, the valiant Mekranoti warriors, the screaming women, and the cowardly enemies, crying for their mothers just before dying. Every once in a while someone from the audience would ask him a question. Teryti would smile quickly at the attention he was getting, before answering with yet another dramatic gesture. He could hold the audience in quiet suspense or make even the chief titter with laughter at his comic antics.

Teryti was charmingly candid and original. When explaining how the Mekranoti sometimes traveled to the east to receive gifts from Claudio Villas Boas, and then west to get presents from Meirelles, he added impishly that the Indians sometimes killed a few Brazilians because they knew this would win them more gifts from the men whose job it was to "pacify" them. I once tried to force Teryti to give me reasons for a visit he and a group of Mekranoti once made to a distant Kayapo village. He kept repeating that the Indians were simply "curious." I was expecting him to say the Mekranoti needed to get wood for bowstaves, or to kill someone in payment for a Mekranoti death, or some other practical excuse. But after rejecting all of my suggestions, he finally smiled wryly at me, knowing he had found the explanation I couldn't reject: "We went to see them for the same reason you came here. Because we were curious."

Another time, when explaining raids on other Indian groups, Teryti rejected the stock Mekranoti reasons for battles, such as revenge killings or the need to steal shotguns, and went right to his own personal motivations. "I went along because I didn't have any children and wanted to steal some." He succeeded.

In one of his battles with the Kreen Akrore Indians, Teryti brought back a young girl that he and his wife managed to raise. A lovely, gentle adolescent, the captured Kreen Akrore now spends a good deal of her time taking care of the children born later to Ngrenhkorre. Perhaps it was her more patient care that made it possible for these children to survive.

Good and bad mothering was a favorite conversation topic for both men and women. Sometimes it came up in unexpected places. Once, when a missionary was explaining Christmas to Kentỳxti, she noticed his horrified reaction to Joseph and Mary's overnight stay in the stable. "What a terrible mother Mary must have been," he exclaimed. "Leaving her baby in a dangerous animal's feeding box!"

This trek gave ample opportunities to talk about bad mothers. One afternoon Jokonōr left her two-year-old daughter alone for a minute while she ran to get some water. In her mother's absence the toddler found a knife and chopped off one of her tiny fingers. The Mekranoti crowded around as one of the Indians tried to tape the finger, hanging by its skin, back on the child. As usual, Kentỳxti was hysterical. "You have to give her a shot or she'll die," he insisted. "This happened once before and the baby died." The others were much calmer. The girl's father looked worried but insisted that the finger would grow back. I tried to tell him this was unlikely, but he was unconvinced.

The women scolded Jokonōr on her return, and the men's conversation that night was dominated by discussions of her bad mothering. Men debated the virtues of watching children closely, of making sure there were no dangerous objects within the child's reach, and of leaving babies in the care of older children only when absolutely necessary. Nhàkngonhti's daughter had dropped her baby sister when left to care for the infant. Although the mother properly punished the girl, she should perhaps not have left the baby in her care in the first place, some men argued. Of course the women did not need to be told by the men about how to care for children, but they had no trouble accepting the men's moral indignation.

There was only one case of extraordinarily bad mothering that seemed to go unnoticed. Karinho'y had let her baby fall into the fire several times. The first time it was so badly burned that the FUNAI medical attendant had to cover it with oil and wrap it in cloth. He was sure the baby would die, but somehow it managed to pull through. Karinho'y seemed indifferent to the infant. She laughed as the medical attendant cared for the child, and then she left the baby fall into the fire several other times as well. It was easy to believe she wanted to kill the baby.

One explanation for their indifference to Karinho'y's poor mothering may be the Mekranoti attitude toward physical disabilities. Probably many people felt that since the baby was so badly burned the first time it fell into the fire, it made no sense to keep it alive. On seeing badly crippled people in cities, Kentỳxti commented that the Mekranoti would have killed them. Life was difficult enough without having to cope with disabilities. The ill treatment Tedjware received when his foot went bad confirms the Mekranoti dislike of permanent physical problems.

Still another reason for their tolerance with Karinho'y was the mother's own disabilities. Karinho'y was once a highly desirable *kurerêr*, but then she fell ill with what seems to have been a stroke. For months she could not talk, and even now she speaks in disconnected phrases, using exaggerated facial gestures to get her point across. The habit of tilting her head to one side and smiling awkwardly after every few words only makes her look more deviant. Her atrophied right arm swings useless at her side, and her right leg is smaller than the left. The Mekranoti were not quite sure how to treat Karinho'y. Some people thought she was stupid, but others, remembering her better days, and observing her actions rather than her words, thought otherwise. People were impressed that she managed to have a baby in the first place. After all, no one could figure out who would want to have sex with her in her present condition. Karinho'y claimed that Nokinh was the child's father, but no one knew for sure.

Good mothering was important because everyone wanted more children. Sometimes the elders nostalgically remembered years long ago when Mekranoti villages were much larger than today. Those were the good days. They hoped, now that there was less disease and fighting, the good times would return. It was no wonder the Indians welcomed new births with delight. When Nhàkno's baby was born one day the word went quickly around that it was a girl, and a long procession filed by the temporary men's house to see the newborn and her mother. The men took advantage of the movement to make ribald jokes with the passers by, and everyone laughed.

Watching women travel was one of the favorite sports of the young men. Every morning when the villagers moved their campsites, the *norny*, *'okre* boys, and sometimes fathers as well would make a clearing at the path's edge to watch everyone else carry belongings. There was even a name for the meetings along the path—*mẽ djy'ã dja*. The men loved to make fun of all those passing by. Because of all their heavy baggage, the travelers had difficulty responding, so the jokes could get very demeaning. When Kamrekti walked by carrying several baskets full of manioc flour and sweet potatoes, the men could not help teasing him about all the women's work he was doing. But Tykre, the woman suspected of prostituting herself in Brazilian cities, had to tolerate more insults than anyone else. She had been behaving more normally recently, but the men still remembered her antics early in the year, and her trip with the men to collect Brazil nuts.

The path meetings reminded me of my need to watch the men more closely. If I wanted to learn about Mekranoti leadership, I would have to observe them as they reacted to each other in groups. When I first arrived among the Indians I understood nothing of the men's meetings and spent little time in the men's house, but now my Kayapo was good enough to catch the fast conversations. From now on I resolved to spend every morning and evening with the men in their meetings, recording everything that happened.

# 16

# IN THE MEN'S HOUSE

Threefold falsetto barks rang through the cold night air, sounding like dogs in the distance, howling at the moon. A few of the men had arrived in the men's house and were announcing the beginning of the morning sing. The music began slowly with a few weak voices trying to encourage the others with confident strains. Every few minutes the sound died away into whispered conversation, spattered with more falsetto barks. Then it began again, a little stronger than before, as men sleepily stumbled into the men's house to join the growing chorus. Gradually the music grew into a powerful masculine roar, reverberating throughout the forest encampment.

The men, whether on trek or in the village, liked to begin their singing around 4:30 in the morning. Guessing the time by the moon's position in the night sky, they usually judged accurately, but when the forest foliage was thick overhead and when the clouds were heavy or the moon new, they often erred by several hours. Several times they began the singing at 1:30 a.m. They would sing for a while, and then quit, some of them, drowsing off again, wrapped arm and leg around their fellows to fend away the cold. Others conversed quietly, or simply stared off into space, feeling miserable at their lost sleep.

Called to join them, I protested that it was too early yet, but the Indians had little confidence in my wristwatch. They liked to tease me, asking me to tell them if it was night or not. I would look at the sky and say it didn't appear so, and they would protest that I had to decide by looking at my watch. After several mistaken morning sings some of the men began to respect watches a bit more and even asked me if I would bring them one. Others remained convinced that time just couldn't be measured with numbers.

At first the men sang perfunctorily, dropping out for a few bars now and then to rest their voices or their arms. A few sang without the arm motions, and a few swung an arm or two without singing. But as the men's house filled they began to sing with more gusto, aggressively swinging their arms to and fro in a cradling motion that rhythmically accompanied all Kayapo melodies. Most of the tunes were in a regular 4/4 time. I suspect 3/4 would have seemed too frivolous. The men sang in the lowest bass they could manage, heavily accenting the first beats and punctuating them with glottal stops that made their stomachs convulse to the music. Each melody ended with the traditional cadence—a sighing downward slide that at first made me feel uncomfortable, as if the music had not quite ended properly. But it did not take long for me to learn that the cadence was as final as the ending dominant-tonic chords of a Beethoven symphony.

Occasionally when the men began a song they could not finish because no one knew the words, they felt ashamed of themselves and asked one of the elders to sing for them. When asked, old and frail Mrytàmti loved to chant the tunes quietly for the others to learn. Once it was Bekwỳnhrax, the spritely old *kupry*, who had to tell the men how to sing their own songs. She sang gustily from her lean-to a good distance from the men's house, and added a few joking insults to the ignorant men for good measure. At least once the men sang the melody that ought to conclude a morning sing long before the gathering was ready to end, but no one worried too much about these mistakes. The important thing was to sing well.

Hounding the men still in their lean-tos was one of the favorite diversions of the singers. "Get out of bed! The Kreen Akrore Indians have already attacked and you're still sleeping," they shouted as loudly as they could. The falsetto barks sprinkled throughout the singing were meant to express anger at those still asleep in their wives' houses or in the *atykbe*, the trekking dormitory for the *'okre* boys, the *norny*, and the fathers observing sex taboos. Sometimes the harassment grew personal as the singers yelled out insults at specific men who rarely showed up.

As they grew tired of the singing, the men looked longingly at the night sky for the first faint signs of dawn. At first it was too dark to see even the treetops overhead, but eventually the men could distinguish the outlines of a few palm trees against the brightening sky. Then they quickly sang the concluding melody and broke into animated conversation. It would not be long before their wives brought them a breakfast of a few cold sweet potatoes or leftover meat pies and then returned to their lean-tos to begin packing for the day's move to a new campsite.

In the evening, if they managed to join together soon enough, the men also sang until sundown, but their songs were generally over quickly. Afterwards, they conversed for several hours until finally going to bed. Every once in a while one of the men decided to spend the night in the men's house. Rik'o complained about large ants back in his wife's hut and decided the men's house would be more comfortable. The night was clear and rain looked unlikely.

To a casual observer it would be difficult to believe the men's-house gatherings were the center of Mekranoti political life. They looked much too informal. Men arrived and departed at will. Sometimes they spent their time weaving a baby sling or making an arrow to sell as native handicrafts to FUNAI, getting up now and then to search for a piece of string, or to look for one of the broken umbrella ribs brought from the village to use as carving tools. Bokrã liked to weave palm leaves into clever snakes that coiled up when you pulled on a small fiber. He gave the toys to little boys, who loved them. Other men sharpened knives or cleaned their shotguns as they talked with their neighbors, sometimes discussing problems back in the lean-tos, as when Amakkry's pet parrot kept falling off the roof.

A few men sat alone, facing away from the crowd, apparently uninterested in the conversations. Some slept, and every now and then someone yelled at a child to stop crying, or told one of the boys to bring food from their relatives' houses. Teryti sometimes told bothersome children that in the past they would have been frightened away from the men's meetings. But mostly the men simply chatted with their neighbors about everything from the taste of their meat pies to a baby's illness, switching topics every few minutes without ever seeming to reach any conclusions. Yet, these meetings were the places where most of the important decisions in Mekranoti life were made.

Since I wanted to know about Mekranoti leadership, I decided to observe these meetings closely. Every morning and every evening, as soon as the first men appeared on the leaves that served as the trekking men's house, I appeared with a hurricane lamp and a notebook. At first I tried to keep track of everything, but I soon realized that there were too many things going on at once—too many side conversations, too many arrivals and departures, and too many gestures full of subtle meanings. I would have to limit my observations to a few people. I decided to use a stop watch, and observe leaders and non-leaders for set periods of time. With a list of those present at any meeting, I followed a regular sequence of names, watching each man for a two-minute period before passing on to the next.

Tàkàkngo showed up for the men's meetings more than anyone else. Always alert, he reveled in the gathering's confusion. Before watching him closely, I had trouble understanding how he managed to wield so much influence in the Mekranoti community. He seemed to act like everyone else. Perhaps he joined in the conversations more often, but he talked about much the same things as the other men. And he never made formal speeches, as influential elders did. Still, it was obvious from the peer ratings that he was a very important man among the Mekranoti.

Watching him every day for over a month, I finally realized why the others listened to him. Brimming with self-confidence, Tàkàkngo hardly seemed the kind of person who would understand the weaknesses of the other men. But he knew just when and how much to scold them, and he was an expert at comforting them if the others grew too hostile. After being heavily criticized for his poor hunting record, Kokony quietly but angrily turned away from the meeting to stare into the forest. Tàkàkngo noticed the subtle change and went up to the young man, to lie down behind him. Gently forcing Kokony to lie down, Tàkàkngo wrapped his leg over the *norny*, holding him in a warm embrace from behind. In this intimate position, he whispered into Kokony's ear. He talked about much the same things the others had said, but Tàkàkngo's comments did not sound like criticisms at all. They sounded instead like fatherly advice. "You can hunt well if you try. Then the others will leave you alone, and will think well of you. You just have to leave the camp a little bit earlier so you can go out farther where the game is. And you have to be careful to watch for peccary footprints. Sometimes you miss them because…" His gentle advice went on and on until Kokony finally relaxed and accepted the suggestions.

When Tàkàkngo entered the men's house, if he was not the first to arrive, the others often asked him to sit in the center, surrounded by all the most talkative young men. They mostly conversed on an equal basis, but Tàkàkngo, and Kute'o if he showed up, were more likely to give advice about everything—how to hunt well, how to arrange tortoises on racks and lug them from one campsite to the next, how to kill and skin jaguars, how to remove thorns from your hands or feet, how to care for pet macaws.

The two young leaders also kept an eye on everyone's behavior to make sure things were going fine. Tàkàkngo asked Rik'o if he had pulled out the teeth from the monkey he brought back to camp. Sometimes the men forgot, or were too lazy to finish the job. Then, when they wanted to make a fine monkey-tooth necklace, they had no materials to work with. After so many men got lost in the forest, Kute'o talked at length one night about how peccary chases can lead hunters astray. He warned the young men not to forget to mark their paths in the passion of the hunt. After looking at the calendar the missionaries had given him he also added a few additional remarks about the approaching dry season which meant hunting would change. The young men would have to listen for different sounds in the forest, and would have to worry about different problems.

Sometimes the men debated about how to deal with the outside world. Here, the information and advice of the two young leaders were essential. One man asked if he should buy a rifle or a shotgun with the money he received from Brazil-nut-collecting. Kute'o and Tàkàkngo summarized the arguments. Rifle bullets were cheaper than shotgun shells, but the gun was more expensive and harder to use when shooting birds. Some men wondered whether they should hold on to money to buy things later. Kute'o carefully pointed out the problem of inflation. "Today, if you spend the one hundred cruzeiros on shells you can get a whole box, but if you wait until next year you'll get only half a box."

Some of these questions involved all of the Mekranoti. FUNAI wanted to move the village to a navigable river so that Brazil nuts could be exported more easily. Paken liked the idea, and argued that the Gorotire-Kayapo were better off than the Mekranoti because they were on a river. But Tàkàkngo complained that he liked airplanes better than boats.

Hunting was a favorite topic of conversation. Everyone knew what everyone else brought back to camp, and loved to talk about it. "Don't get angry," Paken once said, defensively anticipating criticism from Tàkàkngo. "There were armadillos where I was hunting, so it wasn't a bad place to go." The elders were the most severe critics of all. In one of his formal discourses at the edge of the men's house, old Mrytàmti harangued the young men about how shameless they were to speak in the men's house when they brought back no game. "We elders don't like eating the bad parts of meat," he complained one night. "Go out and bring back good game—tapir, deer, and paca." Young, handsome Ropni countered that he had no shotgun to kill animals.

The others wasted no time in jumping on him. "Quick, give Ropni a gun," yelled Rik'o, half jokingly.

"If you don't have a gun, then use a bow and arrow," Mrytàmti scoldingly added to his speech.

"And there are always armadillos to dig up and kill with a club," Bokrã contributed.

Almost every night one of the elders stood at the edge of the men's house to deliver the traditional harangues. Hunting was only one of the topics in their speeches. Mrytàmti once scolded Kaxngri publicly about his morning singing after the sun had already appeared. He was probably angry about Kaxngri's late arrivals for the sings. "You should sing at night, not during the day. Are you afraid of something?" he challenged the other old man.

One night Mrytàmti drew the entire village into his speech. Some of the trekkers were talking about returning to the village to meet the FUNAI medical team scheduled for another visit to the Indians. Mrytàmti thought it nonsense to worry about medicine. "Instead of everyone going back to the village," he suggested," some of the women ought to return to the gardens to fetch manioc and sweet potatoes for everyone else." Kute'o disagreed with Mrytàmti about the medicine, but he concurred with most of the men that the women ought to bring more sweet potatoes. The women felt otherwise. Several of them shouted out their protests to Mrytàmti and the rest of the men. They thought it better to end the trek.

As is usual among the Mekranoti, no one announced any conclusions, but the trekkers continued on for several more weeks, and the women eventually had to go back to the village gardens to fetch more produce.

The closer, more intimate life on trek made Mekranoti political ambitions easier to see. In the village, there were only some six men who gave speeches in the central plaza. The other elders stayed quietly at home. But on trek the discourses were a little less formal. Instead of marching about alone in the empty central plaza with only a speaking club for comfort, speech-givers on trek simply stood at the edge of the men's house. They could easily hear all of the comments people made. The informality of trekking made it a good time for inexperienced men to try out their speech-giving abilities.

One night, Kaxti, recently recovered from his foot injury, won the attention of the entire men's house as he recounted a long story about the past. Impressed by his performance, several of the younger men asked him if he would consider giving a speech. Kaxti smiled shyly at the compliment, but he was taken by surprise and modestly refused. "I'm not good at that kind of thing," he said, nervously looking away from the other men. The men pressed him on, agreeing that he would be a good speech-giver. But Kaxti simply imitated jokingly a few phrases of the stilted language used in the nightly harangues, and pulled away from the others, explaining that he had some important things to do back in his lean-to.

Other older men were less shy. One night Kaxngri decided to try his hand at the traditional Kayapo oratory. Struggling to his feet, the short, fat man made his way to the edge of the men's house. Tàkàkngo handed him a gun to use as a speaking club. Clumsily lifting his legs now and then to swat away flies, Kaxngri falteringly began his speech. At one point he paused and looked with dismay at everyone in the men's house. It seemed no one was listening to him, but he began again just the same.

It did not take long for 'Orwỳkti to begin chuckling at Kaxngri's performance. At first he tried to hide his laughter, but eventually it grew more obvious. Tàkàkngo asked the irreverant young men if he was laughing. Overhearing the question, Kaxngri asked if 'Orwỳkti was mocking him, and glanced angrily at the chortling young man before continuing with his discourse. Finally, 'Orwỳkti grew bolder and asked Kaxngri if he could borrow his pipe. This was too much. Kaxngri threatened 'Orwỳkti and marched into the center of the men's house, grabbing 'Orwỳkti by the arm. Some of the others lightly scolded the young man about his laughter, but to no avail. 'Orwỳkti refused to go with Kaxngri, and refused to stop his giggling. Finally Kaxngri gave up and went back to his speech only to finish early and disappear, embarrassed, into his lean-to.

Kaxngri was not a very respected elder. People though him too greedy, too lazy, and too stupid to pay him much attention. His wife, Tyrre, did not fare much better. A fragile, gentle old lady with a cataract clouding over one eye, she was also considered stupid and greedy by the rest of the villagers. Not even their daughter's marriage to a man as influential as Kentỳxti seemed to help much. Mekranoti elders usually gained influence because they acquired knowledge as they grew older. But those like Kaxngri and Tyrre, who failed to learn with age, actually lost prestige. Even the presence of more sons, sons-in-law and daughters helped them little.

Many of the younger Mekranoti had ambitions about becoming speech-givers one day. Sometimes they bantered with each other in the heavily punctuated language of the nightly harangues. Like most play, the joking was a way of learning about their future roles. Kentỳxti tried harder than most. He joked at length with the men and with me in the stylized talk, and he sometimes tape-recorded Tàkàkrorok's speeches to listen to later for any extra hints the others might miss. Tàkàkngo and Kute'o were more subtle, but just as interested in learning the proper way to give speeches.

The men's house was the main arena for Mekranoti political life, but it was also a place to relax with friends after a hard day's hunting. Usually men got along well with each other as they lay entwined in one another's arms or painted each other sloppily with ashes from the fire, though the men sometimes became irritated with one another. One man would complain about another's farting. Or 'Orwỳkti would yell throughout the camp that old Tyrre had defecated near the men's house, only to discover later that the source of the bad smell was a dead rat nearby.

'Omexti rarely appeared in the men's house, and when he did, he usually sat facing away from the crowd, avoiding the animated discussions. One of the missionaries described him as a loner, but he was a generous man, and well liked by the others. He talked little, but usually had original things to say, so the men liked to talk to him. His wife was the daughter of a captured Kreen Akrore man. At 1.6 meters (5 feet 3 inches), she was the tallest of the Mekranoti women and, seeing her charming and sophisticated smile, many of the non-Indians in the village thought she was also the prettiest. Even though she knew absolutely nothing of her Kreen Akrore ancestors, the Mekranoti still referred to her as a Kreen Akrore's daughter.

Sometimes the night conversation was dominated by one or two themes—bad mothering, hunting success, or deals with FUNAI. Once, the conversation turned to illnesses. Some of the men heard that Wakōkry, who had not come along on trek, was already delirious with malaria. People began to talk excitedly about whether he would live or not. They described all the symptoms he had passed through, and began to compare his case with past illnesses and deaths. Also, earlier in the day I had treated Kokomy, a young *norny*, for malaria, but he went back to the village. Now the men were saying he was lying unconscious along the return path. And then there was Ajoba.

Ajoba had come to me almost every night asking for medicine. One day he complained about a sore neck, another day about sore legs, and still another time about headaches. He wanted me to give him an injection, but I had no idea what was wrong. He never had any fever. I began to suspect that he just wanted an excuse to go back to the village and avoid hunting. Finally, I told him there was nothing I could do because I had no idea what was wrong with him. I suggested he go back to the village to talk to the FUNAI medical attendant.

It did not take long for gossip to trickle into camp about Ajoba as well. He was bleeding from the mouth, one man reported—liters of blood every day. The men's house discussion grew more animated. Everyone listened carefully as people described how close their fellows were to death. Even the women and children were quietly attentive to the stories. In the still, pitch black night, it was easy to believe the accounts, even when the stories of illness grew more and more gruesome as different men added the symptoms they had heard to the growing list.

Finally, Kuture, returning with garden produce form the village, walked briskly into the dark encampment. After dropping off his heavy cargo, he joined the men's house discussion. The reports about Kokomy were sheer rumor, he said. The young *norny* returned safely to the village and was hardly sick at all. Wakõkry was ill, he conceded, but not delirious, and seemed to be getting better. As Kuture carefully answered everyone's questions, I realized how far the warm, silent evening had seduced us into believing the exaggerated stories. I thought of the nights in my childhood as friends and siblings exchanged horror stories. The Mekranoti were enjoying the fear they managed to generate.

But the rumors about Ajoba were not dispelled. The respected oldest son of Tàkàkrorok was bleeding profusely from the mouth, Kuture reported. I asked if he meant that Ajoba was throwing up blood. "No," he responded, "he's bleeding from the gums."

It was several days before we finally learned the truth about Ajoba. He had contracted scurvy. I was surprised at the diagnosis. It seemed the Mekranoti could get plenty of vitamin C from sweet potatoes and papaya during the dry season, and from forest fruits or green bananas in the wet season. Perhaps the disease resulted more from intestinal parasites than from lack of vitamin C. Worms could consume all the valuable vitamin C the Indians ate.

The FUNAI medical assistant tried to help Ajoba with injections of vitamins K and C, but to no avail. Finally, he decided to call in a plane to take the Indian to a hospital. Unfortunately, the FUNAI radio had not been working for several months, so there was no way to communicate with the outside world. Some of the young men decided to make the trip, by foot, and then by canoe, to a neighboring Indian village. With luck they could reach their destination in three or four days.

Ajoba was an important man in the Mekranoti community and people listened carefully for any news about his health. He was the fiercest of Mekranoti warriors and, along with his younger brother Mydjêti, one of the principal ceremonial leaders as well. Perhaps because he was a bit too greedy, he was not as popular or influential as Tàkàkngo, but he was still one of the community's more prestigious men. With luck, the expected arrival of the FUNAI medical team would solve his problem.

Already some four weeks on trek, the Mekranoti talked about continuing in the forest for several more weeks. Things had gone well and everyone, including myself, was enjoying the trip. But I had to think about going back to the main village. Some of the most important leaders had already returned in anticipation of the FUNAI medical team, and long ago I had scheduled a final flight out of the village toward the end of June. My money was too short to afford missing the plane. I tried to get some idea of just how much longer the trip would last, but people disagreed. Some wanted to continue for another week and then return on the same path. Others wanted to continue longer, cutting a new path back to the village. Kute'o finally told me that the trek would continue much longer. I decided to return. Kentỳxti would accompany me.

My decision caused a stir in the encampment. "Who told Beproti [my name] that we would cut a new path?" a few women shouted out angrily at Kute'o. "Who's going to give us medicine now?" Embarrassed at the unexpected reaction, Kute'o tried to calm the women, but to no avail. The damage had already been done. I had always tried to maintain a low profile in the Mekranoti community, but realized now that I had become more important than I wanted to be.

The sky was still dark when we set off for the village the next morning. Kentỳxti, carrying the medicine on a tumpline from his forehead, ambled off in front. His pace seemed to quicken as the day grew warmer. At first I tried to keep up, but his pace was too fast and I fell behind. Kentỳxti didn't think twice about leaving me so far behind. There was nothing unusual about his fast clip, and there was nothing unusual about walking alone in the forest. I felt differently, but said nothing, Especially when the path ran through a clearing, or through an old campsite, I had trouble finding where it continued and was sure I would get lost. I began to resent Kentyxti's abandonment of me in the middle of the forest.

After several hours of walking alone, I finally came across Kentỳxti again. I was angry and in a scolding mood, but the carefree soul was sitting nonchalantly by a fire he had built and was roasting fish he had caught along the way. As I approached him he handed me a leaf with steaming fish and manioc flour and told me he had been waiting for me to eat with him. His easygoing manner and his thoughtfulness at preparing a nice meal quickly dispelled any resentment I had built up.

It was already dark when we arrived in the village. I visited the men's house and FUNAI to find out if there was any news. After receiving the radio message from the other Indian village, a plane had come in and taken out Ajoba while we were walking along the path. The plane also brought a new radio for FUNAI, and told of the imminent arrival of the medical team.

I spent most of the next few days in the men's house, watching the men. The humdrum discussions of the few people who appeared there were a far cry from the excited meetings on trek. During the hot afternoons men either went hunting in the forest or worked on handicrafts in their homes or in the men's house. At night they wandered in and out of the men's house, sometimes visiting FUNAI, sometimes returning to their houses or visiting neighbors.

Old freckled Tedjware was the only unmarried father in the village. Having nowhere else to go, he always slept in the men's house and spent more of his time there than anyone else. Sitting in his corner, he talked on and on in a mumbling voice to the others, who often cut him off in the middle of his sentences to change the subject. Sometimes Tedjware asked a small boy to bring him food from his daughter's house, but to no avail. The youngster usually chose to ignore the requests, and there was nothing Tedjware could do. Tàkàkrorok talked little, but got better responses from the others. Even the children jumped at his requests.

When the medical team finally arrived, most of the villagers were still on trek. As usual in these circumstances, Kentỳxti ran off to the forest to spend the days hunting. He disliked being roped into translating for the foreigners. The Indians were too difficult, he complained. So I ended up acting as middleman between the doctors and the Indians. I soon learned what Kentỳxti meant.

The medical team needed to know the names of all the children in order to avoid revaccinating the same babies against the same diseases. Nhàkkàre and her entire household has always given me problems in the village. I dreaded doing time-allocation studies in her house, because she liked to crack "smart" jokes at the *kubens'* expense. Now she was joking with the doctors, giving them every one of her child's names except the one name she knew they would recognize. Since Mekranoti children inherit many different names from their mother's brothers or father's sisters at various points in their lives, the list of names grew quite long. I explained the problem to Tàkàkrorok, and he took it seriously. Without looking at his ex-paramour, he lectured about the importance of the doctors' not mistaking the children. Nhàkkàre quickly cooperated.

The seriousness of Tàkàkrorok's lecture made me realize how important he considered the medicine. Other aspects of Western culture were also gaining respect among the Mekranoti. Several of the Indians wanted to learn Portuguese, and wanted to know about mathematics so they could keep accounts of Brazil-nut sales and city shopping. They asked me to find them a teacher. Half in jest and half earnestly, Kentỳxti even offered to pay me to teach him about my country's ways. I realized it would not be long before the Indians began to look more and more like Brazilians.

# 17

# GOING HOME

It was June 17, 1977, when the announcement came over the FUNAI radio. I should prepare to leave the Mekranoti village the next day. I was sitting in the men's house when Tedjware excitedly burst in to give me the message. Even though he understood none of the Portuguese, he liked to listen to the radio broadcasts, and ask questions about what was said. Now he asked me why I was leaving. "I need to go to the cities to tell people what I learned here," I told him, feeling sad about my departure.

"When will you come back?" he asked. Some of the other men replied that I would surely return within a couple of weeks, as I had always done. I tried to explain that this time I had no way of knowing, but it certainly would not be within a couple of weeks. Perhaps in a few years, I suggested.

"Why do you want to leave us?" one of the men asked. "Don't you like it here?" "You're going to miss the end of the men's *bijok* ceremony," added another, trying to entice me into staying. Especially after being told of all the orgies and other fun people were expecting, I was looking forward to the ceremonial finale. But I could not afford to miss the flight. I simply told the Indians I had little choice in the matter. I was being called back to Brasília, and would eventually go back to my own country.

The idea of returning to New York after so many months with the Indians made me feel both relieved and anxious. I felt satisfied that I had gathered most of the data I wanted. I had systematic details on the personal qualities and social ties of leaders in one of the few places in the world where leaders are not wealthier than their followers. No one else had this kind of information, and in a few years it would be impossible to acquire, for non-stratified societies are becoming harder and harder to find. I could also contribute to some lively debates in anthropology on the role of such factors as population pressure, protein scarcity, and agricultural work in stimulating customs like warfare, ceremonies, or different kinship systems.

In my naiveté, I sometimes entertained delusions of grandeur about the importance of my studies, while at other times I imagined all my efforts would be worthless. My psychological waverings only accented the anxiety I felt about returning once again to the fast-paced life of New York City. In Brazil I had always been treated with the respect offered to those of high status. Now I would be returning to New York as a penniless student, and would have to lie to my landlord to convince him of my solvency.

I envied the self-confidence the Mekranoti gained from knowing how to live off nature. They could never be left homeless or jobless. I also envied the uncompetitive life of the Mekranoti's daily routine. But I harbored few romantic notions about the Indians' "nobility" or about their "savagery." I had come to see them as ordinary people like the people I had known in the United States. In their egalitarian ideals the Mekranoti even struck me as somehow more "American" than most of the Brazilians I had met. Perhaps more than anything else, my stay with the Mekranoti had made me appreciate the differences between individuals, wherever they may live.

I hated leaving the Mekranoti village while the Indians were still on trek. On learning that the medical team had arrived, a few came back to the village to get teeth pulled, or for other health matters, but I would not be able to say goodbye to most of them.

After confirming the radio announcement with FUNAI, I wandered back to my hut amidst the shouts of the other Mekranoti asking if the message was true. I still had some goods left over, and wanted to give them to the Indians. I thought of simply handing everything over to Tàkàkrorok to pass on to the others, but the Indians preferred that I do the distributing. I would know best what people wanted and deserved, they pointed out. Kute'o told me he wanted my pressure cooker. Like the other Indians, he called it a "shaman's pot" because of the noise it made as the steam escaped, and because it cooked food so fast. I had brought the pot along on one of my later trips into the village, and concluded that it is one of the great inventions of

Western civilization, especially when keeping a fire going and fetching water are chores.

I tried to explain why I was distributing presents as I did. The Mekranoti remembered one incident when a filmmaker visited their village, giving them what seemed like enormous amounts of goods in return for posing for pictures. The Indians saw the gifts as a windfall, and began to invent half-mystical ideas about where manufactured goods come from. They already half idolized the filmmaker, believing in supernatural accounts of his stomping on the moon. I was afraid the Mekranoti might develop a full-fledged "cargo cult," as had happened with other Brazilian Indians who refused to plant gardens and do other normal work in belief that foreign goods could be acquired magically. I had no intention of contributing to this mysticism.

The plane landed as scheduled the next morning. Ropnhỳ grabbed a wheelbarrow to help carry my notebooks, papers, and city clothes to the airstrip. I followed behind, dressed as always in worn blue jeans and a slightly torn T-shirt. Some of the Indians objected that I couldn't appear in the city so poorly dressed. One of the young men ran to his hut to bring out a pair of slacks he kept stored there just in case he ever made a trip to Belém. He offered them to me with a gentle smile, saying he would feel embarrassed to wear the clothes I had on. I was touched by his generosity, but explained that I was not that poor. I had other clothes packed away and promised to change as soon as the plane landed.

As I boarded the plane, Tàkàkrorok asked once again, when I would be coming back. After I told him I didn't know, he insisted that my departure not be for long. The Indians watched gravely from the airstrip as the plane took off. Looking down on the village, I remembered my reaction on landing for the first time. Then the jungle had seemed grand and lonely, and the village with its Indians seemed exotic and frightening. Now the forest looked warm and lively, and the double circle of houses around the central plaza had all the familiarity of home. The people on the ground stood out as individuals with different personalities, ambitions, fears, and loves. They, too, had become as familiar as home and friends.

It was half an hour later before I said anything to the pilots. We had little to talk about. The pilots detested the interior. Sometimes, when they could not make it back to Cuiabá in time, they spent a few nights at the mining company next to the Baú Kayapo village neighboring the Mekranoti. The company asked them to bring in food, medicine, work materials, and sometimes prostitutes.

Beyond giving the workers manioc flour and game, the Indians had little to do with the mining company. Linked to a giant multinational, the firm would have preferred it if there were no Indians at all to create problems over land rights. I was glad the Mekranoti, at least, had still avoided this kind of contact.

The pilots, who would be returning to the mining company, promised to leave me in Sinop, a town in northern Mato Grosso on the new Cuiabá-Santarém highway. Sinop was so new it did not yet appear on any of the area's maps. I expected that, like most of the other frontier towns I had seen, Sinop would have a dusty main street, and maybe even hitching posts for the horses. The lack of law enforcement in the hinterlands, together with the presence of gold miners, cattle ranchers, homesteaders, prostitutes, shoot-outs in bars on Saturday nights, and fights with Indians, all gave a "far west" feel to the Brazilian boondocks. Some of the Mekranoti who had visited the interior towns were appalled by the murders they witnessed after drunken men began fights in the bars.

Getting out of these frontier outposts was usually difficult and expensive, requiring finding and renting a car and driver. Since Sinop did not even appear on the area's maps, I expected transportation problems would be even worse.

The plane followed the bright red dirt of the Cuiabá-Santarém highway. I had seen the road once before from the air—my plane had even landed on its rough surface in order to refuel at a small way-station manned by two or three lonely young Brazilians who took care of the occasional truck that passed by. We had been flying for two hours when the scenery gradually changed from the uninterrupted deep green of the tropical forest to an occasional patch of yellowish savanna. Finally the pilot announced our landing.

My first surprise was at the asphalt landing strip. I had expected a dirt road or at best a well-kept grassy clearing. I was even more impressed on getting out of the plane. A taxicab sat waiting for me a few yards away. Sinop was larger than I expected. After lugging my baggage over to the cab, I opened the door to greet the blond, blue-eyed driver. He looked at me, also fair-haired and blue-eyed, and asked smilingly, "*Wohin?*" A modern town was not totally beyond what I could imagine, but to be greeted in German? At most I had expected a backwoods Portuguese.

As he drove me to the corner of town the cab driver talked with pride, half in Portuguese and half in German, about the town's quick rise. "The northern Brazilians have been here for over a hundred years," he said with disdain, "and they accomplished nothing. But we come here, and in four years we have paved streets, a supermarket, and even a movie theater." Since a bus would not be leaving for Cuiabá until late in the evening, I spent the afternoon talking to some of the town's young men over beer in a local café. Most of them had come from German-speaking communities located in Santa Catarina and Paraná in southern Brazil. They were attracted northward by offers of work on manioc plantations. The Brazilian government had helped establish a factory to turn the starchy tuber into alcohol that they hoped would eventually replace gasoline as the country's automotive fuel. The men were excited about the coming official visit of Brazilian President Geisel to inaugurate the operation.

The young men chatted excitedly all afternoon. They asked me about what I had been doing, and where I was from. When I told them I lived in New York, they said they had heard of the city, but were not quite sure where it was. After a discussion among themselves in German, of which I understood little, they finally decided that New York must lie somewhere between Brasília and Belém, on the new highway. I was charmed by their friendliness and by their unassuming provincialism.

The quick rise of Sinop made me realize how close Western civilization had come to the Mekranoti village. The Indians had been dealing sporadically with the civilized world for a long time. Manufactured goods like pots and guns made their way into their village even before whites appeared—the Kayapo stole them from other Indian groups. But now, mining companies, ranches and even alcohol factories were advancing rapidly on the Mekranoti's homelands.

I felt anxious about how the Mekranoti would react to the changes they were forced to face. Only a few decades before my stay among them, the Mekranoti view of civilization and its products was primarily mythical. There is one story about how monkeys were the original owners of metal axes. The Indians saw them carrying the tools on their shoulders and using them to get honey and hearts of palm. Anxious to replace their old stone axes with the superior metal ones, the warriors threatened the monkeys by shooting arrows at them. The monkeys finally gave in and relinquished their prizes. So for a long time the Kayapo trekked periodically to the land of the monkeys to steal metal axes. But gradually they found it easier to steal the prized tools from whites, whom they still call "the metal people."

Today the Mekranoti often remark how intelligent whites must be because they learn to speak Kayapo and can make so many marvelous things, like radios and airplanes. For a long time, the Indians saw themselves as innately inferior. But this view changed after the young men returned from the April 1977 Brazil-nut expedition with news of the new FUNAI attendant at the other Indian post. He was Japanese, they were told. The Mekranoti had already heard of these fantastic people who made cars and tape recorders even better than whites. Now they saw their first example, and were surprised to find out that he looked just like them—long sleek black hair, "reddish" skin and slightly slanted eyes. Kentỳxti recalled a soccer match he had seen in Belém between Brazilians and Japanese, and confirmed the description. The men were excited about their discovery. "Maybe we're not so dumb," Nokinh suggested. "It's just a matter of learning."

The talk about Japanese manufacturing skills soon launched us into a discussion of the division of labor in modern society. I tried to explain to the young men that no one knew how to make everything—people specialized. I wanted to talk about some of the problems of specialization, like the need to punch a time clock, or the danger of losing one's livelihood at the pronouncement of a superior. I wanted to show that all was not so rosy. But the Indians were not ready for these critiques.

Tàkàkngo held up a pen. "Who makes these?" he asked. I answered that there were probably many different people involved—some to make the ink, others to make the plastic, and others to put them together. "Well!" he exclaimed, impressed by all the specialization. "And what do you make?" he wanted to know. I said I didn't make anything. I just wrote. There was a dead silence. The men were not very impressed. Finally, Tàkàkngo looked at me in that fatherly way he sometimes used when giving advice to the young men. "Maybe if you learned how to make something you would have more money," he suggested as he prepared to leave. Walking out the door, he added one more question. "Do you know when FUNAI will send us a professor to teach us Portuguese and other things?" There was no stopping the Indians' desire to learn about civilization.

Sometimes the Indians' admiration turned to the mystical. Kentỳxti was so impressed with the things city folk did that he was ready to believe almost anything. Once, while walking around Belém with one of the missionaries, he saw a man advertising a circus by walking around on stilts with long baggy pants legs. "It's Kukryt Uire," he told the surprised missionary.

Kukryt Uire was one of the mythical heroes of the Kayapo. As a young boy he and his brother saw their grandmother carried off and eaten by a giant bird. The bird had been menacing the Indians for a long time, so the boys' grandfather decided to do something about the problem. He laid the boys in a riverbed, telling them not to move, and he fed them every day until they grew into giants. Their legs grew so thick that the fish thought they were tree trunks. When the young men had finally grown large enough, they were given spears and clubs and sent out to kill the dangerous bird. They accomplished their task, in the process creating many small birds from the giant bird's feathers.

The missionary explained that the tall man was not the Kayapo cultural hero. She described stilts to Kentỳxti and took him up to the circus performer to show him the wooden struts. Duped once, Kentỳxti was not about to be deceived again. Later in the day the two came across a sidewalk beggar. The man appeared to have no legs, but Kentyxti was not going to be fooled this time. So he walked around and around the cripple, looking for the hole he was sure the beggar was standing in. When the missionary told Kentỳxti that the beggar indeed had no legs, the dazzled young man was horrified. How could Brazilians let people like that live? The Mekranoti would have killed him.

Even some of the foreign customs they had already adopted were not well understood by the Mekranoti. Paken dropped by my hut one day wearing his wife's dress. A large, burly man, he could barely fit into the outfit. He had donned the clothes simply to keep away the black flies that became such a nuisance toward the end of the rainy season. None of the Indians seemed to notice this breach of Western norms. Apparently, clothes had not become so profoundly sex-typed as in our own society.

Despite their fascination with manufactured goods, the Mekranoti were not ready to accept everything civilization had to offer. Once, while sitting in the men's house, 'Omexti asked for a tool to fix an arrowhead. I dug into my pockets and pulled out an elaborate Swiss army knife I had brought along. By the time I opened it and handed it to 'Omexti, he had already fixed his arrow with a twig he pulled from a tree. Out of curiosity he examined my knife for a few minutes, then handed it back. "What good is this?" he asked. "Did you work to get it?" He then spent the next few minutes patiently explaining that some of the things *kuben* made were just not worth the trouble. "It's better to have more time to talk to your neighbors," he lectured.

Tàkàkrorok was also cautious about adopting too much from the outside. He grumbled about the missionaries and sulked conspicuously in his hammock the few times Kute'o attempted to hold an evangelical religious service. Tàkàkrorok's contacts with civilization had always been tentative. He was proud of the decisions he made long ago to isolate his village. Sometimes he talked over the FUNAI radio with the Mekranoti who in 1953 opted to stay with Claudio Villas Boas in the Xingu National Park. After hearing about their land problems Tàkàkrorok gloated openly, hypocritically expressing his sorrow and carefully pointing out that everything in his more isolated village was fine. His people were getting along well with the few whites in the village, and no one had been encroaching on their land. Yet he

did agree to give the Xingu group some shotguns needed to fight the poach-
ers. Since the conversation was entirely in Kayapo, FUNAI had no idea what
it was about.

Tàkàkrorok's optimism was perhaps a bit premature. He had been lucky
so far in choosing fairly out-of-the-way places to live, but the isolation would
not last forever. The Mekranoti were unaware of the plans for new highways
that would pass within fifty kilometers south of their village. The roads would
surely bring in more ranches, farms, and mineral firms. Although they had
been trying for some time to get their territory officially demarcated, so far
they had not been very successful. The Mekranoti would have to fight to
preserve their lands.

I would have liked to help the Mekranoti more with their problems.
Beyond aluminum pots and glass beads, I had given them precious little
compared to what they had given me. In my reports to FUNAI I transmitted
their requests for improvements in the village, including someone to teach
Portuguese and other matters needed to get along in Western society. I also
added a few recommendations of my own about tribal economics. I think the
Indians understood that I had relatively little power with the Brazilian
bureaucracies, and they expected little from me in this regard. But like many
other Indians who had dealt with anthropologists, they did expect me to write
accurately about their lives so that outsiders and future generations of
Mekranoti would know how they had lived. I hope I have at least partially
accomplished this task.

# 18

# Epilogue

Since leaving them in the summer of 1977, I have heard only a few pieces of news about the Mekranoti. In August, 1980, the Mekranoti living in the Xingú National Park appeared in a photograph in the *New York Times* after killing eleven peons who were working on a ranch near their settlement. Dressed in traditional war paint, they carried guns, but had used their clubs as weapons. The Indians claimed they wanted only to scare the whites out of the area, but were provoked into violence by insults. Later in the same month another Kayapó group also attacked ranchers who were trying to clear trees in the Indian area. This time sixteen whites, including women and children, were clubbed to death. Just so someone would recount the terrible story, the warriors left one woman alive to run for help. Since they are considered minors by Brazilian law, the Indians were not held responsible for the murders.

Many other conflicts between *kuben* and the Kayapó have also taken place. Plans to build a huge hydroelectric complex on the Xingú River have threatened many of the Indians and poor Brazilians who live there. In fact, the project would do away with the river, turning it into a series of reservoirs. In 1988 one anthropologist accompanied two Kayapó Indians to the United States where the Indians presented their case before the World Bank. On their return, the anthropologist (an American residing and working in Brazil) and the two Indians were met by the Brazilian police and threatened with deportation, based on a law that prohibits foreigners from meddling with Brazilian politics. The Indians were also placed under this law regarding foreigners, and the resulting scandal made headlines in major newspapers around the world. In 1989 a former Mekranoti leader from the Xingú National Park, and now a nationally recognized leader of Indian groups, Robni (called Rauni by the press) visited several European countries to plead his case for Indian land rights before European leaders.

From Tàkàkrorok's village I have heard very little. Kentỳxti and Kutêo once wrote notes to me answering some questions I had. Gustaaf, who later returned to the village, sent me the letters along with some news of his own. The community had grown to almost 350 individuals, he mentioned. To accommodate the additions, the Indians built a new village circle, much larger than the older one. And at the suggestion of FUNAI, people talked of moving the community to the river so that they could better transport Brazil nuts, although nothing had happened yet.

I also discovered that the Indians had a teacher in their village and were learning Portuguese. According to Gustaaf, they loved hearing about the civilized world and were grateful for the help, but the teacher scheduled the adult classes in the afternoon, which interfered with the men's hunting. Since there was also less game in the area, they were not eating as well as before.

Tribal economics continued much as always. FUNAI bungled a few Brazil nut-collecting expeditions by not showing up on schedule with their boat. The men grew discouraged and returned to their village. So the Indians were not very enthusiastic about FUNAI's economic schemes. Just the same, they were extraordinarily patient. The Kayapó in the neighboring village eventually decided to throw out the mining company, which they had grown to dislike.

Gustaaf also sent more personal news: the Indians adored the pictures I had sent them, and wanted to know when I was coming back. There had also been a bad cold epidemic one rainy season and several people died, including kind old Teptykti, Ne'i, who never did go back to Ngrenhre, and Ireki, who worked so hard to feed the trekkers during the men's *bijok* ceremony. I was saddened to learn of the deaths of these people I had grown so much to like. I realized that the Indians' lives were as fragile as their culture.

Recent government measures have made it increasingly difficult to visit Indian areas in Brazil. Since Gustaaf's letter I have received only the most scanty news of the Mekranoti. Tàkàkrorok, who became deaf, retired from his leadership position, and the village split into two groups—one led by Tàkàkngo, and the other by Kentỳxti. Most of the Indians, at least the young men, now speak Portuguese and are much more involved in Brazilian national life. Many of the features of their culture may be giving way to Brazilian customs, but the Indians continue to distinguish themselves from Brazilians and to affirm their pride in their Kayapó origins.

# AFTERWORD

Sometimes when I think of the academic job market and the low esteem accorded anthropologists in the business world, I question why I ever went into the field, and half-seriously consider pursuing engineering or medicine. Other times, I contemplate the fleetingness of my time on earth, and feel I ought to experience life to its fullest by doing something risky and adventurous. There are days when I feel that anthropological arguments are too vague, too divorced from anything useful, and then I wish I had studied a natural science with clearer and more practical questions and answers. Other days I grow bored with the world of "things" and want to talk about people.

Probably most anthropologists feel as ambivalent as I do about their jobs, caught between orderly caution and romantic abandon; between scientific rigor and human empathy. It may be this ambivalence is what attracts us to the profession. Few fields accommodate so easily our wavering spirits.

When they imagine what fieldwork is like, most people think of the physical hardships—living without plumbing, electricity, and movies, plodding through mud, putting on soggy clothes, stepping on snakes and dangerous insects. In fact, I suspect most anthropologists are little bothered by these problems. Fieldwork is a kind of rite of passage, and anthropologists take pride in surviving it. We gain confidence and we can thrill others with our adventures. We do not go into anthropology in spite of the physical hardships but because of them.

Most anthropologists' complaints about fieldwork have little to do with material difficulties. I imagine my anxieties are typical. I worried most about getting along with informants and about gathering useful data. It was not always easy to tolerate other people's behavior and still remain polite, even though I knew I was totally dependent on the Indians for food as well as information. The tension I feel every time I ask an informant to grant an interview will probably never go away. There is too much at stake in these personal relationships.

Sometimes laymen fail to realize how intimate we become with our informants. Anthropologists live with their informants for months and cannot help but feel a closeness and sympathy with "their people." The danger for anthropologists is to forget the reasons they undertook fieldwork. It is easy to get lost in a culture and to lose perspective on one's research.

I remember those slow summer months with the Mekranoti when I could not figure out how to spend my time. The Mekranoti world had become more immediate and real to me than the one I had left, which seemed at the time as fantastic and faraway as the Mekranoti's seems today. I needed contact with the outside to put my work into perspective, to let me know what would be interesting and important to people in my own culture. If I had not planned beforehand the kinds of data I wanted to collect I would have been lost.

Fortunately, I had decided to limit myself to only a few specific questions that I hoped to answer well. Sometimes this meant I had to measure things more carefully than others had done, often by amassing quantified data, even though the results might have seemed self-evident. I cannot help feeling that those who condemn techniques such as statistics are reacting much as the Mekranoti did to my wristwatch—sure that there is nothing to be gained by measuring something everyone can see, and unaware of all the new things to be learned by making finer measurements.

I do not think anthropology loses its romance when researchers take greater care in preparing their research. The thrill of a peccary hunt, the pageantry of a native ceremony, and the calm of an evening around the campfire with jungle sounds in the distance continue to excite the imagination. If fieldwork is losing any of its romance, I suspect it is because societies are becoming less isolated, cultures less varied, and the fieldworkers' safety less precarious. Perhaps the intellectual thrill of science will substitute for the loss in romantic allure. Intellectual excitement is more difficult to convey than the thrill of travel but it is no less real, and perhaps more enduring.

My own contributions to the science of human behavior are modest, and interesting only when compared with others' studies. Still, I am excited about my work because it is new, and relatively solid, and I realize that larger questions can be answered well only when smaller ones have been addressed. My study of Mekranoti gardening and hunting productivities, together with the studies of dietary intake and work, have been compared to similar studies in other native South American societies. The comparisons show that as Indians are forced to live on less land because of white encroachment, their standard of living decreases. Although they continue to work roughly the same number of hours, the returns on their hunting and gardening decrease and their diets become less satisfactory. With similar studies in different societies we are beginning to piece together a picture of the economic factors that motivate people to work to improve their living standards or encourage them to let their standards drop.

My data on Mekranoti fertility and mortality, when compared with that of other societies, give us a better picture of the reasons people choose to have more children, and the reasons they suffer higher mortality. Often these comparisons are not encouraging. One tenth of Mekranoti babies die within the first year of life. This is high in comparison with U.S. rates, but it pales in comparison with the infant mortality rates of much of the Third World. For example, in Pernambuco, Brazil, one fourth of all newborns die in their first year of life. As civilization intrudes into the isolated parts of the world, those people who inhabit them are brought not into the life of the developed nations, but into the suffering and impoverished Third World. The Mekranoti will resist, but it is unlikely they will succeed. I hope that what I have found will at least help make us in the developed world less arrogant, and more cautious about how we force people into civilization.

My studies of Mekranoti leadership and prestige were more abstract. I wanted to contribute something to the debates about the origin of human inequalities. The question is an old one and I knew I could not solve it, but I hoped at least to provide some needed data that might help us eventually understand why some societies are more unjust than others. In most places in the world, leaders are wealthier than their followers; among the Mekranoti they are actually somewhat poorer. By examining the personal and social characteristics of Mekranoti leaders I could examine arguments about how inequalities occurred even before differences in wealth became important. I hoped to learn something about the nature of human hierarchies. I discovered that much the same persons have high prestige in most areas of Mekranoti life and that all Mekranoti do not have the same opportunities to acquire prestige: males and the chief's descendants are privileged. Equal wealth does not guarantee that people will treat each other equally.

It is difficult to convey the excitement these academic questions can create. Many people feel that they already know why humans behave as they do, and are impatient with what seems like academic nitpicking. But anthropologists remain excited by such questions.

I know of no studies on the personalities of anthropologists. I imagine we are similar to other academics. We have learned to think things through carefully and patiently, to be open to ideas, to be respectful about what we do not know. Still, there are probably some things that distinguish us from other intellectuals. Our habit of choosing to study the world's poorest, most isolated and despised social groups and our fascination with people whose lives are so divorced from our own has given us renown as academic eccentrics. Perhaps most of us are unsatisfied with our own society, or perhaps we are like delinquents, who enjoy breaking the ordinary rules of our culture. Our craving for adventure is very similar to the "stimulus-seeking" behavior common to juvenile offenders.

Many ethnographers have commented that fieldwork puts anthropologists in the position of children who need to be taught how to act and talk. I suspect we are a bit more childlike than other academics—more innocently trustful of others and maybe more gullible. I think this childlike innocence is an advantage. It is better to be deceived and fooled at times through over-trustfulness than to be insensitive because we have grown cold or too sure of ourselves.

Anthropologists have curious ambitions. Probably we are not as interested in accumulating wealth as business people. I suspect that prestige is more important to us. Yet the prestige we acquire is very different from what we study. Like other academics we receive honors from our peers all over the world. Yet many of us devote our careers to studying isolated groups where the game of life and prestige is played out in a small arena in which everyone knows everyone else. We can never hope to achieve the kind of everyday respect given by the Mekranoti to Tàkàkrorok, though I think many of us would like this more intimate kind of esteem.

Perhaps this conflict in anthropological ambitions appears in our writings and explains why many people feel affection toward anthropologists they have never met. The day Margaret Mead died I bought a newspaper at the street corner. The woman who sold it to me had no idea I was an anthropologist, but she handed me the paper with tears in her eyes. "Today Margaret Mead died," she cried. "I feel as if my own mother had passed away." Whenever I feel particularly bad about my profession I remember the newspaper saleswoman, and anthropology seems worth it all.

# PERSONAL NAMES

| | |
|---|---|
| **Ajoba** | Tàkàkrorok's oldest son and Tàkàkdjamti's father |
| **Amakkry** | Teptykti's son-in-law, my "father" while in the village |
| **Angme'ê** | historical Mekranoti chief who made contact with Meirelles |
| **Apikrã** | Kukrytbam's young *norny* friend |
| **Bànhõr** | old man, possibly retarded |
| **Bekwynh'i** | Amakkry's *norny* son |
| **Bekwỳnhnor** | the oldest woman in the Mekranoti village |
| **Bekwỳnhpĩ** | Bekwỳnhry's short son-in-law with many children and a poor hunting record |
| **Bekwỳnhry** | Amakkry's sister |
| **Bepita** | name given by the Mekranoti to Gustaaf Verswijver |
| **Bepnĩ** | one of the *norny* |
| **Beproti** | name given by the Mekranoti to the author |
| **Beptu** | Bekwỳnhrax's likable son |
| **Bokrã** | elderly man, haranguer and warrior |
| **Esther** | missionary |
| **Gustaaf** | anthropologist |
| **Iredjo** | Bokrã's daughter, a *kupry* with many sons, who bore twins during my stay in the village |
| **Ireki** | Amakkry and Kokokà's daughter |
| **Irekĩ** | woman who sponsored the men's *bijok* ceremony |
| **Ireti** | Kute'o's brother, who ran amok many years ago, shooting Kute'o |
| **Jokonor** | mother whose daughter cut off her finger |
| **Kamerti** | Tàkàkrorok's current wife |

| | |
|---|---|
| **Kamrekti** | older hunter who lost his way in the forest |
| **Kamti** | Teptykti's burly son (Kokokà's brother) |
| **Karàrti** | old Tapirapé *kupry* whose relatives were killed by the Mekranoti |
| **Karinho'y** | the crippled *kupry* |
| **Kaxngri** | not very respected old man |
| **Kaxre** | Tàkàkrorok's vain youngest son |
| **Kaxti** | man who cut his foot while clearing the forest for a garden |
| **Kaxtykre** | an older *kupry* |
| **Kenti** | historical Mekranoti chief banished because of his ruthlessness |
| **Kentỳxti** | the only man who spoke Portuguese among the Mekranoti |
| **Kokokà** | Teptykti's daughter, Amakkry's wife, and my "mother" during my stay in the village |
| **Kokokamrek** | Bokrã's daughter, mother of the girl who died before the July trek |
| **Kokomy** | *norny* treated for malaria |
| **Kokonhy** | Bànhõr's wife |
| **Kokonỳ** | *norny* who lost his way in the forest |
| **Kokopa** | Teptykti's fat pretty daughter |
| **Kokory** | Tàkàkngo's beautiful wife |
| **Kokowakõ** | Kute'o's son |
| **Kotjaka** | Kentyxti's wife |
| **Kukrytbam** | Tedjware's son, who helped me set up house |
| **Kute'o** | one of the leaders of the younger section of the larger men's society; one of the missionaries' helpers |
| **Kuture** | Kamerti's son, song leader for the women's and men's *bijok* ceremonies |
| **Kwỳrdjo** | one of the ceremonial "anteaters" for the *koko* festival |
| **Mary** | missionary |
| **Mateu** | FUNAI attendant |
| **Meirelles** | well-known Brazilian Indianist |
| **Mrotityk** | *kupry* whose baby died during the men's *bijok* ceremony |
| **Mrytàmti** | old man who spoke quietly |
| **Mydjêti** | one of Tàkàkrorok's sons, owner of the ceremonial privilege of taking women out of the women's *bijok* ceremony |
| **Ne'i** | Ngrenhre's husband, who later left his wife |
| **Nemyti** | one of the *norny* who helped repair author's house |
| **Netire** | Kwỳrdjo's brother and fellow "anteater" during the *koko* festival |
| **Ngrenhkà** | Bekwỳnhpi's boisterous young wife |
| **Ngrenhka** | Kokokà's niece (Teptykti's adult granddaughter) |
| **Ngrenhkangro** | Apikrã's sister |
| **Ngrenhkorre** | Teryti's rugged wife |
| **Ngrenhrĩ** | Mrotityk's sister |
| **Ngrenhre** | Kamerti's niece and Ne'i's wife |
| **Ngrwany** | one of the Mekranoti *kupry* from another Kayapo village |
| **Ngrwa'o** | one of the village *kupry*, Kentỳxti's paramour |
| **Nhàkkamro** | Kaxti's wife |
| **Nhàkkàre** | Tàkàkrorok's paramour during my stay in the village |
| **Nhàkkruw** | Kaxre's wife |
| **Nhàkmroti** | Nokinh's wife—younger woman who passed her *pytê* ceremony shortly after the July season trek |
| **Nhàkngonhti** | woman whose baby's beads were stolen |
| **Nhàkno** | woman who gave birth on the May trek |
| **Nhàkrop** | Ireki's younger sister and co-sponsor of the men's *bijok* ceremony |
| **Nhàkry** | Tàkàkrorok's ex-wife |

| | |
|---|---|
| Nokinh | Kute'o's younger brother who became a "father" by passing the *pytê* ceremony after the July trek |
| 'Okàre | Kokokà's infant daughter |
| 'Oken | Kute'o's wife |
| 'Omexti | respected shaman and loner |
| 'Orwỳkti | sponsor of a samba festival |
| Paken | coarse old man |
| Pãxajk | old woman |
| Pãxkê | leader of smaller men's society |
| Pãxmry | Ajoba's wife |
| Pãxtu | Tàkàkrorok's middle son, ceremonial sponsor for the men's *bijok* ceremony |
| Pedro | black man who worked for FUNAI and brought his family to the village |
| Pirã | Bokrã's wife and Ireki's mother |
| Rik'o | man who built house during my stay |
| Ronaldo | FUNAI medical attendant |
| Ropnhỳ | quiet lip-disked friend of the village's outsiders |
| Ropnĩ | one of the *norny* |
| Ropti | Ngrenhkangro's husband, one of Bokrã's sons |
| Ryti | woman who gave birth during the July trek. Kentỳxti's sister-in-law |
| Tàkàkdjamti | Tàkàkrorok's grandson who ran amok |
| Tàkàkngo | Tàkàkrorok's son, one of the leaders of the younger section of the larger men's society |
| Tàkàkrorok | village chief, leader of the larger men's society |
| Tàkàkta | Ngrenhre's paramour |
| Tàkàk'y | Kokokà's energetic ten-year-old son |
| Tedjware | old white man stolen as a child by the Mekranoti |
| Tep'i | Kokokamrek's husband, father of the girl who died before the July trek |
| Teptykti | elderly grandmother and matron of a large household |
| Teryti | one of the distinguished elders, and a fine dramatist |
| Tykre | Tàkàkrorok's deviant daughter |
| Tyrre | Kentỳxti's mother-in-law |
| Villas-Boas | well-known Brazilian Indianist |
| Wakõkry | one of the "fathers" |
| Wakõni | Ngrenhnĩ's husband, man with poor sense of direction, bitten by snake |
| Wakõte | Teptykti's short, thin son |
| Wore | Ryti's brother |

# GLOSSARY

**atykbe**   while on trek the dormitory for boys, young men, and fathers observing postpartum sex taboos

**bijok**   a Mekranoti naming ceremony, for either men or women

**bô**   the masks used during the men's *bijok* ceremony

**bokti**   young boys, from the time they can walk until about ten years old

**koko**   one of the Mekranoti naming ceremonies; also, the "stationary" masks used during this ceremony

**krabdjwỳ**   ceremonial friends

**kuben**   foreigners

**kupry**   single women who have had children with men who are not their husbands, and who provide sexual services for the men, receiving gifts in return

**kurerêr**   postpubescent girls who have not yet had children

**mẽ djy'ã dja**   men's path meetings while on trek

**mẽ krare**   men and women who have had children but are not yet old

**nekrêx**   ceremonial and other privileges inherited from one's mother's brother or one's grandfather in the case of boys, or from one's father's sister or one's grandmother in the case of girls

**ngà**   the Mekranoti men's house where meetings are held and where boys, young men, and fathers observing postpartum sex taboos sleep while in the village

**norny**   young men who have already received the penis sheath but have not yet had children

**'okre**   prepubescent boys who sleep in the men's house (or *atykbe*) but who have not yet received the penis sheath

**pytê**   the ceremony marking a young man's and a young woman's passage to the parents' age-grade

# ADDITIONAL
# INFORMATION
# ON THE KAYAPO

## DEMOGRAPHY AND ECOLOGY

FLOWERS, NANCY, D. R. GROSS, M. L. RITTER and D. WERNER. "Variation in Swidden Practices in Four Central Brazilian Indian Societies." *Human Ecology* 10(2)1982:203–217.

GROSS, DANIEL R., G. EITEN, N. FLOWERS, F. LEOI, M. L. RITTER, and D. WERNER. "Ecology and Acculturation Among Native Peoples of Central Brazil." *Science* 206(4422)1979:1043–1050.

POSEY, DARRELL. "Wasps, Warriors and Fearless Men: Ethnoentomology of the Kayapo Indians of Central Brazil." *Journal of Ethnobiology* 1(1)1981:165–174.

WERNER, DENNIS. "Fertility and Pacification among the Mekranoti of Central Brazil." *Human Ecology* 11(2)1983:227–245.

———. "Why Do the Mekranoti Trek?" In *Adaptive Responses of Native Amazonians*, by R. Hames and W. Vickers, pp. 225–238. New York: Academic Press, 1983.

———. "Trekking in the Amazon Forest." *Natural History* 87(9)1978:42–55.

———, N. FLOWERS, M. L. RITTER and D. GROSS. "Subsistence Productivity and Hunting Effort in Native South America." *Human Ecology* 7(4)1979:303–315.

## SOCIAL AND POLITICAL LIFE

BAMBURGER, J. "Naming and the Transmission of Status in a Central Brazilian Society." *Ethnology* 13(4)1974:533–560.

GROSS, DANIEL R. "Village Movement in Relation to Resources in Amazonia." In *Adaptive Responses of Native Amazonians*, by R. Hames and W. Vickers, pp. 429–449. New York: Academic Press, 1983.

VIDAL, LUX. *Morte e Vida de Uma Sociedade Indígena Brasileira*. São Paulo: Editora da Universidade, 1977.
WERNER, DENNIS. "Child Care and Influence Among the Mekranoti of Central Brazil." *Sex Roles*, 1984. (in press)
―――. "Solteiras entre os Mekranoti-Kayapor." *Anuário Antropológico*, 182. (in press)
―――. "Leadership Inheritance and Acculturation Among the Mekranoti of Central Brazil." *Human Organization* 41(4)1982:342–345.
―――. "Chiefs and Presidents: A Comparison of Leadership Traits in the United States and Among the Mekranoti-Kayapo of Central Brazil." *Ethos* 10(2)1982:136–148.
―――. "Are Some People More Equal than Others? Status Inequality Among the Mekranoti Indians of Central Brazil." *Journal of Anthropological Research* 37(4)1981:360–373.
―――. "Gerontoracy Among the Mekranoti of Central Brazil." *Anthropological Quarterly* 54(1)1981:15–27.

## CEREMONIAL AND MYTHICAL LIFE

BANNER, HORACE. "Mitos dos Indios Kayapo." *Revista de Antropologia* 5 1957:37–66.
LUKESCH, ANTON. *Mito e Vida dos Indios Caiapós*. São Paulo: Biblioteca Pioneira de Estudos Brasileiros, 1976.
VERSWIJVER, GUSTAAF. "Les Hommes aux Bracelets Noirs: Un Rite de Passage Chez les Indiens Kayapo-Mekragnoti du Bresil Central." *Naitre, Vivre et Mourir*. Neuchatel, 1981.

# Index

## A

Abduction, 92
Abortions, 136
*Açai, see* Enterpepalm berry
Age-grades, 122–23, 149
Agriculture
  and bees, 131–32
  open-field
  slash-and-burn, 105, 111
Amazon jungle
  area of, 1
  dangers in, 2
  mystery in, 1–2
  population of, 3–4
  sounds of, 2
  temperature in, 27
  vision in, 2
  *see also* Forest
Amazon river, 2–4, 11

Amazon valley, and settlers, 3
American Protestants, 156
"*Amijo*" (Kayapo word), 43
Ancestors, 50–53
Andes mountains, 2–3
Anteater masks, 121–22
Anteaters, 95
Anthropologists
  personalities of, 199
  and prestige, 199
Anthropology
  and fieldwork, 196–97, 199
  measurements by, 197
Antibiotics, 134
Ants, 79, 131–32
  leaf-cutting, 111
  stinging, 142–43
Apache Indians, 75
Araguaia River, 12–13
Argentina, 3

ending